The American Kennel Club's

Meet the Breeds

Dog Breeds from A to Z

™

An Official Publication of the

AMERICAN
KENNEL CLUB®

SPORTING

HOUND

WORKING

TERRIER

TOY

NON-SPORTING

HERDING

Lead Editor: Amy Deputato
Associate Editor: Jennifer Calvert
Contributing Editor: Amy Fernandez
Design Manager: Véronique Bos
Senior Art Director: Brian Bengelsdorf
Book Designer: Kari Wirtz
Production Supervisor: Jessica Jaensch
Production Coordinator: Tracy Burns
Publishing Coordinator: Karen Julian

Vice President, Chief Content Officer: June Kikuchi
Vice President, Kennel Club Books: Andrew DePrisco
BowTie Press: Jennifer Calvert, Amy Deputato, Lindsay Hanks, Karen Julian, Elizabeth L. McCaughey, Roger Sipe, Jarelle S. Stein

American Kennel Club: Cynthia Beagles, Gina DiNardo, Jennifer Herzog, Rebecca Mercer, Lisa Peterson, Daphna Straus
AKC Photo Editor: Meghan Lyons

Cover main image (Labrador Retriever puppy): Cioli & Hunnicutt/BowTie/courtesy Ron Morelos
Page 4: Russell Bianca © AKC; **page 6:** Carol Ann Johnson; **page 8:** © 2010 Jeremy Kezer/courtesy Irish Water Spaniel Club of America; **page 9:** Diane Hoy/Otterhound Club of America; **page 10:** Isabelle Francais for AKC; **page 11:** © Derek Glas/courtesy Norfolk Terrier Club; **page 12:** Leanne Bertani/courtesy Japanese Chin Club of America; **page 13:** courtesy Bichon Frise Club of America; **page 14:** Chet Jezierski © AKC; **page 15:** courtesy American Bullmastiff Assocation

BowTie Press
3 Burroughs, Irvine, CA 92618, USA
www.bowtiepress.com

Library of Congress Cataloging-in-Publication Data

The American Kennel Club's meet the breeds : dog breeds from A to Z / author, The American Kennel Club.
    p. cm.
 Includes bibliographical references and index.
 ISBN 978-1-935484-59-2 (alk. paper)
 1. Dog breeds. 2. Dogs. I. American Kennel Club.

SF426A534 2010
636.7'1--dc22

2010036360

Printed and bound in the United States
14 13 12 11 10   1 2 3 4 5 6 7 8 9 10

Contents

A Letter from American Kennel Club
    President/CEO Dennis B. Sprung   **5**

Are You Ready to Be a Dog Owner?   **6**

Dog Breed Profiles: Affenpinscher
    to Yorkshire Terrier   **16**

Photo Credits   **194**

Resources   **196**

Index   **198**

AKC President and CEO Dennis B. Sprung and Pomeranian Blue Moon's Back in the USSR, RN ("Lennon").

AMERICAN KENNEL CLUB®

Dennis B. Sprung
President and
Chief Executive Officer

For more than 125 years, the American Kennel Club has celebrated the wonderful world of purebred dogs and their diversity, predictability, and beauty. Owners of purebred dogs know what to expect regarding the full-grown size, body type, coat, and temperament of their dogs. They can also predict whether it will need special grooming, as well as its energy level and exercise needs. Purebreds also possess specific traits common to their breeds and have natural, instinctive aptitudes for different jobs and dog sports. With 167 AKC-recognized breeds and more on their way to recognition, there is a purebred dog to fit every family!

Since 1884, the American Kennel Club has maintained the largest registry of purebred dogs in the world, and today the AKC governs more than 20,000 canine competitions annually. Along with over 5,000 licensed and member clubs and its affiliated organizations, the AKC advocates for the purebred dog as a family companion, advances canine health and well-being, works to protect the rights of all dog owners, provides fun and educational opportunities for owners of dogs, and promotes responsible ownership. For more information, visit us at www.meetthebreeds.com and www.akc.org.

This book was created in honor of the 2nd annual Meet the Breeds™, presented by PetPartners, Inc., a provider of top-quality pet healthcare, and hosted by the American Kennel Club and Cat Fanciers' Association. As the world's largest dog and cat showcase, Meet the Breeds is truly a one-of-a-kind event, allowing spectators the opportunity to meet more than 200 dog and cat breeds, gain knowledge first-hand from AKC Parent Clubs and CFA Breed Councils, talk with top experts in every pet-related field, shop the latest pet products, and watch dogs and cats show off their skills in the demonstration rings. Meet the Breeds truly fulfills the missions of AKC and CFA to promote purebred pets and educate the public about responsible ownership. We hope you enjoy the book, which is dedicated to all the Parent Clubs and Breed Council members and volunteers at Meet the Breeds.

Sincerely,

Dennis B. Sprung

Dennis B. Sprung

Are You Ready to Be a DOG OWNER?

Some purebred litters are more difficult to find, such as this irresistible tricolor trio of Swiss pups. The Entlebucher Mountain Dog, one of the newer additions to the AKC Miscellaneous Class, is the smallest of the four Swiss Mountain Dog breeds.

The multifaceted responsibilities of dog ownership have been well publicized in recent years. We are vigorously cautioned to investigate all aspects of care and training before acquiring a dog. But this isn't as easy as it sounds. A dog's demands vary drastically by breed, and even individual puppies in the same litter can have different needs. Long-held notions about dog care are constantly revised with innovations such as dog parks, dog whisperers, and dog walkers. If you are prepared to manage some complication and inconvenience, large energetic dogs can live contentedly in small apartments, and hairless dogs can live happily in frigid northern climates.

Dogs are some of the world's most adaptable creatures. They have been acclimating themselves to human lifestyles for thousands of years. We should never underestimate their ability to do this. Dogs have some basic and essential requirements, and we must honestly evaluate our ability to provide them with what they need.

Today most dogs are destined to spend their lives as pets, regardless of their instinctive abilities or heritage. Dogs come in every imaginable shape and size, and these differences comprise a lot more than superficialities of appearance. Mental and physical traits are inseparable. Inherited tendencies, sensory abilities, and energy levels will profoundly influence a puppy's chances of acclimating to certain lifestyles. Every puppy's personality is ultimately a combination of genetics and environment, but there are clear differences in canine temperament traits, based on a dog's ancestry and intended function. A hound and a terrier not only look different, they think and act differently. Their perceptions, energy levels, and responses to training will differ. Many temperamental differences are easily predicted, but they may not be obvious without some breed knowledge or research. For instance, toy dogs come from a variety of backgrounds. They are all little and cute, but they are not all equally sweet, cuddly, and biddable. The Boxer and the Neapolitan Mastiff are both Working breeds, both watchdogs, but their basic temperaments differ drastically.

Knowing something about a breed's history and innate temperament greatly improves the odds of choosing a good canine match. It also makes it easier to anticipate potential problems to which a puppy may be prone. Better yet, all of this information is available at the click of a mouse.

For every breed, in-depth information about temperament, health, and general care can be instantly accessed through a network of local and national dog clubs and from the American Kennel Club. Long before you bring your new Great Pyrenees puppy home, you will know that he is going to need more than average amounts of socialization, training, and exercise and that he is likely to demonstrate strong guardian instincts at maturity. Taking the time to discover these details before acquiring a puppy makes all the difference in the world.

MEET THE PUREBRED DOG

The American Kennel Club (AKC) has grouped all of the breeds that it registers into seven categories, or groups, roughly based on function and heritage. Breeds are grouped together because they share traits of form and function or a common heritage. You probably have some idea of which traits you really want in a puppy, which unanticipated traits you are prepared to cope with, and which traits you really want to avoid. Specific qualities associated with the breeds in these groups provide some idea of where to begin your search.

Sporting Breeds

First developed in thirteenth-century Iberia, sporting dogs were bred to work closely with hunters to assist with hawking, netting, and especially shooting. Rather than capturing or killing their quarry, they helped locate it, retrieve it, or both, as they still do today. As soon as they were introduced to the rest of Europe, sporting breeds became immensely popular, and they have remained so ever since. Their intelligence and natural versatility make them easy to train for a wide range of activities. Many Sporting dogs are still used for hunting. They also compete in organized field trials. But the majority of them live as companions. Some of the most popular breeds, such as the Labrador Retriever, Golden Retriever, and Cocker Spaniel, are found in this group.

Sometimes referred to as "bird dogs" or "gundogs," there are four basic types of sporting dog. Spaniels are used to flush birds and game into the open, setters and pointers locate game, retrievers fetch game, and water retrievers retrieve dead and wounded game specifically from the water. Some Sporting breeds have been further specialized to hunt certain types of game or work in particular kinds of terrain. For instance, the Clumber Spaniel is a slow, steady hunter, easy to follow on foot. The Chesapeake Bay Retriever was

Sporting dogs are eager to please, very responsive, and great fun for the whole family. This smiling youngster is an Irish Water Spaniel.

Is a Sporting Dog for You?

- Puppies and adult dogs are likely to be available from breed rescues.
- Sporting dogs are bred to be highly responsive to human direction, which makes them easy to train.
- They are noted for their ability to get along well with children and other dogs.
- Sturdy and athletic, with plenty of energy and stamina, a Sporting dog is a good choice for someone with an active lifestyle.
- Their protective coats allow many of these breeds to spend a lot of time in outdoor activity.
- They need a substantial amount of regular exercise.
- They need plenty of social interaction.
- Some Sporting breeds shed extensively, while others require significant grooming.
- Some Sporting breeds are prone to doggy odor.

designed to retrieve game from the frigid waters of the Chesapeake Bay. A number of sporting breeds are also classified as multipurpose breeds, known as "HPR" breeds because they hunt, point, and retrieve.

In general, Sporting dogs are friendly, sociable, and highly responsive to humans. They are tireless workers with tremendous energy. Many of them, especially the water-retrieving breeds, have well-insulated water-repellent coats, which are quite resistant to environmental conditions.

Hound Breeds

Hounds are the world's oldest specialized hunting dogs, documented for thousands of years. Their gracefulness, beauty, and superlative hunting skills inspired ancient Egyptian hieroglyphics and Greek literature. Hounds are not good at everything, but they are extremely talented at the things they are bred to do. In medieval times, owning a Greyhound often meant the difference between survival and starvation. Today hounds are used for recreational hunting, racing, performance competition, therapy work, and police and customs-inspection work, and, of course, as pets. The Beagle and the Dachshund are among the popular breeds found in this group.

Hound breeds vary drastically in size, shape, and proportion, from smooth-coated, short-legged Dachshunds to huge, rough-coated, leggy Irish Wolfhounds. There are two basic hound types: sighthounds and scenthounds, so named for the primary sense by which they hunt. Examples of sighthounds include the Borzoi, Afghan Hound, Greyhound, and Whippet. Some sighthounds are short-coated and some are long-coated, but all of them have extremely keen eyesight and are built for speed to find, chase, and catch prey. These are the fastest breeds, pursuing their quarry with single-minded determination. They run mute, using all their breath to gain speed.

Examples of scenthounds include the Bloodhound, Basset Hound, Beagle, and foxhounds, as well as the coonhounds—the Black and Tan Coonhound,

American English Coonhound, and Redbone Coonhound. They follow their prey primarily by scent rather than by sight. With large nostrils and long ears to help them gather scents, they are truly built to sniff. All scenthounds are also noted for their tremendous endurance and perseverance.

Unlike sighthounds, who hunt silently, scenthounds instinctively bark or howl when they pick up a scent. When hunting, they move more slowly than sighthounds do. Some are short-legged, making them easy to follow on foot rather than on horseback. Probably the most renowned scenthound is the Bloodhound, prized for centuries for its trailing abilities. Working Bloodhounds remain indispensable to police departments and search and rescue teams all over the world.

Perhaps the most unique of the scenthounds is the Dachshund, so much so that the breed competes in a group of its own in Europe. The Dachshund does possess some traits that set it apart from other hounds and make it seem more like a terrier; Dachshunds are permitted to compete in earthdog events along with the Terrier breeds.

Regardless of specialized abilities, all Hounds are mentally and physically designed to find and catch prey. Whether they are hunted singly or in packs, they rely primarily on their instincts and senses rather than on human direction. They have been selectively bred to work independently and persistently, qualities

When you think of the Hound breeds, you often think of packs such as this rare but wonderful gathering of Otterhound puppies.

Is a Hound for You?

- Hounds are sturdy and hardy.
- Hounds are sensitive, even-tempered, gentle, and highly affectionate.
- The short- and smoothhaired breeds require very little coat care.
- Many Hounds are fairly inactive indoors, making them good house dogs.
- Their strong predatory drive makes them very playful.
- Some Hounds are notably quiet; others are not.
- Their strong hunting drive can cause hounds to be easily distracted during training.
- Because of their strong predatory instinct, hounds may not be reliable with small animals and other pets unless they are well socialized to them at a young age.
- Their instinct to chase things can make Hounds unreliable off lead.
- Digging and jumping breeds can be escape artists.
- Leash training, obedience training, and a securely fenced yard are mandatory.
- Smooth- and shorthaired breeds may need extra weather protection.
- Long-coated breeds may experience extensive seasonal shedding.

highly desired in a hunting dog. But these traits can complicate training, which is why Hounds are sometimes described as being aloof or independent in nature. Their affection and devotion to their owners may be balanced by a reserve toward strangers.

Working Breeds

This is a broad category, including breeds that perform a wide variety of roles, such as those of police dog, sled dog, guard dog, and search and rescue dogs. They are some of the world's oldest breeds. Mastiffs have been used since Roman times as house guards and war dogs. Draft dogs have been used to pull carts and sleds since the thirteenth century. Many of these breeds are still used as working dogs today. Rottweilers and Doberman Pinschers are preferred breeds for military work. Others

Large-breed puppies from the Working Group tend to grow very quickly but mature slowly. Most of these large breeds require experienced owners who are able to provide leadership and consistent training, along with ample space and care.

are favored as guide dogs and drug-detection dogs. Because Working breeds are so versatile, many of them have traditionally been used for multiple functions, such as hunting, guarding estates and livestock, tracking, hauling freight, and serving as companions.

The common denominator is that all Working breeds assist humans in some capacity or another. They vary in appearance, but they are all known for their tremendous strength, endurance, and intelligence. Many have been bred to appear menacing, which belies their gentle, loving nature. They tend to be naturally protective toward their household "pack" and home territory.

Terrier Breeds

Rugged, courageous, and self-sufficient, Terriers were developed in England centuries ago. They were expected to hunt, eradicate vermin, guard their families' homes, and serve

Is a Working Dog for You?

- They have plenty of strength, stamina, and endurance.
- They are extremely loyal to and protective of their families and make excellent watchdogs.
- Their weatherproof coats provide good protection in hot and cold weather.
- They are responsive to training.
- Some large Working breeds have only modest exercise requirements despite their size.
- Many Working breeds are fairly inactive indoors, making them well-behaved house dogs.
- Working instincts can veer in unwanted directions without adequate training and socialization.

- Owners must be prepared to supply firm and consistent training.
- Some Working breeds can be very slow to mature, retaining puppy traits longer than some smaller breeds do.
- Because of their strong protective instincts, Working dogs tend to be tolerant but suspicious of strangers. Don't expect these breeds to behave as fun-loving extroverts.
- Giant-breed puppies require careful dietary management and have some exercise restrictions as they grow.
- Some breeds in this group can be targets of breed-specific legislation.

as companions. Although all Terriers originally served as working dogs, many of the functions that Terriers once performed are now obsolete, and most terriers today live primarily as companions.

Modern-day terriers still retain the working traits of their ancestors. Short-legged terriers, such as the Scottish Terrier and Cairn Terrier, were bred to pursue prey such as foxes and badgers underground. Long-legged terriers, such as the Airedale Terrier and Fox Terrier, were developed to tackle larger prey and keep up with fast-running packs of foxhounds during a hunt. The bull-and-terrier breeds were designed to be strong, agile, and tenacious for bull-baiting.

All Terriers are tough and resilient. They have high energy levels and enhanced reactivity, responding instantly to anything unusual in their environments. Their moderate sizes simplify many aspects of routine care, but their headstrong, energetic natures can pose training challenges. Without appropriate outlets for their mental and physical energy, they may devote their time to barking, digging, and chewing.

Is a Terrier for You?

- Vigilant and fearless, they make great alarm dogs.
- They are adaptable to small living spaces and city life.
- Their moderate sizes and extroverted temperaments can make well-trained Terriers good companions for children.
- Shorthaired and wirehaired coats are protective and low maintenance.
- Sturdy structures make them less prone to many common orthopedic disorders and injuries.
- Terriers require firm, consistent training to discourage rough play and biting.
- Without early, comprehensive socialization toward other dogs, some Terriers have the potential to become dog-aggressive.
- They may not be reliable around small animals due to their strong predatory instinct.
- If neglected or bored, they can become prone to digging, chewing, and barking.
- Bull-and-terrier breeds may be subject to breed-specific legislation.

The Norfolk Terrier, a breed known for its gregarious personality and loyalty to its family, is the Terrier Group's smallest tyke.

Toy Breeds

Toy breeds come from a wide range of backgrounds. Some of them, such as the Chinese Crested and Maltese, were developed solely as companions. Others, such as the Toy Manchester Terrier, Pomeranian, and Italian Greyhound, are miniaturized versions of other breeds, and they retain many of the traits associated with their larger counterparts. Regardless of their origins, all Toy breeds are naturally attuned to human interaction. They are affectionate, sociable, and adaptable to a wide range of lifestyles. Because they are so affectionate, toy breeds are temperamentally suited to children but might not be sturdy enough for rough play, and thus caution must be taken.

Today most Toy dogs live as companions. They are also popular for therapy work, competitive obedience, and agility. Despite their size, many Toy breeds are very energetic, requiring quite a bit of daily exercise. Of course, everything is relative. A Japanese Chin can get a good workout just by running around the living room.

The Toy breeds were designed to be companions, and the Japanese Chin shines as an example of an affectionate and responsive pet.

Is a Toy Dog for You?

- Smaller dogs are less expensive to keep.
- Easily portable, Toy dogs make great travel companions.
- Smaller breeds are noted for their longevity.
- Some Toy breeds, such as the Papillon, Miniature Pinscher, and Pug, have very low-maintenance, easy-to-groom coats.
- Many Toy dogs are surprisingly tough, athletic, and energetic. They are, indeed, big dogs in small packages.
- Small size decreases a dog's resistance to weather conditions.
- Small size increases a dog's risk of accidental injuries and escapes.
- Some Toy dogs have a higher than normal incidence of vaccine, anesthesia, and drug reactions.
- Some Toy breeds, such as the Maltese and Havanese, require complex regular grooming.

Some Toy breeds, such as the Chihuahua and Yorkshire Terrier, have strong protective instincts, requiring consistent training and socialization to prevent associated behavior problems. Others, such as the Shih Tzu and Toy Poodle, need substantial grooming unless they are kept in pet clips. Toy breeds have a reputation for being difficult to train. However, many of these problems are caused by indulgent owners rather than due to any particular traits of Toy-breed temperament.

Non-Sporting Breeds

When the American Kennel Club was founded more than a century ago, all breeds were classified as either Sporting or Non-Sporting. Gradually, as new groupings were added, most breeds were moved out of the Non-Sporting Group. Eventually, it became a sort of catch-all group for breeds that simply did not fit anywhere else. The breeds comprising the AKC's Non-Sporting Group vary drastically in size, type, and heritage. They come from a wide range of backgrounds, making it difficult to generalize about them.

Some Non-Sporting breeds, such as the Chinese Shar-Pei, Tibetan Spaniel, and Lhasa Apso, are among the world's oldest breeds, traditionally used as guardians. Others, such as the Dalmatian, Bulldog, Keeshond, and Schipperke, were bred for working functions that are now obsolete. A few, such as the water-retrieving Standard Poodles, are still used occasionally in their traditional jobs. There are also several breeds in this group that were bred strictly to serve as companions, such as the Boston Terrier, French Bulldog, and Bichon Frise.

Although their temperaments vary considerably due to their range of origins, all Non-Sporting breeds were designed to interact with humans in some capacity. Not all of them can be classified as extroverts, but they are known for outstanding loyalty and devotion to their owners. Some, such as the

Is a Non-Sporting Dog for You?

- All Non-Sporting breeds have fascinating histories.
- Some Non-Sporting breeds, such as the Dalmatian and Shiba Inu, combine exotic appearance and low coat maintenance.
- Some, such as the Bulldog and Chow Chow, have moderate exercise requirements.
- Most are good watchdogs and house dogs.
- Their eclectic backgrounds necessitate careful research of each breed to understand typical traits and temperament; you cannot generalize about the breeds in this group.
- Some, such as the Chow Chow, Bichon Frise, and Lhasa Apso, require extensive grooming.
- Some, such as the Bulldog, Boston Terrier, and French Bulldog, have a low tolerance to heat.

Standard and Miniature Poodles and the Bichon Frise, are quite outgoing. Others, such as the Tibetan Terrier and Chow Chow, are naturally reserved. Some of them, such as the Dalmatian, possess fairly high energy levels, and others, such as the Lhasa Apso, require extensive grooming.

Like the Toy breeds, the members of the Non-Sporting Group excel as companions. Each of these breeds has a diverse background, such as the Bichon Frise, which derived from Spanish Poodle-like dogs transported to the Canary Island of Tenerife.

Herding dogs are generally easy to train and devoted to their families, yet are driven to work. The Canaan Dog is territorial and proves to be a reiiable watchdog.

Herding Breeds

In many parts of the world, Herding dogs continue to gather, herd, and protect livestock, functions that they have performed since prehistoric times. But that's far from all they do. Today, some Herding breeds, such as the German Shepherd, are commonly trained for police and protection work. Others, such as the Border Collie, excel at competitive performance events. Because of their outstanding loyalty and intelligence, Herding dogs are prized as house dogs, watchdogs, and companions.

Herding dogs specialize in rounding up livestock, finding strays, and moving animals from one grazing area to another. They are designed to tirelessly stalk and chase. Their high working drive and boundless energy are great for rounding up sheep, but dogs with these traits do not easily adapt to an undemanding lifestyle. Barking, heel nipping, and nudging are normal herding behaviors that may be seen as problems in a house pet.

Is a Herding Dog for You?

- They are loyal, intelligent, and extremely affectionate toward their owners.
- Their weatherproof coats are good for all types of climates.
- They are versatile and have plenty of stamina for participating in all kinds of activities with their owners, and they excel at dog sports.
- Herding dogs are sturdy and rugged and make good watchdogs; many work as police and military dogs.
- They require consistent training and socialization as puppies.
- Instinctive herding behaviors such as barking, nudging, stalking, and heel nipping are part of the package.
- Some can require extensive grooming to keep them clean and to minimize doggy odor.
- Eager to please though independent-minded, herding dogs are easily trained.

What's in a Group?

That's 167 dog breeds in seven Groups, and 10 more breeds on the way! Since selecting the right breed can be overwhelming and exciting, a good understanding of the basic characteristics of each group can lead a new owner toward the perfect purebred dog.

Most owners have a good idea about what they want and don't want in a companion dog. If you are certain that you want a dog that's suitable for jogging with you in the morning, rain or shine, you should be looking more at the Sporting and some of the Hound breeds and likely less at the Toy and most of the Non-Sporting breeds. If, on the other hand, you're looking for a snazzy, head-turning but less energetic pet, you'd likely go directly to the Toy and Non-Sporting Groups. Activity level is just one of the many things to think about. Other important considerations are size, grooming demands, and temperament.

Many large breeds are categorized as Working and Herding breeds, though some of the Hounds are huge. The smallest breeds are grouped as Toys, though there are also a few pint-sized companions in the Non-Sporting Group. The Hounds generally have the easiest coats to groom, though any small shorthaired dog is fairly undemanding to maintain.

Temperaments vary significantly from group to group, from breed to breed, and even from dog to dog. Even though temperament is fairly predictable in most breeds, generalizations are not always helpful: you can encounter a high-strung Saluki or Bulldog as readily as you can find an easygoing Border Collies and Brittany.

The forthcoming breed profiles, in alphabetical order, shed light on the temperaments, general descriptions, and requirements of each of the 177 AKC breeds. Good luck, and enjoy this exciting opportunity to *meet the breeds*.

A Bullmastiff puppy will be alert and confident, and owners should seek a puppy that appears healthy, eager to meet them, and unafraid of new experiences.

AFFENPINSCHER

Year of AKC recognition: 1936

Group: Toy

Size: 9–11½ inches, 7–10 pounds

Coat: Affenpinschers have a rough, harsh wire coat of approximately 1 inch in length on the shoulders and body. The breed has a shaggy mane and a longer, slightly softer coat on the head, neck, chest, abdomen, and legs. The longer, shaggy coat on the head and the beard enhance the Affen's monkeylike expression.

Color: Black, gray, silver, red, black and tan, belge (red mixed with black, brown, and/or white)

Life expectancy: 12–15 years

Activity level: Moderate. They are active indoors and will get some exercise, but they should have daily walks and some outdoor play.

Grooming: The coat should be stripped regularly to maintain its hard texture and neatened occasionally with thinning shears. The goal is a "neat but shaggy" appearance.

Temperament: The Affenpinscher personality is an irresistible blend of the self-assurance and courage of its terrier forebears and the playful, affectionate nature of a companion breed. Affens are all business when protecting their families, but they are equally famed for their playfulness and comical, fun-loving nature.

Parent club: Affenpinscher Club of America (www.affenpinscher.org); founded in 1965

Buyers' advice from parent club: This is a very rare breed, and buyers should not get frustrated if they must wait for a puppy.

Rescue: Affenpinscher Rescue (www.affenrescue.org)

Affenpinscher-type dogs have existed for over four centuries, and they trace their ancestry to Germany's schnauzers and pinschers. For hundreds of years, these farm dogs controlled rodents in barns, kitchens, and stables. These sturdy, scruffy, self-reliant little dogs were later crossed with breeds including the Brussels Griffon and Pug to perfect the "monkey terrier." The breed first came to America in the 1930s.

The Affenpinscher is often described as a big dog in a small package. This is a toy-sized, compact, sturdy, balanced dog with a hard, wiry, protective coat. The breed's uniquely appealing monkeylike expression is produced by round, dark, luminous eyes; a prominent lower lip; a short muzzle; and a broad jaw. Ears can be cropped, natural, erect, semi-erect, or dropped.

This ancient sighthound is one of the world's oldest breeds. It was developed in Afghanistan as a hunting dog and came to the attention of European dog lovers in the nineteenth century. Afghans are no longer used to hunt, but they are versatile. Even though the earliest records of Afghan Hounds in the United States date to the 1920s, it was the import of Ghazni dogs from Britain that established the breed in America. Today, they function as companions, therapy dogs, show dogs, and canine athletes.

The Afghan Hound is a true canine aristocrat—elegant, dignified, and aloof. This athletic hound is squarely proportioned, with long legs; prominent hip bones; a flowing ring tail; and a long, silky coat. The breed's long head is refined, with a slightly Roman appearance to the

muzzle, a strong underjaw, a profuse topknot, and a black nose. The long ears are covered with silky hair. One of the Afghan's most arresting features is its exotic expression, with eyes that "gaze into the distance as if in memory of ages past."

Year of AKC recognition: 1926

Group: Hound

Size: 25–27 inches, 50–60 pounds

Coat: Long, thick, and fine-textured, with shorter hair on back and a silky topknot

Color: All colors

Life expectancy: 12–18 years

Activity level: High. Afghans are generally quiet indoors, but they need daily outdoor running time. They have a high prey drive and will chase moving objects, so they must be exercised on lead or in a fenced area.

Grooming: Afghans should be thoroughly brushed, bathed, and blown dry regularly.

Temperament: Afghan Hounds are bred to work independently rather than taking cues from people. Although they seem aloof, Afghans are extremely affectionate with their owners. This is a spirited and sensitive, though at times strong-willed, breed. This independent streak, coupled with the breed's high prey drive, can lead to training challenges. An Afghan Hound needs a consistent pack leader, ready to approach training with patience, determination, and a sense of humor.

Parent club: Afghan Hound Club of America (http://clubs.akc.org/ahca); founded in 1937

Buyers' advice from parent club: Visit dog shows to research the breed. See the puppy before purchase, and be prepared for a dog with an independent nature. The Afghan Hound Club of America has a mentoring program for new owners who need advice on grooming, training, and general care.

Regional clubs: The AHCA works with regional clubs in twenty-five states; for information, select "Regional Clubs" from drop-down menu on the parent club's Web site.

Rescue: Afghan Hound Club of America Rescue (http://afghanhound.net)

AFGHAN HOUND

AIREDALE TERRIER

Year of AKC recognition: 1888

Group: Terrier

Size: 23 inches, 50–70 pounds

Coat: Dense, wiry outer coat with a shorter, softer undercoat

Color: Tan with black or dark grizzle (black mixed with gray and white) markings on the body

Life expectancy: 11–14 years

Activity level: This breed loves activity.

Grooming: Twice-weekly brushing is advised, and the beard should be washed regularly. Stripping or professional grooming four times per year is recommended.

Temperament: Airedales possess an interesting combination of hound and terrier personality traits. They are intelligent, self-assured, and somewhat aloof. These qualities can make for an incomparable companion, but they can lead to bad habits if an Airedale is deprived of exercise and attention. Airedales are highly trainable, and their playfulness and versatility can be channeled into many activities and dog sports. However, they can be strong-willed and assertive, so consistent leadership is essential.

Parent club: Airedale Terrier Club of America (www.airedale.org); founded in 1900

Buyers' advice from parent club: Buy from a dedicated hobby breeder who has his or her dogs health-tested. Look for a well-socialized, self-assured puppy.

Regional clubs: For information on over twenty regional Airedale clubs, click on "Important Links" on the parent club's Web site.

Rescue: National Airedale Rescue, Inc. (www.airedalerescue.net)

The now-extinct English Terrier and the Otterhound were two of the breeds used to create the Airedale Terrier. The breed was developed in the region of northern England's Aire River and was known as the Waterside or Bingley Terrier in the nineteenth century. The hound ancestry added another dimension to the breed's hunting aptitude. In addition to terrier pursuits, Airedales were used to track and course game. They have also been used for police work, as wartime sentries, and as messengers, in addition to their role as family companions.

The Airedale is the largest AKC-recognized terrier, and the breed easily lives up to its reputation as the "king of terriers." This is a sturdy, athletic dog with a hard, wiry, protective wash-and-wear coat. The skull is long and flat; the button ears are small and V-shaped; the nose is black; and the eyes are dark and full of terrier fire. The breed has a moderately long neck, a deep chest, and a short, level back. The tail is set high and carried gaily but not over the back.

The Akita was developed in Japan as a versatile guardian and hunting dog. Early references to the breed date from the seventeenth century on the island of Honshu. At one time, Akita ownership was restricted to Japan's imperial family and ruling aristocracy. It is one of seven Japanese breeds designated as a Natural Monument in its native land. The breed came to America's attention in 1937 when Helen Keller received an Akita puppy as a gift while visiting Japan, and the breed's popularity increased in the United States following World War II, possibly as a result of the dogs' returning home with US troops.

This is a powerful, imposing, working dog with heavy bone; slightly rectangular proportions; a wide, deep chest; and a level back. The long, bushy tail is set high and curled over the back.  The head is broad and triangular. The Akita's small eyes and erect ears create a keen, alert expression.

Year of AKC recognition: 1972

Group: Working

Size: Males—26–28 inches; females—24–26 inches

Coat: Double coat with a harsh outer coat and a dense undercoat

Color: All colors, including brindle and pinto (white with colored patches on the head and body)

Life expectancy: 10–13 years

Activity level: Moderate. Akitas need daily exercise, but use caution in hot weather. They should be exercised on leash or in a secured area, as their hunting instincts cause them to roam.

Grooming: Akitas are noted for their fastidious habits and will groom themselves like cats. They should be brushed daily during heavy shedding in spring and fall; brush weekly at other times.

Temperament: The Akita possesses the courage, perseverance, and fortitude to hunt large, dangerous quarry such as boar and bear. The breed is equally skilled at hunting small prey and retrieving waterfowl, and it has been used in its native Japan to drive fish into nets. Akitas are typically loyal and devoted to their families but reserved and dignified with strangers. They are strong willed and protective, with good guardian instincts. Puppy socialization is essential to ensure that they are tolerant of strangers. Akita temperament varies from calm to dominant, and care should be taken when introducing them to children and other pets.

Parent club: Akita Club of America (www.akitaclub.org); founded in 1956

Buyers' advice from parent club: Akita ownership is a responsibility that should not be taken lightly. Be prepared to invest time and effort into training and socializing your dog.

Regional clubs: There are over thirty-five US breed clubs listed on the parent club's Web site on the "Akita Clubs" page under "Akita Info."

Rescue: The Akita Club of America lists rescue group information on its Web site under "Rescue."

AKITA

ALASKAN MALAMUTE

Year of AKC recognition: 1935

Group: Working

Size: Males—25 inches, 85 pounds; females—23 inches, 75 pounds

Coat: A harsh, dense, double coat

Color: All white or predominantly white with markings in shades of gray, silver, red, black, sable (black or gray with red in undercoat), or Alaskan seal (black with cream undercoat)

Life expectancy: 10–14 years

Activity level: High. Malamutes should be exercised on lead or in a securely fenced area.

Grooming: The breed needs daily brushing during heavy seasonal shedding in the spring and fall and twice-weekly brushing at other times.

Temperament: This is the largest of the Arctic breeds, noted for its strength and endurance. Malamutes are quite affectionate and devoted to their families, but owners should not overlook the fact that these are powerful dogs with independent natures. Early training and socialization are essential to ensure that a Malamute is a well-behaved pet. Originally bred as sled dogs, Malamutes today need jobs to do, and many activities will fit the bill, such as hiking, backpacking, swimming, and participating in organized dog sports. Without an outlet for its mental and physical energy, a Malamute will resort to habits like digging and chewing to alleviate boredom.

Parent club: Alaskan Malamute Club of America (www.alaskanmalamute.org); founded in 1935

Buyers' advice from parent club: Avoid impulse buying. Find a reputable breeder who will advise you whether your lifestyle can comfortably accommodate a high-energy dog that sheds extensively and requires a great deal of personal attention.

Rescue: Alaskan Malamute Assistance League (www.malamuterescue.org)

The Alaskan Malamute is one of the world's oldest breeds and one of the first developed in North America. Inuit tribes of western Alaska relied on these powerful dogs to hunt and carry freight through the region's deep snow. The breed came to worldwide attention in the nineteenth century during the Alaskan gold rush. During these years, Malamutes were crossbred to a variety of other breeds to increase their size and to fill the endless demand for big, powerful sled dogs. The pure-bred Malamute had nearly disappeared when sled-dog racing emerged as a popular amateur sport, attracting a new generation of fanciers to the breed. In 1926, breeders began developing purebred strains from native Alaskan stock.

This is a large, powerful Nordic breed, noted for its heavy bone, its great substance, and the impressively plumed tail that is carried over the back. The breed's double coat is thick and protective, standing slightly off the body. The head is large, broad, and triangular. The small, deep-set, triangular eyes and small, erect ears create an alert expression that conveys calmness and great courage.

The American English Coonhound was developed from the English Foxhound and shares its ancestry with other treeing coonhound breeds. It is known variously as the American English Fox and Coonhound, English Coonhound, Redtick Coonhound, or Virginia Hound. The breed was traditionally used for a wide range of game, including fox, raccoon, possum, deer, boar, bobcat, and bear. It is used today for hunting and competitive coonhound sports.

This is an athletic, sturdy, muscular, and confident hound. Its neck is of moderate length; its chest is deep; and its broad, muscular back slopes slightly from shoulder to hips. The feet are round with well-arched toes and thick pads. The tail is moderately long, set high, and carried high. The breed has a broad, slightly domed head; a square muzzle; and low-hung, fine-textured ears that reach almost to the tip of the black nose when pulled forward. Dark brown, wide-set eyes give American English Coonhound a gentle houndy expression.

Entered into Miscellaneous Class in 2010

Size: Males—24–26 inches; females—23–25 inches

Coat: Hard, protective, medium length

Color: Red and white ticked, blue and white ticked, tricolor with ticking, red and white, white and black

Life expectancy: 11–12 years

Activity level: High. The breed is renowned for its strength, speed, and endurance, and must have daily vigorous exercise such as hunting, running, swimming, or interactive play. American English Coonhounds can become hyperactive or destructive without sufficient exercise. They must be exercised on lead or in a secure area, as they will chase and roam and may not heed commands to come back.

Grooming: Weekly brushing is recommended.

Temperament: The breed has a typical easygoing and sociable hound nature. Friendly and pleasant, American English Coonhounds are instinctively focused on hunting, and training requires persistence and patience. They are versatile and can be wonderful house dogs as long as owners provide plenty of exercise and firm, fair, consistent training. They are protective and make good watchdogs. American English Coonhounds are famed for their voices but may bark and howl excessively if confined or neglected. They are tough, stoic, and good at masking illness and injury, so owners must be watchful. They get along well with people and other dogs but are not recommended for homes with small pets.

Parent club: American English Coonhound Association

AMERICAN ESKIMO DOG

Year of AKC recognition: 1995

Group: Non-Sporting

Size: This breed has three sizes: Toy—9–12 inches, 6–10 pounds; Miniature—12–15 inches, 10–20 pounds; Standard—15–19 inches, 25–35 pounds

Coat: The breed has a dense, harsh, stand-off double coat with a noticeable ruff, feathering on the backs of the legs, and long hair on the tail.

Color: Solid white; biscuit cream (off-white) shading is permitted in conformation showing.

Life expectancy: 13–15 years

Activity level: Moderate. Eskies should be exercised in an enclosed area such as a fenced yard.

Grooming: The Eskie's voluminous coat must be brushed daily during heavy seasonal shedding in spring and fall. Twice-weekly brushing at other times will prevent mats and control shedding.

Temperament: Eskies are noted for their happy, playful demeanor. The breed was developed from a combination of working and companion dogs, resulting in dogs that are energetic, eager to please, and versatile. They crave companionship and attention, and they can be ideal pets for those who are prepared to devote time and attention to socialization, training, and regular activity. Without training, interaction with its owners, and a structured routine, the naturally alert and protective Eskie can develop behavior problems.

Parent club: American Eskimo Dog Club of America (www.aedca.org); founded in 1985

Buyers' advice from parent club: Owners should be prepared for an active breed that requires plenty of attention and frequent grooming to control shedding.

Rescue: American Eskimo Dog Club of America Rescue (www.aedca.org)

The American Eskimo Dog was developed from strains of various European Spitz breeds. These forebears included all-purpose farm dogs, family companions, and performing dogs. Thanks to this heritage, the American Eskimo is a supremely versatile breed. Spitz breeds were brought to America by European immigrants in the nineteenth century and soon became popular as pets, watchdogs, and farm dogs. Small Spitz dogs were widely used as circus performers in the 1930s, which also broadened their public appeal. Breeders began the process of AKC recognition for the breed in 1985 and achieved that goal a decade later. It was accepted by the Canadian Kennel Club in 2006.

This is a small to medium-sized Nordic breed that is sturdy, compactly built, and covered by a voluminous double coat with a long, plumed tail carried loosely over the back. The white coat is contrasted with the breed's deep black eyes, nose, and lips. The head is wedge shaped with a broad muzzle, and the ears are erect and triangular.

English Foxhounds and Staghounds arrived with early settlers in the 1600s to hunt large game from bear to bison. Over time, these large, heavy hounds were modified to better suit American terrain and quarry. George Washington is often cited as the "father" of the breed, as dogs bred at his Mount Vernon kennel in the mid- to late 1700s were instrumental in the creation of the American Foxhound, which is a lighter, racier version of its English cousin.

This is an athletic, muscular hound with a deep chest; long, sturdy, straight legs; and a long, high-set tail that is carried in a slight curve. Its close-fitting coat is hard and protective. The moderately long, houndy head has a straight, square muzzle. The ears are long and set low, and the large, wide-set eyes in brown or hazel convey a gentle expression.

Year of AKC recognition: 1886

Group: Hound

Size: Males—22–25 inches; 65–70 pounds; females—21–24 inches; 60–65 pounds

Coat: Medium length, hard, and close

Color: The breed standard indicates "any color." Typical colors include tricolor, red and white, tan and white, and lemon and white.

Life expectancy: 11–13 years

Activity level: Moderately high. Owners must be prepared for a hound that loves to run and must provide sufficient exercise in a safe area. Foxhounds should be exercised on lead or in a safely fenced yard, as they will chase small animals and roam in search of interesting scents.

Grooming: Weekly brushing will control moderate shedding.

Temperament: Like other hounds, the American Foxhound is hardwired to search for prey. It instinctively follows, and can become preoccupied with, scents. This is a very sociable breed, equally fond of human and canine companionship. American Foxhounds are an energetic and slow-maturing breed, and owners should be prepared to provide consistent training and supervision. These dogs have a rather independent nature, and training requires patience and perseverance. Ongoing socialization will curb any tendency to be reserved toward strangers.

Parent club: American Foxhound Club (www.americanfoxhoundclub.com)

Buyers' advice from parent club: Foxhounds are bred to perform different jobs, and this will be reflected in the characteristic temperament of each particular strain. Hounds raised in a home setting tend to be more easygoing, mild tempered, and likely to get along well with children and other pets. An American Foxhound should be closely supervised with small pets until the owners are confident of the dog's behavior.

AMERICAN FOXHOUND

AMERICAN STAFFORDSHIRE TERRIER

Year of AKC recognition: 1936

Group: Terrier

Size: Males—18–19 inches, 55–70 pounds; females—17–18 inches, 40–55 pounds

Coat: Short, hard, flat, and glossy

Color: Any color—solid, parti-colored, or patched—but certain colors and combinations are discouraged in competition, namely black and tan, liver, solid white, or more than 80 percent white.

Life expectancy: 12–16 years

Activity level: High. The AmStaff has plenty of endurance and will enjoy activities done with its owners. It should be exercised on leash or in a securely fenced area.

Grooming: Weekly brushing will control moderate shedding.

Temperament: Despite the breed's formidable ancestry as a fighting dog, the AmStaff is famed for its affectionate disposition. AmStaffs are quite sociable and extremely loyal, courageous, and protective toward their families. However, these are strong, athletic dogs that must be introduced to basic training at an early age. With proper socialization, most AmStaffs can learn to accept other dogs and household pets.

Parent club: Staffordshire Terrier Club of America (www.amstaff.org); founded in 1936

Buyers' advice from parent club: Anti-dog legislation has made it illegal to own this breed in some parts of the country. Check your local ordinances before acquiring an AmStaff. Buy only from a reputable breeder. Research carefully before choosing a puppy, and consider adults and rescue dogs, which can also make fine pets.

Rescue: Information about the Staffordshire Terrier Club of America Rescue Committee is available on the parent club's Web site under "Committees."

Bulldog and terrier mixes were bred for pit fighting and bull-baiting in Britain until the country banned baiting sports in 1836. These "bull and terriers" then gained popularity as show dogs and were gradually standardized into several different breeds. The American Staffordshire Terrier descended from a bull and terrier strain bred in Staffordshire, England, where it was called the Staffordshire Bull Terrier. As the breed became established in America, it evolved into a larger, heavier type of dog and was renamed American Staffordshire Terrier, while the Staffordshire Bull Terrier remained a separate breed. The breed's athletic conformation, intelligence, and versatility made it suitable for a variety of jobs during World War I; in fact, an AmStaff named Stubby became a decorated war hero. Today, the breed excels in a variety of sports, including agility, obedience, and tracking.

This is a well-balanced, athletic dog. The AmStaff's body is muscular with a deep, broad chest and sturdy legs. The tail is short, low-set, and tapered. The head is broad, with pronounced cheek muscles, a medium-length muzzle, well-defined jaws, and a black nose. The eyes are dark, round, and wide set. The ears are set high on the skull and may be cropped or natural. The coat is hard, glossy, and close fitting.

The American Water Spaniel was developed in Wisconsin in the mid-1800s from an ancestry of Irish Water Spaniel and Curly-Coated Retriever. Because of its versatility, the breed was widely popular as a working gundog long before it was officially recognized. The American Water Spaniel is the official state dog of Wisconsin and remains popular with sport hunters, particularly in the Great Lakes region. It is one of the rarest breeds, with a population estimated at approximately 3,000 dogs.

This little brown spaniel was bred as a dual-purpose sporting dog to flush and retrieve all types of game. Its compact size makes it ideal for working in close quarters. It is a solidly built dog with rectangular  proportions, covered in a crisp water-repellent coat. The tail is tapered with moderate feathering and is carried slightly above or below the back. The ears are long and wide, and the eye color can range from light to dark brown.

Year of AKC recognition: 1940

Group: Sporting

Size: 15–18 inches; males—30–45 pounds; females—25–40 pounds

Coat: A crisp-textured, water-repellent, wavy or curly outer coat with a dense undercoat

Color: Shades of brown ranging from dark chocolate to liver, with or without a small amount of white on the toes and/or chest

Life expectancy: 10–14 years

Activity level: High. American Water Spaniels need a daily outlet for their mental and physical energy.

Grooming: The coat should be brushed weekly to prevent matting and can be trimmed occasionally for a neater appearance. The ears should be cleaned regularly. Detailed grooming information is available on the parent club's Web site.

Temperament: This is an energetic, friendly, playful spaniel that is generally easygoing and tolerant of other pets. American Water Spaniels are noted to be excellent watchdogs, but they can become overly protective and possessive if these instincts are not guided by training. They are responsive and willing to please, and they respond enthusiastically to positive training methods.

Parent club: American Water Spaniel Club (www.americanwaterspanielclub.org); founded in 1985

Buyers' advice from parent club: Choose a puppy from a breeder who screens his or her dogs for health disorders and provides a health guarantee.

Rescue: American Water Spaniel Rescue, Inc. (www.awsrescue.com)

AMERICAN WATER SPANIEL

ANATOLIAN SHEPHERD

Year of AKC recognition: 1996

Group: Working

Size: Males—29 inches, 110–150 pounds; females—27 inches, 80–120 pounds

Coat: There are two coat types: short (minimum of 1 inch long) and rough (around 4 inches long); both types have a thick undercoat. There is slightly longer hair around the neck, and there may be some feathering on the ears, legs, and tail.

Color: All colors are acceptable in conformation showing, but the traditional color is fawn (cream to red) with a black mask. Other colors include white, pinto (irregular patches of secondary color), brindle (fawn or gray marked with darker stripes), and wolf sable (a light gray undercoat with darker steel gray guard hairs that end in black tippings).

Life expectancy: 11–13 years

Activity level: Moderate. Anatolians should be exercised on lead or in a yard with at least 6-foot-tall fencing.

Grooming: Brush daily with a slicker brush during seasonal shedding in the spring and fall. Weekly brushing will control shedding at other times.

Temperament: Bred to work independently as a livestock guardian, Anatolians are dignified, calm, self-possessed house dogs. With their families, they are extremely affectionate and loyal. Anatolian Shepherds have a strong territorial and protective instinct, and they are vigilant, courageous watchdogs. As they are naturally reserved, they require ongoing training and socialization to manage their guardian instincts and ensure that they are tolerant of strangers.

Parent club: Anatolian Shepherd Dog Club of America (www.asdca.org); founded in 1970

Buyers' advice from parent club: Purchase your dog from an experienced breeder who belongs to the national parent club. Make sure that the puppy's parents are AKC-registered and have been health-tested. This breed is recommended for experienced owners with the time and physical resources to train and manage a large, strong dog.

Rescue: Anatolian Shepherd Dog Rescue League, Inc. (www.asdrl.org)

The Anatolian Shepherd originated in Turkey around 6,000 years ago. The breed was used by nomadic herders to move and protect livestock, and was selectively bred for strong working drive and hardiness, making it impervious to Asia Minor's harsh climate. Over the centuries, these dogs developed a consistent appearance, similar in size and color to the flocks they protected. This camouflage gave them an advantage in defending their flocks from predators. The Anatolian Shepherd was introduced to America in the 1950s. These dogs continue to be used as livestock guardians on small hobby farms and large working ranches, where they protect species ranging from llama to ostrich.

This big, sturdy, rugged dog is strictly functional in appearance. Its expression is calm and intelligent, characterized by dark, almond-shaped eyes; dropped ears; and a strong, blocky muzzle. The Anatolian Shepherd has a muscular, athletic appearance; rectangular proportions; long, sturdy legs; and a long tail, held high in a distinctive "wheel carriage" when alert.

After Europeans arrived in Australia, sheep and cattle became the mainstay of the Australian economy. Smithfield Collies imported from Britain proved unsuitable for the job, as they lacked stamina and weather resistance and barked excessively. Smooth merle Collies imported from Scotland in 1840 were crossed with Dingoes to produce a regional breed; these crosses were further crossed with Dalmatians and black and tan Kelpies. The blue became the more popular of the two colors, so the breed was known as the Blue Heeler, a name that is sometimes still used today.

This is a sturdy, compact dog with the stamina to work all day in the harsh conditions of Australia's vast ranches. The body is rectangular, well-proportioned, and muscular with sturdy, round bone and a  deep chest. The long, low-set tail is carried low or level with the back. The hard, weather-resistant coat is colored in red or blue with distinctive markings. The skull is broad with muscular cheeks, a broad foreface, a medium-length muzzle, and a black nose. The eyes are oval in shape, and the erect ears are wide set on the skull, moderately pointed, and very sensitive.

Year of AKC recognition: 1980

Group: Herding

Size: Males—18–20 inches; females—17–19 inches

Coat: This breed has a short, harsh, weather-resistant double coat. The outer coat is short, hard, and close; the undercoat is dense. Body hair should be around 1–1½ inches long.

Color: Blue, blue mottled, or blue speckled and may have black, blue, or tan markings. Reds are speckled all over and may have darker red markings on the head.

Life expectancy: 12–16 years

Activity level: This is a high-energy working dog that needs plenty of exercise and mental challenges. It excels in many types of dog sports.

Grooming: Weekly brushing and occasional bathing to keep the ACD neat and clean, with more frequent brushing during spring and fall shedding.

Temperament: Extremely alert, vigilant, and courageous, Australian Cattle Dogs were bred to work, and they must have a job to satisfy their need for mental and physical activity. This can range from herding livestock to chasing a Frisbee. They are wonderful family companions as long as owners are committed to training and socialization; otherwise, the breed's strong instincts can lead to problems such as herding children or other pets, nipping at heels, or barking excessively.

Parent club: Australian Cattle Dog Club of America (www.acdca.org); founded in 1968

Buyers' advice from parent club: Join a breed-related email list to learn about training and care before acquiring an ACD. Choose a puppy that has been with his dam and littermates for at least eight weeks, learning bite inhibition. Owners must continue this training to discourage inappropriate nipping and, more importantly, be willing to take the role of benevolent pack leader.

Regional clubs: Information can be found under "Regional ACD Clubs" on ACDCA's Web site.

Rescue: Australian Cattle Dog Rescue, Inc. (www.acdrescueinc.com)

AUSTRALIAN CATTLE DOG

AUSTRALIAN SHEPHERD

Year of AKC recognition: 1991

Group: Herding

Size: Males—20–23 inches, 50–65 pounds; females—18–21 inches, 40–55 pounds

Coat: Coats range from short with less undercoat to longer with feathering and a dense undercoat.

Color: Black, blue merle, red merle, and red, with or without white markings

Life expectancy: 12–15 years

Activity level: High. This breed has a strong working drive and requires daily vigorous exercise and mental challenges.

Grooming: Daily brushing with a slicker brush is needed during heavy seasonal shedding in spring and fall. Weekly brushing with a pin brush at other times will keep the coat free of dirt and tangles.

Temperament: Aussies possess the mental drive and physical stamina to work all day, and this energy can be channeled in many directions. They are intelligent, trainable, and versatile, making them excellent candidates for dog sports. Their pronounced herding instincts can get out of hand without proper training and guidance; if neglected, Aussies will become bored and frustrated, which generally leads to bad habits.

Parent club: United States Australian Shepherd Association (www.australianshepherds.org); founded in 1990

Buyers' advice from parent club: This is a demanding, high-energy breed that needs time and attention. Owners must be willing to provide outlets for their dogs' energy through regular activities such as interactive play, jogging, hiking, or organized dog sports. Before buying a puppy, prospective owners should inquire about any incidence of hereditary diseases in the line.

Rescue: Second Time Around Aussie Rescue, Inc. (www.staar.org)

Contrary to the breed's name, the Australian Shepherd didn't originate in Australia. It is generally agreed that it developed in America from dogs brought there by Basque shepherds who came from Australia in the nineteenth century. The breed was formerly known as the Spanish Shepherd, New Mexican Shepherd, or California Shepherd. After World War II, Aussies became a familiar sight at rodeos and horse shows, where their intelligence and trainability earned them widespread admiration. Aussies are still used as working ranch and farm dogs. They also excel at competitive dog sports and have been trained as guide dogs, therapy dogs, search and rescue dogs, and drug-detection dogs.

This is a sturdy, athletic, medium-sized dog with rectangular proportions and a short stub tail. Its triangular, semi-prick ears fold over at the tips, producing an attentive, intelligent expression. The moderate-length neck is strong; the back is level and firm; the chest is deep and broad; and the legs are straight and strong. The eyes are the Aussie's most remarkable feature, ranging from blue to amber to hazel to all shades of brown.

The Australian Terrier was the first officially recognized breed developed in Australia; this happened in 1868. It was created from a combination of breeds imported by settlers in the 1800s: the Yorkshire Terrier, Irish Terrier, Cairn Terrier, Dandie Dinmont, and Black and Tan Terrier. This mixture resulted in small, black-and-tan, rough-coated dogs used to control snakes and rodents and guard homesteads. Their popularity in Tasmania soon spread to the rest of the continent. The breed was exported to Britain in 1887 and came to the United States in the 1940s.

This is one of the smallest working terriers. Despite their size, Aussies are athletic, with excellent jumping and climbing skills. They are quite versatile, possessing a combination of terrier confidence and the hardiness to meet the demands of Australia's  Outback. Their rectangular proportions provide the flexibility to jump, climb, and squeeze into holes. In addition to these talents, they possess a charming, mischievous look. The small, wide-set, dark eyes; small, pricked ears; and black nose create a keen, intelligent expression that is topped by a rakish topknot of hair.

Year of AKC recognition: 1960

Group: Terrier

Size: 10–11 inches

Coat: A harsh, wire outer coat with a softer undercoat

Color: Blue and tan, solid sandy, or solid red

Life expectancy: 11–15 years

Activity level: This high-spirited, high-energy terrier needs daily activity and interaction to keep its busy mind and body occupied. Walks, jogs, and games of fetch are all ideal.

Grooming: Weekly brushing will keep the coat clean and neat. Aussies should not be bathed too frequently, as this can soften the coat. A grooming booklet is available from the national parent club.

Temperament: Aussies love outdoor adventures, but they are definitely house dogs. They need close contact with their owners as well as supervision to prevent bad habits. Without training and attention, they can become bossy and demanding. They were bred to go to ground and rout out vermin, and that strong prey drive is still present in the breed today. This not only makes them dedicated diggers but also gives them a propensity to chase small animals. They should be introduced to other dogs and pets under supervision.

Parent club: Australian Terrier Club of America (www.australianterrier.org); founded in 1957

Buyers' advice from parent club: Study the breed standard before selecting a puppy. Buy from a responsible breeder, and realize that you may need to place your name on a breeder's waiting list.

Rescue: Australian Terrier Rescue (www.australianterrierrescue.org)

AUSTRALIAN TERRIER

BASENJI

Year of AKC recognition: 1944

Group: Hound

Size: Males—17 inches, 24 pounds; females—16 inches, 22 pounds

Coat: Smooth, flat, and glossy

Color: Chestnut red, black, tricolor, and brindle. All colors may have white markings on the feet, chest, and tail tip; white legs; and a white blaze and collar.

Life expectancy: 13–14 years

Activity level: Basenjis should be exercised on lead or in a securely fenced yard. Although small, they are extremely fast runners when they take off in pursuit of prey. Their problem-solving abilities also make them talented escape artists.

Grooming: Weekly brushing will control minimal shedding. Basenjis are noted for their clean, fastidious habits.

Temperament: The Basenji is an independent hunter with sharp senses, quick reflexes, and a strong hunting drive. A Basenji needs regular mental and physical activity as well as training and ongoing socialization; these dogs may be aloof with strangers. They are resourceful problem solvers and may get into trouble if left to entertain themselves.

Parent club: Basenji Club of America (www.basenji.org); founded in 1942

Buyers' advice from parent club: Basenji puppies are available only in the spring because the breed has only one annual reproductive cycle.

Regional clubs: Information on close to twenty affiliated regional clubs can be found on the parent club's Web site under "About BCOA."

Rescue: A list of rescue volunteers can be found on the parent club's Web site by clicking on "Basenji Rescue" under "About Basenjis."

The breed originated as a general-purpose hunting dog in Central Africa; its ancestors can be traced back to ancient Egypt. Basenjis are still used for this work in the Sudan and Zaire. The breed arrived in England in 1937 and was first seen in North America the following year. The first litter born in America was produced from African imports in 1941.

This is a small, short-backed, light-boned, somewhat leggy hunter with a smooth, glossy coat and a tightly curled tail. The Basenji's wrinkled brow gives it a quizzical, worried expression. The ears are small, erect, and set well forward on the top of the flat, well-chiseled skull. The almond-shaped, obliquely set eyes range in color from dark hazel to dark brown. The Basenji is known as the "barkless dog," but it has a range of sounds, including yodeling, growling, crowing, and howling.

Short-legged scenthounds were developed in the hunting kennels of the French aristocracy, intended for the hunters to follow on foot, dating back to the sixth century. They caused a sensation when they were introduced to the British public at the earliest dog shows in the 1860s. Interest in the breed in both Britain and America led to the establishment of Basset Hound breeding programs in the late nineteenth century, and they have remained popular as hunting dogs, show dogs, and family companions.

The Basset Hound is long, low, and dignified. This is a sturdy, muscular dog with a long, straight, and level back. The chest is full; the sternum extends in front of the forelegs and is noticeable in silhouette. The breed's short,  heavy-boned legs are powerful, and the paws are massive. The long tail is carried high. A long muzzle; a large nose; distinctive loose wrinkles; and long, glossy ears characterize the Basset's large head.

Year of AKC recognition: 1885

Group: Hound

Size: Up to 15 inches

Coat: The short, hard-textured coat densely covers the Basset's distinctively loose-fitting, elastic skin.

Color: Any recognized hound color is allowed in competition; common colors in the Basset are classic tricolor (black, tan, and white), red and white, and tan and white.

Life expectancy: 12–13 years

Activity level: Moderate. Bassets have the stamina for a day in the field but also live contentedly as house pets as long as they have two or three outings a day. They will pursue prey and should be exercised on lead or in fenced areas.

Grooming: Weekly brushing will maintain the coat in good condition; bathe as needed. The Basset's long, heavy ears need weekly cleaning; they are prone to infection, as they do not allow air to circulate well. Owners should pay attention to the droopy areas around the eyes and should trim the nails regularly.

Temperament: The Basset is famed for its easygoing, good-natured demeanor. As a pack hound, it easily accepts the companionship of other dogs. Bassets are gentle and patient with children and completely devoted to their families. However, this is a scenthound, hard-wired to search for prey. Maintaining a Basset Hound's attention during training requires creativity and patience.

Parent club: Basset Hound Club of America (www.basset-bhca.org); founded in 1935

Buyer's advice from parent club: Bassets can be prone to obesity and may need some encouragement to get up and moving; be prepared to walk your Basset at least once daily to maintain a healthy weight. With their long backs and heavy bone, puppies are prone to strain and injury, so owners must take caution with growing puppies and not allow them to jump or climb during the first year.

Rescue: Information about Basset rescue can be found under "Rescue" on the BHCA's Web site.

BASSET HOUND

BEAGLE

Year of AKC recognition: 1885

Group: Hound

Size: This breed has two sizes: 13-inch Beagle—up to and including 13 inches, usually under 20 pounds; 15-inch Beagle—over 13 up to and including 15 inches, about 20–30 pounds

Coat: Short, hard, double coat

Color: The standard specifies "any hound color." Typical hound colors include tricolor (black, tan, and white), blue or liver tricolor, red and white, tan and white, and lemon and white.

Life expectancy: 10–15 years

Activity level: Moderate. Beagles should have daily outdoor exercise and interactive play. They will roam and chase small animals and must be kept on lead or in a securely fenced yard.

Grooming: Brush once or twice a week to control shedding. Bathing when shedding starts will help remove the dead hair. Regular ear cleaning and nail trimming are necessary.

Temperament: Cheerful and adaptable, Beagles get along well with other dogs and are typically friendly with people. They are quite intelligent, but hunting is their priority. The Beagle's sense of smell is second only to that of the Bloodhound. It can be challenging to keep a Beagle focused on formal training, but most Beagles enjoy dog sports, such as flyball, that give them a chance to utilize their instinctive prey drive.

Parent club: National Beagle Club (http://clubs.akc.org/NBC); founded in 1887

Buyers' advice from parent club: Purchase your dog from a reputable breeder.

Regional clubs: The National Beagle Club maintains a list of around twenty-five regional Beagle specialty clubs, as well as an extensive list of field-trial clubs, on its Web site.

Rescue: The National Beagle Club lists rescue information under "Beagle Rescue" on its Web site.

Small hounds have been bred to hunt rabbits since ancient times, and Beagles can trace their ancestry back many centuries in England. Originally, Beagles came in two varieties, rough and smooth coated, although the rough-coated Beagle eventually disappeared. These quick little hunters were equally popular in America, and type in the breed was established with the importation of quality stock from Britain in the mid-1800s. In 1888, the National Beagle Club held its first Beagle field trial. From the twentieth century on, Beagles have earned a place as one of the most popular pet breeds, therapy dogs, and detection dogs.

The Beagle is a small, sturdy hound with what the AKC standard describes as a "wear-and-tear look." The back is short and muscular, the neck is medium length, and the chest has adequate depth and breadth. The tail is high set and carried gaily, but not over the back. The muzzle is straight and square, and the nose has large, open nostrils for gathering scent. The large brown or hazel eyes and long, soft, houndy ears combine to create the sweet, gentle expression of a devoted companion.

The Bearded Collie was developed in Scotland, likely descended from Continental European herders, as a working sheepdog adapted to the cold, wet climate and rocky terrain. Beardies were first exhibited at dog shows in Victorian times, but there were no serious efforts to seek recognition for the breed until the 1950s. In 1959, the Bearded Collie was recognized in Britain, and the first American-bred litter was born in 1967.

This is a medium-sized working dog who is long, lean, and athletic, covered by a long, protective shaggy coat. The tail is long and may be carried low or level with the back. The skull is broad and flat, with hanging ears that lift slightly when the dog is alert. The eyes are large and wide set to create a bright inquiring expression. Longer hair on the cheeks, lower lips, and chin form the breed's distinctive beard.

Year of AKC recognition: 1976

Group: Herding

Size: Males—21–22 inches; females—20–21 inches; 45–55 pounds

Coat: Harsh, shaggy, flat double coat

Color: Beardies come in black, blue, brown, or fawn, and may have white and tan markings. The color typically lightens as the dog matures so that the adult Beardie can be seen in various shades of the aforementioned colors.

Life expectancy: 12–14 years

Activity level: Moderate to high. The Beardie is a dog that requires daily exercise. This is a playful, bouncy breed, but some individuals are more active than others. Their energy should be directed into structured activities, such as dog sports.

Grooming: Daily brushing will keep the coat free of mats and dirt. Many pet owners opt to have their Beardies' coats clipped for easier maintenance.

Temperament: The Bearded Collie is famed for its bouncy, carefree attitude. This is an affectionate, outgoing breed, and individual temperaments within the breed range from sweet and low-key to lively and rambunctious. Beardies respond well to positive training methods; they are sensitive to correction. They typically get along well with other pets.

Parent club: Bearded Collie Club of America (www.beardie.net/bcca); founded in 1969

Buyers' advice from parent club: Owners must be committed to grooming and tolerant of muddy pawprints and wet beards. Before buying a puppy, ask the breeder about health certifications on the puppy's parents. The parent club warns that Beardies are like peanuts—you can't stop with just one!

Regional clubs: There are seventeen regional Bearded Collie clubs listed under "Regional Clubs" on the parent club's Web site.

Rescue: Bearded Collie Club of America Beardie Rescue can be found under "Rescue" on the parent club's Web site.

BEARDED COLLIE

BEAUCERON

Year of AKC recognition: 2007

Group: Herding

Size: Males—25½–27½ inches; females—24–26½ inches; 70–110 pounds

Coat: Short double coat

Color: Black with tan markings or harlequin (blue merle with red markings)

Life expectancy: 10–12 years

Activity level: Moderate to high. Beaucerons were bred to move large flocks of sheep up to 50 miles a day. They have exceptional endurance and must have an outlet for this energy.

Grooming: Weekly brushing is recommended.

Temperament: This is a highly versatile working dog that needs both physical activity and mental challenges. Beaucerons are extremely intelligent, self-confident, and highly trainable. Training should commence early. They are sensitive and slow to mature and can be strong-willed. Owners must be prepared to provide consistent leadership. The breed has strong guardian instincts, being fiercely devoted and protective toward its family but generally aloof toward strangers. Ongoing socialization will ensure that these protective, territorial instincts are well-balanced.

Parent club: American Beauceron Club (www.beauce.org)

Buyers' advice from parent club: Buy from a reputable breeder. Meet the dam and evaluate her temperament before choosing a puppy. Owners with limited space should choose a smaller female rather than a large, energetic male. Experienced trainers seeking a dog for work or sport should take on a dominant male puppy. This is not a breed for novice owners. Beaucerons require physically active owners who are dedicated to training.

Rescue: Information on American Beauceron Club Rescue is available under "Rescue" on the parent club's Web site.

Closely related to the Briard, the Beauceron is a traditional French herding dog, developed in the La Beauce region near Paris. It is believed that mentions of the breed date back to the late sixteenth century. Beaucerons were selectively bred to possess great endurance. Originally used to drive and protect livestock, they were also trained as military and police dogs. The first national club for the breed was established in France in 1922, but Beaucerons did not become popular outside France until more recent decades, closer to the turn of the century. Today, they are also used for search and rescue work and participate in dog sports such as agility, obedience, and tracking.

This is an athletic, powerful, well-balanced dog with rectangular proportions and covered by a short, protective coat. The neck is of good length; the chest is wide and deep; the legs are straight and strong; and the feet are large and round. The long tail is carried low. The chiseled head reveals courage and confidence. The high-set ears may be natural or cropped.

The Bedlington was developed as a vermin hunter in the town of Bedlington in Northumberland, England, in the early 1800s. Possible ancestors include the Dandie Dinmont Terrier, Kerry Blue Terrier, and Whippet. The breed also became popular as a racing dog and a poaching dog. It was promoted by Lord Rothbury and was subsequently known as the Rothbury Terrier or Rothbury Lamb at one point in its history. Britain's Bedlington Terrrier Club was founded in 1877. In America, the breed attracted fanciers including the Rockefeller family, who owned some of the breed's prominent show dogs of the time.

The breed's lamblike appearance is deceiving. This is a well-balanced, athletic dog with a lithe, graceful outline, similar to a sighthound. The back has a distinctive arch, and the front legs are set close together at the feet and wider apart at the elbows,  giving the front a triangular appearance. This unique construction enables the dog to sprint and pivot on a dime. The tail is long, low set, and scimitar shaped. The head is described as pear shaped. The jaw is proportionally longer than the skull, which is topped with a thick, curly topknot. The eyes are small, bright, and almond shaped, and the ears are long and low set, with tasseled tips. The outline of the body is evident beneath the thick, curly coat.

Year of AKC recognition: 1886

Group: Terrier

Size: Males—16–17½ inches; females—15–16½ inches; 17–23 pounds

Coat: A mix of hard and soft hair results in a coat that is crisp to the touch and typically curly.

Color: The breed's colors include blue, sandy, liver, blue and tan, sandy and tan, and liver and tan. Puppies are born darker and fade to a lighter color as they mature.

Life expectancy: 11–16 years

Activity level: Moderate. Bedlingtons need daily exercise, especially interactive play. They also do well in dogs sports such as agility, earthdog, and obedience.

Grooming: The coat should be brushed and combed twice a week, and trimmed professionally every eight weeks. The coat sheds only minimally.

Temperament: Game and tenacious, the Bedlington lives up to its terrier heritage. The breed is also prized for its fun-loving, people-loving, cheerful disposition. Bedlingtons are quite intelligent and adaptable, and they respond well to positive training. If bored or neglected, they can develop bad habits such as digging, excessive barking, or chasing small animals.

Parent club: Bedlington Terrier Club of America (www.bedlingtonamerica.com); founded in 1936

Buyers' advice from parent club: Buy from a reputable breeder. Choose a puppy from lines that are health-tested.

Regional clubs: There are four regional clubs listed under "Resources" on the parent club's Web site.

Rescue: Bedlington Terrier Club of America Rescue can be found under "Rescue and Placement" on the parent club's Web site.

BEDLINGTON TERRIER

BELGIAN MALINOIS

Year of AKC recognition: 1959 (registered as Belgian Sheepdogs from 1911 until 1959)

Group: Herding

Size: Males—24–26 inches, 60–80 pounds; females—22–24 inches, 40–60 pounds

Coat: Short, hard, double coat

Color: Body color ranges from fawn to mahogany, with black tipping, black mask, and black ears

Life expectancy: 14–16 years

Activity level: High. The Malinois is an agile dog that enjoys doing things with its owner, such as jogging, hiking, and interactive play.

Grooming: The coat needs daily brushing during seasonal shedding in spring and fall. Weekly brushing will control shedding at other times.

Temperament: Malinois have a strong working drive. Along with regular physical activity, this highly intelligent breed thrives on mental challenges such as dog sports or advanced obedience training. Loyal, devoted, and courageous, these dogs bond strongly to their owners and make excellent watchdogs. However, they can become protective and territorial without ongoing socialization. Personalities can range from aloof to bold. Malinois require confident owners who are mindful of the breed's sensitive nature.

Parent club: American Belgian Malinois Club (www.malinoisclub.com); founded in 1978

Buyers' advice from parent club: This breed is not recommended for novice owners. Owners should be prepared for the breed's intense personality. Malinois require plenty of training, socialization, and daily interaction with their families.

Rescue: American Belgian Malinois Club Rescue (www.malinoisrescue.org)

Over the centuries, several types of working sheepdogs were developed in France and Belgium. The Malinois evolved in the region of Malines, Belgium, where it became noted for exceptional strength and stamina. The breed was imported into the United States before World War I and shown in the AKC's Miscellaneous Class until it was fully recognized in 1959. Malinois have excelled as working military dogs, being used as messenger dogs, as ambulance dogs, and for other tasks.

The Belgian Malinois is a sturdy, well-balanced, agile dog, ready for action. The breed is moderately heavy boned, stands squarely on its feet, and carries itself proudly. The topline is level, and the chest is deep, with a smooth, graceful curve from chest to abdomen. The tail is long enough to reach the hock and is carried in a curve. The strong, clean-cut head; triangular, erect ears; and dark, almond-shaped eyes reveal the breed's thoughtfulness and intelligence.

The Belgian Tervuren, Belgian Malinois, and Belgian Sheepdog were originally grouped together as three varieties of Belgian Sheepdog. The long-coated black variety originated in the late 1800s. It became known as the Groenendael, named after the kennel that was mainly responsible for breeding this variety. In addition to herding and guarding livestock, Belgian Sheepdogs were used on World War I battlefields as messenger dogs, ambulance dogs, and draft dogs. Today, they are used for search and rescue and as guide and therapy dogs. The AKC separated the varieties and approved separate standards for the Malinois, Tervuren, and Belgian Sheepdog in 1959.

The Belgian Sheepdog is a well-balanced, moderately heavy-boned dog with a square outline, covered by a gleaming black coat. Its long tail is heavily coated and reaches to the hock. The top of the skull is flattened and the head is clean-cut and  strong, with medium-sized, triangular, erect ears; a black nose; dark brown eyes; and an alert, intelligent, questioning gaze.

Year of AKC recognition: 1911

Group: Herding

Size: Males—24–26 inches, 55–75 pounds; females—22–24 inches, 45–60 pounds

Coat: The breed has a long, straight, abundant outer coat with an extremely dense undercoat. The Belgian Sheepdog's weather-resistant coat makes the breed adaptable to temperature extremes.

Color: Black. A small amount of white is permitted in competition.

Life expectancy: 12–14 years

Activity level: High. Belgian Sheepdogs need vigorous daily exercise in the form of interactive play and activities such as swimming, dog sports, and hiking.

Grooming: The breed needs regular weekly brushing with a slicker brush. The coat should be brushed more often during seasonal shedding, which lasts about a week in the spring and fall.

Temperament: Belgian Sheepdogs require a great deal of personal attention. They adapt well to life as house dogs but do not cope well in a kennel environment. They have a strong protective instinct and make excellent watchdogs. Noted for their intelligence, they learn quickly and respond well to positive training methods. They will become bored and frustrated without daily exercise and attention.

Parent club: Belgian Sheepdog Club of America (www.bsca.info); founded in 1949

Buyers' advice from parent club: Owners should be prepared for a very smart, very active dog. Never underestimate the Belgian Sheepdog's intelligence and intuitiveness. Develop and maintain a good working relationship with your breeder and your veterinarian and join a Belgian Sheepdog club to continue your education.

Regional clubs: Contact information for nine regional breed clubs can be found on the parent club's Web site under "Regional Clubs."

Rescue: Belgian Sheepdog Rescue Trust (www.bscarescue.com)

BELGIAN TERVUREN

Year of AKC recognition: 1959 (registered as Belgian Sheepdogs from 1911 until 1959)

Group: Herding

Size: Males—24–26 inches, 55–75 pounds; females—22–24 inches, 45–60 pounds

Coat: This breed has a moderately long, protective double coat of straight guard hairs and a dense undercoat. Males tend to have more abundant furnishings than females.

Color: Fawn to mahogany with black tipping and a black mask

Life expectancy: 12–14 years

Activity level: High

Grooming: Daily brushing is needed during heavy shedding in the spring and fall; brushing twice weekly is advised at other times.

Temperament: This is an intelligent, devoted, versatile working dog. Highly adaptable and trainable, Tervs excel at police work and obedience. They can be possessive and demanding of attention, but it is generally agreed that they have a great sense of humor.

Parent club: American Belgian Tervuren Club (www.abtc.org); founded in 1960

Buyers' advice from parent club: This is an active breed and not the dog for everyone. The ideal Terv owner wants a dog that can be trained for a variety of challenges.

Regional clubs: Under "Area Clubs" on the parent club's Web site are links to eleven regional breed clubs.

Rescue: Belgian Tervuren Rescue, Inc. (www.belgiantervurenrescue.com)

Several varieties of Belgian Shepherd became popular in the late nineteenth century. The Tervuren takes its name from the Belgian village where the breed was originally developed for both herding and protection work; it soon became equally prized as a companion dog. Interest in the breed outside France and Belgium developed after World War II. The AKC registered its first Terv in 1918 as a variety of Belgian Sheepdog. The breed was not classified separately from the Belgian Sheepdog until 1959. Today Tervs compete in a wide range of dog sports. They also work as service dogs and therapy dogs in addition to serving their original purpose as herding dogs. The AKC's first Herding Champion was a Belgian Tervuren.

This breed is medium-sized, squarely built, sturdy, and elegant. The coat is dense and protective, with longer hair on the neck, backs of the forelegs, hindquarters, and  tail. The head is carried proudly and the long tail is raised. The well-set triangular ears and dark brown eyes create an intelligent, inquisitive expression.

One of the four varieties of Swiss Mountain Dog, the Bernese Mountain Dog was developed in the canton of Bern, Switzerland, as an all-purpose farm dog, draft dog, and watchdog. For years, the breed was largely neglected in its homeland until Franz Schertenleib and Albert Heim made efforts to revive it in the 1890s. The first club was formed in Switzerland in 1907. The breed was first imported to America in 1926.

A large, handsome dog, the Berner is sturdy, balanced, and athletic. It has slightly rectangular proportions and sturdy bone, making it ideally suited to the demands of farm work. Other distinctive features include a long, bushy tail; round, compact feet; and a tricolor coat. The head is characterized by a flat, broad skull; dark brown, oval-shaped eyes; high-set triangular ears that hang close to the head; a black nose; and an animated, gentle expression.

Year of AKC recognition: 1937

Group: Working

Size: Males—25–27½ inches, 80–115 pounds; females—23–26 inches, 70–95 pounds

Coat: The moderately long, thick coat is straight to slightly wavy.

Color: Tricolor—black with rust and white markings

Life expectancy: 7–10 years

Activity level: Moderate. Berners are quiet and well mannered indoors, but they must have daily outdoor activity. Owners must keep exercise limited in hot weather.

Grooming: Brush daily during shedding in the spring and fall and twice weekly at other times.

Temperament: Berners possess the typical temperament of a steady, reliable working dog. They are gentle, intelligent, self-confident, and quite responsive, which makes them good candidates for advanced training. They are naturally vigilant and protective and should have ongoing socialization and training to discourage dominant or protective tendencies. Today the breed is used for herding, carting, therapy work, agility, obedience, and rally.

Parent club: Bernese Mountain Dog Club of America (www.bmdca.org); founded in 1968

Buyers' advice from parent club: Research the breed and breeders carefully before purchasing a puppy. The Bernese Mountain Dog Club of America maintains a list of breed stewards who can advise prospective owners and novice owners on care, health, and training. Reputable breeders pay close attention to health issues, and they screen their dogs for inherited conditions. Contact several breeders and spend time talking to them before selecting a puppy.

Regional clubs: The BMDCA's "Regional Clubs" page lists over twenty-five breed clubs throughout the United States.

Rescue: Information on Bernese Mountain Dog rescue is available under "Rescue" on the parent club's Web site.

BICHON FRISE

Year of AKC recognition: 1972

Group: Non-Sporting

Size: 9½–11½ inches

Coat: The breed is famed for its plush, curly double coat, made up of a soft undercoat and a coarser outer coat. The coat is springy to the touch and stands away from the body, giving the dog a "powderpuff" appearance.

Color: White. A small amount of buff, cream, or apricot shading is permitted in competition.

Life expectancy: 14-15 years

Activity level: Moderate. Bichons enjoy long walks and interactive play.

Grooming: Daily brushing and combing are needed; visit a groomer once a month for bathing and trimming.

Temperament: Bichons are cheerful, playful, and highly sociable, but they must have regular socialization to develop confidence. They are quick learners but are quite sensitive and cannot tolerate harsh training methods. Bichons are meant to be companions, and their families are very important to them. They love to spend time with their people.

Parent club: Bichon Frise Club of America (www.bichon.org); founded in 1964

Buyers' advice from parent club: This is considered to be a very healthy breed if purchased from a reputable breeder.

Regional clubs: There are fifteen regional breed clubs listed on the "National and Local Clubs" page under "Bichon Frise Information."

Rescue: Bichon Frise Club of America Rescue Effort (www.bichonrescue.org)

Originally known as the Bichon Tenerife, the breed originated in the Mediterranean, where it likely developed from early water spaniels. It first gained popularity in the fourteenth century as a prized pet of Italian nobility and then spread to France in the fifteenth century, where it met with similar favor. It remained a favorite aristocratic companion and performing dog into the nineteenth century. After World War I, four French breeders established foundation breeding programs to document Bichon lineage, and the breed was recognized in France in 1934. The breed began gaining popularity in America in the late 1950s. Since AKC recognition in 1972, Bichons have been consistently popular as pets and show dogs. They also distinguish themselves in dog sports and therapy work.

This is a small, sturdy, rectangular dog whose hallmark traits are a plush, white, powderpuff coat; a plumed tail that is carried over the back; a jet-black nose; and sparkling black eyes. The expression is soft, inquisitive, and alert. The neck is long and arched; the back is level; and the chest is well developed.

The Black and Tan Coonhound traces its ancestry back to the scenthounds of medieval Europe. Foxhounds and Bloodhounds imported to America before the Revolutionary War were used to develop a hound to hunt possum and raccoon in the Ozark and Smoky Mountain regions. This is a versatile breed, and today Black and Tans are used to hunt many types of game.

This is a hardy trail and tree hound, athletic and moderately built, with a smooth-fitting, glossy black-and-tan coat. The head is cleanly modeled, with an oval-shaped skull. The shoulders are powerfully constructed; the back is strong

and level; and the legs are strong and well boned. The breed has a friendly, alert expression; brown eyes; long, low-set ears; and a long tail that is carried high when on the move.

Year of AKC recognition: 1945

Group: Hound

Size: Males—25–27 inches; females—23–25 inches; 65–110 pounds

Coat: Short, hard, and dense

Color: Coal black with rich tan markings above the eyes, on the sides of the muzzle, and on the chest, legs, and breeches. There are black pencil markings on the toes.

Life expectancy: 10–12 years

Activity level: Moderate. Black and Tans are well-behaved house dogs as long as they have adequate daily exercise. They love long walks, but they have a strong prey drive and will follow interesting scents, chase small animals, and roam if not leashed or securely fenced.

Grooming: Five to ten minutes of brushing three times per week will minimize shedding, and regular bathing is needed to eliminate houndy odor.

Temperament: Individual temperament can range from outgoing to aloof, but as a rule, Black and Tan Coonhounds have the characteristic easygoing nature of scenthounds. They are gentle, calm, and tolerant, and typically get along well with other dogs. They are quiet house dogs but have a strong prey drive and may not be trustworthy with small pets. Their territorial instinct and deep bark make them excellent watchdogs. They are extremely intelligent and superb problem solvers; these traits may complicate training. Black and Tan Coonhounds do things their own way.

Parent club: American Black and Tan Coonhound Club (www.abtcc.com); founded in 1973

Buyers' advice from parent club: Take time to educate yourself about the breed and search for a healthy, well-bred puppy.

Rescue: American Black and Tan Coonhound Rescue Inc. (www.coonhoundrescue.com)

BLACK AND TAN COONHOUND

BLACK RUSSIAN TERRIER

Year of AKC recognition: 2004

Group: Working

Size: Males—27–30 inches; females—26–29 inches; 80–130 pounds

Coat: Slightly wavy double coat from 1½–6 inches in length with longer facial furnishings

Color: Black

Life expectancy: 10–12 years

Activity level: Moderate. BRTs need two half-hour-long exercise sessions daily. They enjoy walking, hiking, jogging, swimming, interactive play, and dog sports. They are not very tolerant of heat or being exercised in hot weather.

Grooming: Brush and comb thoroughly once a week; trimming or professional grooming every four to eight weeks, depending on coat length, is recommended. A grooming DVD is available from the parent club.

Temperament: The Black Russian Terrier was selectively bred for intelligence and trainability. This is an alert, confident dog; a loving and devoted family dog; and a fearless, determined watchdog. As this is a large, powerful breed, ongoing training and socialization are essential. The breed's strong guardian instincts begin to emerge during adolescence and become more pronounced by maturity. Without guidance, this trait can result in an overly protective dog. BRTs must have plenty of attention and human companionship. BRTs are not always reliable with other dogs, and they should be supervised with young children.

Parent club: Black Russian Terrier Club of America (www.brtca.org); founded in 1997

Buyers' advice from parent club: This breed is recommended for experienced owners. Buy only from a breeder who has done health clearances on his or her dogs. You must be prepared for a dog that will snore, track in dirt, and require crating when guests or repairmen come into your home. Join the BRTCA to learn more about the breed.

Rescue: Black Russian Terrier Rescue (www.brtrescue.org)

The Black Russian Terrier was developed after World War II in Russia as an all-purpose, hardy, trainable military and police dog that could withstand the Russian climate. The breed was created at the state-operated Red Star Kennel in Moscow, and seventeen breeds contributed to the BRT's ancestry, including the Giant Schnauzer, Airedale Terrier, Rottweiler, and Newfoundland. Black Russian Terriers started to be bred privately in 1956, and an official standard was published in 1958. The breed gradually gained a following in Eastern Europe and was exported to America in the 1980s.

The Black Russian Terrier is a large-boned, muscular dog with slightly rectangular proportions and a high-set tail that may be long or docked. This is a self-assured, powerful dog that moves with a strong, ground-covering gait. The breed's head emphasizes the overall impression of power and strength. It has a wide skull and a broad muzzle, which is further accentuated by the moustache and beard; the large, black nose; and medium-sized, high-set, triangular ears.

The Bloodhound was developed in medieval Europe from a combination of ancient Greek and Roman hounds brought to France by returning Crusaders. The breed's ancestor, the St. Hubert's Hound, dates back to the seventh century. Bloodhounds were carefully bred and kept "pure-blooded," which is thought to have led to the breed's name. Bloodhounds were used for centuries to trail game. Today, the Bloodhound is acknowledged as the premier scenthound, making it a favorite of police departments and search and rescue teams.

This is a big, powerful hound. Its most notable feature is its solemn, dignified expression, created by a combination of deep-set eyes; long, low-set ears; and deep folds of loose skin over the head and neck. The head is narrow and long; the neck is long; and the chest forms a deep keel. It is a well-proportioned dog with good muscling and sturdy bone. On the move, the long tail is carried high.

Year of AKC recognition: 1885

Group: Hound

Size: Males—25–27 inches, 90–110 pounds; females—23–25 inches, 80–100 pounds

Coat: Short, hard, and flat

Color: Black and tan, liver and tan, and red

Life expectancy: 7–9 years

Activity level: Moderate to high. Although Bloodhounds are sometimes portrayed as slow and lazy, this is not true! In contrast, this is a working dog with exceptional strength and stamina to tirelessly follow scent trails for miles. Puppies especially require a great deal of daily exercise. Bloodhounds must be supervised outdoors because they can climb over or dig under many fences.

Grooming: Weekly brushing will maintain the coat. Clean and check the long ears regularly.

Temperament: Bloodhounds are noted for their gentle, easygoing nature. They typically get along well with other dogs and enjoy the company of most people. However, following scents will always be their priority. They will wander and roam if not leashed or securely fenced. Keeping them focused for formal training can be challenging, which can make them seem stubborn at times. This is a sensitive, slow-maturing breed that requires patience and perseverance from owners.

Parent club: American Bloodhound Club (www.bloodhounds.org); founded in 1952

Buyers' advice from parent club: Visit as many breeders as possible. Discuss your expectations with your breeder and ask to see the puppy's parents. Puppies should not go to new homes before they are ten to twelve weeks old. Bloodhounds can be high-maintenance pets. They drool and track mud into the house, and puppies require a great deal of exercise.

Regional clubs: Information on seven regional breed clubs is listed on the parent club's Web site under "The Club."

Rescue: The parent club lists rescue-group information on its Web site under "Where Can I Get One?"

BLOODHOUND

BLUETICK COONHOUND

Year of AKC recognition: 2009

Group: Hound

Size: Males—22–27 inches, 55–80 pounds; females—21–25 inches, 45–65 pounds

Coat: Short, glossy, hard, and protective

Color: The body coat is dark blue mottled with white, and there are black spots on the back, ears, and sides. A Bluetick may have tan points over the eyes, on the cheeks, on the chest, and below the tail, and may have red ticking on the feet and legs.

Life expectancy: 11–12 years

Activity level: High. This is a high-energy hound that requires room to run. Like other scenthounds, the Bluetick Coonhound will wander or chase if allowed off lead in an open area.

Grooming: Occasional bathing and brushing are recommended.

Temperament: This is a steady, athletic working dog that must have daily mental and physical challenges in the form of hunting, dog sports, or another activity. A slower, determined worker, it is sometimes compared to a rangy Bloodhound. Blueticks are very intelligent, with great problem-solving ability. They are gentle and affectionate and typically friendly toward people and other dogs, but they are not recommended for homes with cats or small pets. The breed is famed for its bugle voice.

Parent club: American Bluetick Hound Association

Buyers' advice from parent club: Choose a dog from a line that is AKC registered and from a breeder who belongs to a national club and is knowledgeable about the breed. This breed can be a lot of work. Blueticks must have access to a large yard and have plenty of socialization and human companionship.

Developed in America, the Bluetick Coonhound was bred to trail and tree raccoons. It is descended from a combination of English Foxhounds and French Staghounds (Grand Bleu de Gascogne) that were imported centuries ago to hunt American game. These breeds were later refined and specialized for the American climate, terrain, and game. Unlike in other coonhound breeds, many traits of the French hound ancestry were preserved in Bluetick Coonhounds, which had been classified as English Coonhounds until 1945.

The breed takes its name from the unusual dark blue ticking of its coat. This is a muscular, athletic hound—compact, well built, and covered in a glossy coat. Its long tail is carried high in a half-moon curve. It has a broad, slightly domed head; a long, broad muzzle; a large black nose; large, wide-set, round eyes; and long, thin, low-set ears.

Originally known as the Scotch Sheepdog, the breed was developed from local strains of drover dogs along the border of England and Scotland, hence the eventual name Border Collie. Documentation of dogs resembling Border Collies dates back to the mid-1800s. They were selectively bred for working ability, trainability, and stamina. The breed entered the AKC's Miscellaneous Class in 1955 and gained full recognition forty years later. Intelligent, athletic, and focused, today the Border Collie is considered among the premier breeds for dog sports.

This is a medium-sized, well-muscled dog with balance, good bone, and a smooth, pleasing outline. Its athletic conformation is matched by its keen expression, which is produced by wide-set, oval-shaped eyes and sensitive, mobile ears. When working, the Border Collie is noted for its distinctive style of crouching with the head down and the tail carried low or level with the back.

Year of AKC recognition: 1995

Group: Herding

Size: Males—19–22 inches; females—18–21 inches

Coat: Rough and smooth varieties, each with a dense, weather-resistant double coat. The coarser outer coat may be straight or wavy; the undercoat is soft, short, and dense. The rough coat is medium length with feathering on the forelegs, haunches, chest, and underside. The smooth coat is short and slightly coarser with slight feathering in these areas.

Color: Most prevalent is black with white markings, but all colors or combinations are allowed in competition except solid white. This includes solid colors, bi- and tricolors, merle, and sable.

Life expectancy: 12–15 years

Activity level: Very high. A fenced yard is essential. However, running in a fenced yard is not sufficient exercise for a dedicated working dog like this.

Grooming: Weekly brushing, with more frequent brushing during times of seasonal shedding.

Temperament: The Border Collie is considered one of the most intelligent breeds, but this doesn't mean a minimal need for training. Border Collies are strong-willed and easily bored. They observe and analyze everything they encounter, are extremely reactive to sound and movement, and have a strong herding instinct. Provide consistent training, socialization, and plenty of personal attention, as Border Collies are very devoted and want to be included in every activity. They also can be quirky, moody, and territorial and tend to be reserved toward strangers. They should be introduced to other dogs under supervision.

Parent club: Border Collie Society of America (www.bordercolliesociety.com); founded in 1993

Buyers' advice from parent club: Find a responsible breeder who selects dogs for health, herding instinct, temperament, and soundness.

Regional clubs: BCSA affiliate clubs can be found on the BCSA's Web site under "Club Info."

Rescue: The BCSA Rescue Program is on the club's Web site under "Rescue."

BORDER COLLIE

BORDER TERRIER

Year of AKC recognition: 1930

Group: Terrier

Size: Males—13–15½ pounds; females—11½–14 pounds

Coat: A harsh, wiry outer coat with a short, dense undercoat

Color: Red, grizzle and tan, blue and tan, and wheaten

Life expectancy: 12–15 years

Activity level: Moderate to high. Border Terriers are working dogs with plenty of energy and stamina. They need daily activity, but they must be exercised on lead or in a fenced yard, as they will run off in pursuit of small animals. Fencing may be reinforced to prevent them from digging underneath.

Grooming: Weekly brushing is advised. The wire coat should be stripped twice a year to maintain its harsh, protective texture.

Temperament: The breed is inquisitive, intelligent, and quite affectionate while also possessing the typical determination and hardiness of terrier breeds. These dogs may be compatible with cats and other dogs, but introductions should be closely supervised.

Parent club: Border Terrier Club of America (www.btcoa.org); founded in 1949

Buyers' advice from parent club: Research the breed carefully before purchasing a dog, as the Border Terrier can be a wonderful companion but is not the breed for everyone. For example, owners must be aware that Border Terriers shed, bark, and dig. Joining a local breed club is an excellent way to meet other Border Terrier fanciers and find information on care and training.

Regional clubs: The BTCOA lists information for eleven regional clubs on its Web site under "US Regional Clubs." There are also pages for Canadian and international breed clubs.

Rescue: North American Border Terrier Welfare (www.borderterrierrescue.com)

The breed was developed along the border of England and Scotland and is considered one of Britain's oldest terriers. Bred to hunt vermin, they had to be rugged, resourceful, and small enough to squeeze into a foxhole but large enough to keep up with a horse. Today the breed excels in earthdog, obedience, agility, flyball, and rally. Border Terriers also work as therapy dogs.

This is a medium-sized terrier with moderate bone, a rather narrow build, and a close-fitting, hard, wiry coat. The tail is moderately short and tapered. The breed is noted for its distinctive "otter head"—a broad, flat skull; full cheeks; and a short, well-filled muzzle with distinctive whiskers. The ears are small and lie close to the cheeks; the eyes are dark and full of fire with a look of implacable determination.

The Borzoi was developed to hunt wolves and big game and has been maintained by Russian nobility for centuries. The breed became popular as pets and show dogs in Britain and America in the nineteenth century and was known as the Russian Wolfhound in the United States until 1936. Today, they are companions, show dogs, and therapy dogs, and they compete in a variety of dog sports, including obedience, agility, lure coursing, and tracking.

The hallmark traits of this large, powerful sighthound are its unmistakable elegant outline and long, aristocratic head. The Borzoi is built to run, with powerful running gear. Its flexible

back allows it to sprint and turn in response to a quarry's evasive maneuvers. The profuse coat and long tail add another touch of glamour to the breed's look.

Year of AKC recognition: 1891

Group: Hound

Size: Males—28 inches and up, 75–105 pounds; females—26 inches and up, 60–85 pounds

Coat: Long and silky; not woolly. Hair is flat, wavy, or curly. The coat is shorter and smooth on the head, ears, and fronts of legs, and longer and heavier on the neck, body, and hindquarters. The hair on the tail is long and profuse.

Color: All colors and combinations

Life expectancy: 9–14 years

Activity level: Moderate. Borzoi must be exercised on lead or in a fenced area and supervised carefully, as they have a strong drive to chase prey and can climb over and dig under fences. Borzoi are sensitive to heat and must be kept cool in summer.

Grooming: Daily brushing will minimize shedding. Borzoi do not need frequent bathing.

Temperament: This is a strong, energetic hound as well as a slow-maturing breed. Borzoi are independent and can be stubborn, so keeping them focused on training requires patience, creativity, and a good sense of humor. This is a very sensitive breed; they do not tolerate harsh training methods. Puppies need supervision and a structured routine. Obedience training is essential; choose a trainer who has experience working with sighthounds. Borzoi should be supervised around small dogs and cats, and they are not recommended for homes with birds and small pets.

Parent club: Borzoi Club of America (www.borzoiclubofamerica.org); founded in 1903

Buyers' advice from parent club: Research the breed carefully. Visit dog shows to meet Borzoi and talk to breeders, or contact a local Borzoi club or rescue group for detailed information on the breed. A reputable breeder is the only source from which you should buy a puppy.

Regional clubs: The Borzoi Club of America lists fourteen American clubs and one Canadian club under "Regional Clubs" on its Web site.

Rescue: National Borzoi Rescue Foundation, Inc. (www.nbrf.info)

BORZOI

BOSTON TERRIER

Year of AKC recognition: 1893

Group: Non-Sporting

Size: The breed has three weight ranges: under 15 pounds, 15 to under 20 pounds, and 20 to 25 pounds.

Coat: Short, smooth, fine-textured, and close-fitting.

Color: Black, brindle, or seal (black with a red cast) in combination with the breed's typical white markings.

Life expectancy: 11–13 years

Activity level: Low to moderate. Bostons require regular activity, but this is not an outdoor breed. They are sensitive to both hot and cold weather.

Grooming: Weekly brushing will maintain the coat.

Temperament: Dapper and charming, the Boston has earned the nickname of "American Gentleman." Personalities within the breed range from energetic to sedate. Bostons are sensitive, so gentle training is essential. This is a first-class companion dog that is also noted for its versatility. Bostons are vigilant watchdogs and wonderful therapy dogs, and they excel at many dog sports, including agility and flyball. They are generally good with other pets.

Parent club: Boston Terrier Club of America (www.bostonterrierclubofamerica.org); founded in 1891

Buyers' advice from parent club: Study the official breed standard. Choose your breeder carefully and buy only from a reputable breeder.

Regional clubs: Affiliate club information is listed on the parent club's Web site under "The BTCA."

Rescue: Boston Terrier Club of America Rescue information is located on the parent club's Web site under "About Bostons."

This is one of America's native breeds, created from a combination of Bulldogs and White English Terriers imported to Massachusetts after the Civil War. Fanciers originally sought to have their breed recognized as the American Bull Terrier. They regrouped as the Boston Terrier Club of America in 1891, and two years later the first American breed was accepted into the AKC studbook.

The Boston has the sturdiness and determination of its Bulldog and terrier forebears. It is lively, spirited, and compactly built, with a clean-cut, square outline and a short, low-set tail. The short muzzle; broad jawline; and large, round, wide-set eyes create an alert, intelligent expression. Ears are small and erect, either natural or cropped. The breed is distinctively marked with a white muzzle band, white blaze between the eyes, white forechest, and white on the forelegs and hindlegs below the hocks.

The Bouvier was developed in Belgium as an all-purpose farm dog with ancestors that include local sheepdogs and water dogs. The Royal Society of St. Hubert in Belgium took note of the breed when M. Paret of Ghent exhibited a male and a female at a show in Brussels. The breed was revived after World War I by Captain Barbry's dog Nic, to whom most European pedigrees can be traced. The first breed standard was drawn up for the Bouvier in 1912 in its homeland, and the Bouvier was first seen in the United States in the 1920s.

This is a big, sturdy, short-coupled dog with strong bone; a rugged, shaggy coat; and a high-set, short, docked tail. Its head is accentuated by an impressive beard and mustache; a broad muzzle; powerful jaws; a large, black nose, and keen, oval-shaped eyes.

Year of AKC recognition: 1931

Group: Herding

Size: Males—24½–27½ inches; females—23½–26½ inches; 70–110 pounds

Coat: A combination of a rough, harsh outer coat and a soft undercoat that is fine but dense. The double coat protects the dog in all types of weather.

Color: Shades ranging from fawn to black, including salt and pepper, gray, and brindle

Life expectancy: 10–12 years

Activity level: Moderate to high. This is a calm, well-behaved house dog, but it is also a working breed, and adequate daily exercise is essential. A Bouvier should have thirty minutes of exercise three or four times per day.

Grooming: Brush the coat twice a week to prevent matting. The beard should be washed daily.

Temperament: The Bouvier was developed for working ability and versatility. The breed standard describes it as "steady, resolute, and fearless." Bouviers are quick learners and vigilant watchdogs. They can be strong willed and do best with confident owners. Bouviers have been used to pull carts, drive cattle, and guard livestock and homes. They also have a distinguished record as guide dogs for the blind, police dogs, and war dogs. The breed also competes in herding events, agility, tracking, and obedience.

Parent club: American Bouvier des Flandres Club (www.bouvier.org); founded in 1963

Buyers' advice from parent club: Purchase your Bouvier from a breeder and confirm that the puppy's parents have been health-tested. A Bouvier needs confident owners who sincerely want to share their lives with a devoted canine companion and are prepared to devote time to training.

Rescue: American Bouvier Rescue League (www.abrl.org)

BOUVIER DES FLANDRES

BOXER

Year of AKC recognition: 1904

Group: Working

Size: Males—23–25 inches, 65–80 pounds; females—21½ to 23½ inches, about 15 pounds less than males

Coat: Short, shiny, and lying smooth and tight to the body

Color: Fawn or brindle, with or without white markings

Life expectancy: 10–12 years

Activity level: Moderate to high. The Boxer should be exercised on leash or in a securely enclosed area.

Grooming: Weekly brushing is recommended; bathe as needed.

Temperament: A guard dog by instinct, the Boxer is keen and alert, but perhaps its most remarkable trait is its need for human companionship and to be part of the family. The Boxer is confident and dignified yet playful and affectionate with its people. It is initially wary of strangers but seems to have the ability to distinguish friend from foe and will respond in like manner to those it deems friends. Bred as a working dog, the Boxer is intelligent, trainable, and loyal—a desirable companion.

Parent club: American Boxer Club (www. americanboxerclub.org); founded in 1935

Buyers' advice from parent club: Locate breeders at local dog shows or through the national breed club. When purchasing a puppy, the breeder should provide you with a three- or four-generation signed pedigree; the AKC registration application, which you will use to register the puppy; vaccination and worming records; and information and advice on the puppy's current diet and future feeding.

Regional clubs: There are over fifty regional clubs in the United States, listed on the parent club's Web site under "US Clubs."

Rescue: The parent club has a list of "Boxer Rescue-Related Web sites," which can be found under "Information" on the club's home.

Developed in Germany in the late nineteenth and early twentieth centuries, Boxers became successful cattle dogs and butcher's dogs. The breed may have derived its name from its propensity to use its front feet in a playful way, suggesting its title as the "middleweight athlete of dogdom." The breed first came to America after World War I, and the breed's foundation in the United States was based on dogs of top-quality German breeding from the famous Von Dom kennels of Friederun Stockmann.

The Boxer is a medium-sized, well-muscled dog of square proportions, good substance, and overall elegance, with a short back; strong, straight legs; and energetic, ground-covering movement. The high-set tail is docked and held up. The Boxer is known for having an expressive face, with soulful, dark brown eyes and a wrinkles on the forehead when the dog is alerted to something; the overall expression is described as "intelligent and alert." The muzzle is blunt, making up one third of the head's total length, and the jaw is undershot. The nose is black, and the ears are high set and usually cropped.

The Boykin Spaniel was developed by hunters in South Carolina in the early twentieth century as an all-around hunting dog to flush and retrieve game. The breed's foundation sire was found as a stray in Spartanburg, South Carolina. The dog, christened Dumpy, displayed exceptional talent as a waterfowl retriever and was given to "Whit" Boykin, who mated him to another small spaniel of unknown origin. The Chesapeake Bay Retriever and other spaniel breeds were also used to develop the Boykin Spaniel. The breed was designated as the official state dog of South Carolina in 1984.

This is a no-nonsense versatile hunting dog characterized by a neat, compact body; slightly rectangular proportions; moderate bone; and a waggy spaniel tail.

Eyes are a shade of brown, the nose is fully pigmented in dark liver, and the hanging ears lie close to the cheeks. All features of the head combine to give the Boykin an alert, smart, and confident expression.

Year of AKC recognition: 2009

Group: Sporting

Size: Males—15½–18 inches, 30–40 pounds; females—14–16½ inches, 25–35 pounds

Coat: This breed has a medium-length outer coat with a short, dense undercoat. The outer coat can be flat to wavy, and there is feathering on the legs, ears, and belly.

Color: A solid shade ranging from liver to chocolate brown

Life expectancy: 10–15 years

Activity level: Moderate. Boykins should have daily exercise to maintain proper weight and condition.

Grooming: The coat should be brushed weekly. Hunting dogs can be clipped to minimize damage from burrs and foxtails. A Boykin should not be bathed more than once a month.

Temperament: Loving and affectionate, Boykins make great family pets. They are friendly, sociable, and inquisitive and are enjoyable and entertaining companions. This breed is not recommended as a watchdog. Boykin Spaniels have a strong natural hunting aptitude, but as this is a slow-maturing breed, they require training to become good hunting dogs

Parent club: Boykin Spaniel Club and Breeders Association of America (www.boykinspanielclub. org); founded in 1997

Buyers' advice from parent club: Do not buy impulsively. Meet several breeders, look at many dogs, and choose a puppy from lines that have been health-tested. Temperament and personality vary within the breed. Check out the sire, dam, and other related dogs to get an idea of the puppy's personality.

Regional clubs: Information can be found on the parent club's Web site under "Local Boykin Clubs."

Rescue: Boykin Spaniel Rescue (www. boykinrescue.org)

BOYKIN SPANIEL

BRIARD

Year of AKC recognition: 1928

Group: Herding

Size: Males—23–27 inches; females—22–25½ inches

Coat: The outer coat is coarse, hard, healthy looking, and dry. It is slightly wavy and lays flat. The undercoat is fine and tight. The hair on the head forms a natural middle part, and the hair of the eyebrows partially veils the eyes.

Color: Black, shades of gray, and shades of tawny

Life expectancy: Around 12 years

Activity level: Moderately high. Briards are agile and energetic, requiring regular exercise, but they are calm house dogs. They do well in sports such as obedience, tracking, herding, flyball, and agility.

Grooming: At least two hours per week brushing and combing to minimize matting and shedding.

Temperament: The Briard is an excellent companion and home guardian. It is a quiet, adaptable house dog as long as its exercise needs are met. Briards remain quite playful throughout their lives, and they want attention and to be included in all of their people's activities. They are naturally territorial and protective, so early and ongoing socialization is strongly encouraged. Briards are reserved with strangers but can become excessively wary without regular socialization. They can also be headstrong, so obedience training should commence early. Briards learn best with consistent, positive training methods. The breed is highly intelligent and can learn to understand around 200 words.

Parent club: Briard Club of America (www. briardclubofamerica.org); founded in 1928

Buyers' advice from parent club: Research the breed thoroughly before purchasing a puppy. Owners must be prepared to give a puppy plenty of attention, love, and training from the outset.

Regional clubs: There are seven regional clubs listed under "Regional Clubs" on the BCA's Web site.

Rescue: Briard Club of America Rescue Trust (www.briardrescuetrust.org)

The Briard's ancestry dates back to the eighth century in France. It is reported that both Charlemagne and Napoleon kept Briards. The breed was used in medieval France as a general-purpose working dog and later became better known as a flock guardian and herding dog, specifically after the French Revolution. It's not certain whether the Marquis de Lafayette or Thomas Jefferson first introduced the breed to the United States, as both brought Briards to America around the same time in the late 1700s. It's even been suggested that Lafayette gave Jefferson two Briards as gifts. At that time, America's growing wool industry created a demand for reliable flock guardians, and the Briard proved to be an excellent choice. The breed is still used for herding and guarding in France and America but is also prized for its companion qualities.

This is a powerful, well-muscled dog with good bone and a long, protective, shaggy coat. Its well-feathered, long tail has a distinctive J-shaped crook at the tip, and the hind legs have double dewclaws. In motion, the Briard has the look of gliding. The head gives the impression of length, made up of two rectangles: the skull and the muzzle. The eyes are large and dark, with dark pigmentation; the ears are high set, thick, and firm, either cropped or uncropped, and covered with long hair. The square-shaped nose is black.

The Brittany takes its name from the French province where the breed originated. Early in the twentieth century, the spaniel type developed in Brittany was crossed to English pointing dogs, which intensified the breed's pointing ability. They were first introduced to America in the 1940s and quickly became popular with hunters. The breed was registered with the AKC as the Brittany Spaniel until 1982.

Year of AKC recognition: 1934

Group: Sporting

Size: 17½–20½ inches, 30–40 pounds

Coat: The coat is dense, either flat or wavy, with a small amount of feathering on the legs.

Color: Orange and white or liver and white in a clear or roan pattern. Tricolored dogs (liver and white with orange markings) are sometimes seen.

Life expectancy: 12–14 years

Activity level: High. This is an energetic, athletic breed. Brittanys can become hyperactive or develop bad habits without regular exercise. If you don't plan to hunt with your Brittany, try hiking, jogging, or dog sports.

Grooming: Brushing and combing twice a week is recommended.

Temperament: This is an extremely versatile breed, equally popular as a hunting dog and a house pet. Brittanys also excel in competitive dog sports. Noted for their sweet, friendly dispositions, Brittanys get along well with people and other dogs. This is primarily a people-oriented breed, willing to please and easy to train. Personalities range from rather aloof and calm to very outgoing and intense.

Parent club: The American Brittany Club (www.theamericanbrittanyclub.org); founded in 1942

Buyers' advice from parent club: This is not an outdoor breed, and it does not fare well in a kennel environment. Before buying a puppy, look at the parents and close relatives to gauge basic temperament. Only buy from a reputable breeder.

Regional clubs: Over eighty breed clubs are listed on the parent club's Web site on the "Find a Regional Club" page under "Inside the ABC."

Rescue: American Brittany Rescue (www.americanbrittanyrescue.org)

The Brittany is a compact, square, medium-sized dog. It is leggy and moves with a long, free stride. The Brittany appears square, as the height at shoulders equals the length of its body. The neck is of medium length; the chest is deep, reaching the elbows; the back is short and straight; and the feet are small, with well-arched toes. Some dogs are naturally short tailed; others are docked.

BRUSSELS GRIFFON

Year of AKC recognition: 1910

Group: Toy

Size: 8–12 pounds

Coat: There are both rough and smooth coat types. The rough coat is hard, dense, and wiry. The smooth coat is short, flat, glossy, and close fitting.

Color: Red, black and tan, black, belge (mixture of black and reddish brown, usually with a black mask and whiskers)

Life expectancy: 12–15 years

Activity level: Moderate. Brussels Griffons do not require a lot of exercise, but they should have daily walks or interactive play to stay fit.

Grooming: Maintain the coat by brushing twice a week.

Temperament: This is an extremely devoted house dog. Griffons require a great deal of personal attention. They can be wary with strangers, which makes them excellent watchdogs, but they can become introverted without ongoing socialization. They are quite courageous and will not hesitate to confront larger dogs, so careful supervision is essential at dog parks. They are intelligent and trainable but are known to have a stubborn streak. Owners should approach training with patience and a sense of humor. Brussels Griffons have proven their mettle in most dog sports.

Parent club: American Brussels Griffon Association (www.brussels-griffon.info); founded in 1945

Buyer's advice from parent club: This is a sensitive, affectionate, long-lived breed. Be prepared for a twelve- to fifteen-year commitment. Crate training is highly recommended. The club maintains a referral guide of breeders, groomers, and veterinarians on its Web site.

Rescue: National Brussels Griffon Rescue, Inc. (www.brusselsgriffonrescue.org)

The breed was developed in Brussels, Belgium, from the local stable dogs, known as Griffons D'Ecurie, and breeds including the Affenpinscher, Pug, and English Toy Spaniel. Initially, the two coat varieties were registered separately as the Griffon Bruxellois (rough coat) and Griffon Brabancon (smooth coat). The Brussels Griffon became extremely popular as a pet and show dog in the early 1900s, and was first registered with the AKC in 1910. The first specialty for the breed in the United States was in 1918.

This is a compact, toy-sized dog with square proportions and sturdy bone. The high-set tail is docked short and carried high. The breed has a jaunty, self-important attitude and is especially renowned for its almost human expression. The head is large and round, the forehead is domed, and the prominent lower jaw has a distinctive upward sweep. The eyes are large, black, prominent, and wide set with long, black eyelashes. The small, high-set ears can be cropped or natural.

The Bull Terrier was developed as a fighting dog from a combination of Bulldog, the extinct White English Terrier, and several other breeds. After dog fighting was banned in Britain, this smart-looking dog easily transitioned to become a popular show dog. The Colored Bull Terrier was developed through crosses with brindle Staffordshire Bull Terriers and became classified as a separate AKC variety in 1936. The Bull Terrier is a fixture of popular culture. In addition to advertising beer and department stores, the Bull Terrier has been showcased as Bodger, the wandering Bull Terrier in *The Incredible Journey* and as General Patton's beloved pet, Willie. Willie was at Patton's side throughout World War II, and a statue commemorating both Patton and Willie can be seen at the General Patton Memorial Museum.

This is a sturdy, well-balanced, muscular dog with plenty of bone and muscle but never coarse. It has a long, muscular neck and a broad chest. The feet are round and compact, and the tail is fairly short, low-set, tapered, and carried level with the back. The head is the breed's most distinctive feature, described as "egg shaped" in profile; there is a gentle convex curve from the top of the skull to the tip of the nose, and the jawline is strong and well defined. The dark eyes are small, obliquely set into the head, and triangular. The ears are small, high set, and held erect.

Year of AKC recognition: 1885

Group: Terrier

Size: Not specified in the standard, but many are in the range of 21–22 inches and 50–70 pounds

Coat: Short, flat, harsh, and glossy

Color: There are two varieties: White and Colored. Brindle is preferred in the Colored variety, but any color other than white or any color with white markings is permitted in competition.

Life expectancy: 12–13 years

Activity level: Moderate. This is an active, agile dog, with surprising strength and endurance.

Grooming: Maintain the coat with weekly brushing.

Temperament: The standard describes the Bull Terrier as having a "sweet disposition" but also "full of fire." Friendly, affectionate, and willing to please, Bull Terriers are famed for their sense of humor. They are also strong willed and can be possessive with food and toys. Guarding behavior should be discouraged in puppies.

Parent club: Bull Terrier Club of America (www.btca.com); founded in 1887

Buyers' advice from parent club: This is a slow-maturing breed. Bull Terriers often behave like puppies until around age three.

Regional clubs: Information on approximately thirty clubs is listed under "Regional Clubs" from the parent club's home page.

Rescue: Bull Terrier Club of America Rescue Committee is located under "Rescue" on the parent club's Web site.

BULL TERRIER

BULLDOG

Year of AKC recognition: 1886

Group: Non-Sporting

Size: Males—50 pounds; females—40 pounds

Coat: Short, flat, glossy, and smooth

Color: The Bulldog's colors are preferred in the following order in the show ring: red brindle; other shades of brindle; white; red, fawn, or fallow (cream to light fawn); and piebald (large patches of two or more colors).

Life expectancy: 8–10 years

Activity level: Low. Bulldogs have a low tolerance for heat and should not be exercised in hot weather. They are poor swimmers and must be carefully supervised around water.

Grooming: Bulldogs should be brushed weekly, and their facial wrinkles must be cleaned daily. They must be trained to accept regular grooming at a young age, as an uncooperative Bulldog will make routine chores such as brushing, ear cleaning, and nail trimming nearly impossible.

Temperament: Despite its formidable appearance, the Bulldog is described in the breed standard as "kind" and "pacific" along with "resolute and courageous." Personalities range from reserved to outgoing, but as a rule, Bulldogs are easygoing and affectionate dogs. They can be stubborn, though, so training should begin early. Bulldogs respond best to short, positive training sessions.

Parent club: Bulldog Club of America (www.thebca.org); founded in 1890

Buyers' advice from parent club: Bulldog owners should be prepared to keep their dogs in air-conditioned environments.

Regional clubs: There are around sixty local Bulldog clubs, organized into eight divisions by the BCA, whose information is listed on the BCA's Web site on the "Histories of Divisions and Clubs" page under "The Club."

Rescue: Bulldog Club of America Rescue Network (www.rescuebulldogs.org)

England's national breed was perfected over many centuries for the unsavory sport of bull-baiting. Bulldogs abruptly declined in popularity when baiting sports were banned in Britain in 1835, but within a few decades, this beloved breed found a new niche as a companion and a show dog, and they remain one of the most popular breeds in America. The Bulldog is the official mascot of the US Marine Corps as well as of many American schools and universities, and is one of the most recognizable breeds.

The Bulldog is a massive, low-slung dog with sturdy, heavy-boned legs; a short neck; a broad chest; and a short tail. The head is large, with a flattened muzzle; a broad, square, upturned lower jaw; wide-set eyes; small, high-set, typically "rose" ears; and a resolute, dignified expression.

The Bullmastiff was developed in its present form from a combination of 40 percent Bulldog and 60 percent Mastiff. The breed was first known as the "gamekeeper's night dog," and it came to prominence in the mid-1800s as a deterrent to poachers on large estates. The breed was recognized in Britain in 1924 and ten years later in the United States.

This is a powerfully built, squarely proportioned, substantial dog with a wide, deep chest and a keen, alert expression. The tail is set high and tapers to the hocks; it can be straight or curved. The head is large, with well-developed cheeks; a flat forehead; a broad, deep muzzle; and characteristic wrinkles when alert. The eyes are dark, and the small ears lie close to the head.

Year of AKC recognition: 1934

Group: Working

Size: Males—25–27 inches, 110–130 pounds; females—24–26 inches, 100–120 pounds

Coat: Short, flat, dense, protective coat

Color: Red, fawn, or brindle, each with a black mask

Life expectancy: 7–9 years

Activity level: Moderate. They should have daily outdoor activity, but they cannot tolerate hot weather. This is a territorial guard-dog breed that should be exercised in a fenced area and never permitted to roam.

Grooming: Weekly brushing

Temperament: The Bullmastiff has the courage and confidence of a guardian combined with the affectionate, devoted nature of a loving companion. Bullmastiffs do well in many dog sports, such as obedience, agility, tracking, and carting, and also make excellent therapy dogs. This is a slow-maturing breed. Puppies can be rambunctious, and early training and socialization are essential. Bullmastiffs learn quickly, but they are sensitive, and harsh training methods will backfire.

Parent club: American Bullmastiff Association (www.bullmastiff.us)

Buyers' advice from parent club: Typical pet-care costs are usually higher for large breeds like the Bullmastiff. Owners should have a strong commitment to training and socialization, and they should consider an adult or rescue dog if not prepared to cope with the demands of raising a Bullmastiff puppy. Breed mentors can be found through the parent club's Web site to advise novice owners on care and training.

Regional clubs: Fifteen regional clubs are listed on the parent club's Web site under "Regional Clubs."

Rescue: American Bullmastiff Association Rescue is located under "Rescue" on the club's Web site.

CAIRN TERRIER

Year of AKC recognition: 1913

Group: Terrier

Size: Males—10 inches, 14 pounds; females—9 ½ inches, 13 pounds

Coat: A harsh, wiry outer coat with a short, soft undercoat.

Color: Any color except white

Life expectancy: 13–15 years

Activity level: Moderate. Although they are active and playful, Cairns are versatile and easily adapt to an urban lifestyle. This is a hardy breed with a strong predatory drive; Cairns must be exercised on lead or in a fenced yard.

Grooming: The low-shedding coat needs thorough brushing and combing once a week. Hand stripping will maintain the coat's proper texture. Some Cairns suffer from flea allergies, so special attention must be paid to keeping them flea-free. A grooming booklet is available from the parent club.

Temperament: Personalities range from gregarious to dignified, but overall the breed is noted for its gameness and spirit. Cairns are self-assured, inquisitive dogs and can become bossy or possessive of food and toys if owners fail to maintain house rules. Cairns were bred to work independently and are noted for their intelligence and problem-solving skills. However, to be happy, a Cairn must be part of the family. Cairns should have jobs to do, and the breed excels at obedience, agility, earthdog, and tracking. If bored or neglected, a Cairn may resort to digging and barking. Cairns are not suited to living outside.

Parent club: Cairn Terrier Club of America (www.cairnterrier.org)

Buyers' advice from parent club: Choose a puppy from a conscientious breeder and trust the breeder to help you choose a puppy that will suit your lifestyle. Many owners say that the only thing better than owning a Cairn is owning two.

Regional clubs: The CTCA lists eleven regional clubs on its Web site under "Affiliate Clubs."

Rescue: The CTCA provides rescue information on its Web site under "Rescue Contacts."

The Cairn Terrier's history traces back to working terriers of Scotland that were used for hunting, vermin control, and companionship. Wirehaired terriers were exhibited at Britain's early dog shows as Scotch Terriers. Gradually, multiple variations were separated into the Scottish, West Highland White, and Skye Terrier breeds. For several years, Cairns were shown as shorthaired Skye Terriers until they were officially recognized as a separate breed in 1912. The breed was recognized by the AKC the following year. Most Americans were first introduced to the breed by Toto from *The Wizard of Oz.*

The Cairn is a rugged, no-nonsense working terrier, sturdy, well proportioned, and covered with a hard, weather-resistant coat. The Cairn is short-legged and strong but not heavily built, with a medium-length, level back and a feathered tail that balances the head. The breed's head is shorter and wider than that of other terriers. Wide-set eyes, shaggy eyebrows, and small, pointed, erect ears produce a keen and foxy expression.

The Canaan Dog, also known as the Kelev K'naani, was developed from the pariah dog, which has existed for thousands of years and was used as a guard and herding dog by the Israelites. As the Israelites were displaced, many of these feral dogs took up residence in the Negev Desert, where they lived for centuries. Dr. Rudolphina Menzel domesticated the breed from this feral stock in the 1930s. Canaan Dogs were bred and trained to be Israeli military dogs, and a breeding program was established to train them as guide dogs. They were first seen in America in 1965, with the arrival of four Canaan Dogs, and the breed was admitted to the AKC's Miscellaneous Class in 1989. Today, in the United States, they compete in agility, herding, and obedience.

This is a medium-sized, moderately built, athletic, graceful dog with square proportions and a bushy tail carried over the back. The head is wedge shaped with a tapered muzzle and a  slight furrow between the brows. The low-set ears are carried erect, and the eyes are dark and almond shaped. The Canaan Dog's expression is watchful and inquisitive.

Year of AKC recognition: 1997

Group: Herding

Size: Males—20–24 inches, 45–55 pounds; females—19–23 inches, 35–45 pounds

Coat: The harsh, flat, straight outer coat is ½–1½ inches in length. The undercoat is straight, soft, short, and flat, and of varying density. The coat is longer on the ruff, back of thighs, and tail.

Color: There are two color patterns. The first is white with a mask, with or without patches on the body. The mask is the same color as the body patches and covers the eyes and ears, sometimes the entire head. The second is solid colored—black or any shade of brown, some with white trim.

Life expectancy: 12–15 years

Activity level: Moderate. A Canaan Dog needs two long walks per day.

Grooming: Brush weekly to maintain the coat.

Temperament: The Canaan Dog is only recently descended from desert pariah dogs, having been developed into a breed around the time of World War II. This is a breed molded by natural, rather than artificial, selection, with pronounced canine instincts. Canaan Dogs are alert and cautious, with keen senses, and are vigilant about protecting their territory. They are very loyal and affectionate toward their families, but they may become overly protective without consistent socialization. They are typically reserved with strangers and may not get along well with other dogs of the same sex. They are not recommended for homes with small pets. Canaan Dogs are intelligent, inquisitive, and easily trained. Their naturally clean habits make them easy to house-train. They respond best to short, positive training sessions.

Parent club: Canaan Dog Club of America (www. cdca.org); founded in 1965

Buyers' advice from parent club: This is an extremely rare breed. Approximately fifteen to twenty litters are born in the United States each year, and potential buyers may wait up to a year for a puppy. Consider an older dog or rescue dog.

Rescue: Canaan Dog Rescue Network (www. canaandogrescue.com)

CANE CORSO

Year of AKC recognition: 2010

Group: Working

Size: Males—25–27½ inches; female—23½–26 inches

Coat: Short, stiff, shiny, and dense with a light undercoat

Color: Colors include black, shades of gray, shades of fawn, and red; the latter two have a black or gray mask. Brindling may be seen in any of these colors.

Life expectancy: 9–12 years

Activity level: Moderate. A Cane Corso must have daily exercise but should never be left unattended in a yard for long periods.

Grooming: The coat should be brushed weekly.

Temperament: This is a guardian breed with strong territorial and protective instincts. It is quiet, docile, and affectionate, but can become bossy if the owners do not establish themselves as pack leaders from the start. Puppies must have extensive early training and socialization to become tolerant, well-mannered adults. Owners must provide firm, consistent training with treats and rewards while the puppy is still small and manageable. The breed is sensitive, and harsh training methods will not get results.

Parent club: Cane Corso Association of America (www.canecorso.org)

Buyers' advice from parent club: Potential buyers must research the breed and breeders carefully, shop wisely, and not buy on impulse. This is a large, dominant dog and not the breed for everyone.

Rescue: Cane Corso Rescue (www.canecorsorescue.org)

This is an Italian molosser breed. Its ancestors were used as hunting, guard, and farm dogs throughout Italy, particularly in the south. The breed suffered a decline during and after the two World Wars, but a small group of breeders began to revive the breed in the 1970s, eventually leading to breed recognition in Italy in 1994. The Cane Corso was first imported to America in 1988.

This is an athletic, muscular, large-boned dog with rectangular proportions. Well balanced and with substantial bone, the Cane Corso is courageous, self-confident, and majestic in demeanor. It has a slightly arched neck; a broad, muscular chest; and a wide, strong, level back. The tail is carried horizontally or slightly above the back and can be docked or undocked. The head is large, broad, and square when viewed from the top, with a broad, square muzzle that is equal in width and length. There is some wrinkling on the forehead. Medium-sized, almond-shaped eyes contribute to the breed's alert, attentive expression. The ears may be cropped or uncropped. Cropped ears are triangular and erect, while uncropped ears are carried near the cheeks.

Descended from the Teckel family of dogs, from which the Dachshunds also came, Cardigans were brought to Wales by Celtic tribes more than 3,000 years ago. Over the centuries, they were used for general purpose farm work, guarding, and flushing game. They became famed for their ability to drive cattle by nipping at their hocks, and the term 'corgi' came into usage in the 1920s to describe these long and low "heelers." In 1925, the Cardigan and its cousin, the Pembroke Welsh Corgi, were shown at British dog shows as the same breed; the breeds were split in 1934. The first two Cardigans were imported to the United States in 1931.

"The Corgi *with* a tail" is a long, low-set dog with the appearance of power and endurance. It is moderately heavy boned, with a deep chest and a long, low-set tail. The skull is moderately wide and flat, and the tapered muzzle is slightly shorter than the length of the skull. The Cardigan's watchful expression is produced by its trademark large, erect ears and wide-set eyes.

Year of AKC recognition: 1935

Group: Herding

Size: 10 ½–12½ inches; males—30–38 pounds; females—25–34 pounds

Coat: The outer coat is medium length, smooth, harsh, and weather resistant. The undercoat is short and dense. The coat is somewhat shorter on the ears, head, and legs, and longer and thicker on the ruff, back of the thighs, and underside of the tail.

Color: All shades of red, sable, and brindle; black with or without tan or brindle points; and blue merle (black and gray marbled). White markings are common.

Life expectancy: 12–15 years

Activity level: Moderate. Cardigans must have exercise, whether daily walks on lead or romps in a nearby field or just play around the house and yard. They can become expert ball-chasers. Young pups should not be allowed to jump down, given their heavy front assemblies. Cardigans excel in herding trials, tracking, agility, and obedience.

Grooming: Brush daily during twice-annual shedding; brush weekly at other times.

Temperament: The Cardigan is even-tempered, loyal, and affectionate. It is an adaptable breed that is very attentive to its owners and quick to learn commands and manners. Nonetheless, Cardigans have an independent nature and the fleet-footed mental acuity of a herding dog. The parent club's Web site states, "A big dog in a small package….who wants to be truly involved with his family….He is full of fun and will shower that family with devotion and sensible affection…"

Parent club: Cardigan Welsh Corgi Club of America (www.cardigancorgis.com)

Buyers' advice from parent club: Great care is warranted when buying a puppy. A responsible, knowledgeable breeder is your only puppy source.

Regional clubs: Nine regional breed clubs are listed on the CWCCA's Web site under "The Club/Regional Clubs."

Rescue: Cardigan Welsh Corgi National Rescue Trust (http://cardiganrescue.org)

CARDIGAN WELSH CORGI

CAVALIER KING CHARLES SPANIEL

Year of AKC recognition: 1995

Group: Toy

Size: 12–13 inches, 13–18 pounds

Coat: This breed's coat is moderate in length and silky, ranging from straight to slightly wavy, with longer feathering on the ears, chest, legs, feet, and tail.

Color: Blenheim (white with chestnut markings), Tricolor (white with black markings and tan points), Ruby (solid red), Black and Tan (black with tan markings)

Life expectancy: 12–15 years

Activity level: Moderate. Some Cavaliers will chase small animals and should be exercised on lead or in a fenced yard.

Grooming: Brush twice a week; the ears must be cleaned frequently.

Temperament: Cavaliers are very sociable, adaptable, willing to please, and easy to train. Their cheerful nature and trainability make them naturals at dog sports, such as agility and obedience, as well as wonderful therapy dogs. This is a family companion who gets along with people and other animals alike.

Parent club: American Cavalier King Charles Spaniel Club (www.ackcsc.org); founded in 1994

Buyers' advice from parent club: Because of the breed's popularity, potential owners must research diligently to find a reputable breeder. It is unwise to answer ads in the newspaper or on the Internet listing puppies for sale.

Regional clubs: Information for approximately thirty regional clubs are listed on the parent club's Web site on the "Regional Clubs" page under "The Club."

Rescue: American Cavalier King Charles Spaniel Rescue Trust (http://www.cavalierrescuetrust.org)

The Cavalier descended from Britain's English Toy Spaniel, which was one of the most popular breeds in the late nineteenth century. In the 1920s, a group of breeders began selecting for a more moderation, crossing English Toy Spaniels with other spaniel and toy breeds to revive a type seen centuries earlier. This type was a little larger in size, with a longer muzzle and a less-domed head. In 1928, a club was formed in Britain to promote this new type, and it was recognized there as the Cavalier King Charles Spaniel in 1944. The first Cavaliers were seen in America in 1952.

The Cavalier possesses the hallmarks of its sporting spaniel ancestors. It is athletic and well balanced, with slightly rectangular proportions; a long, arched neck; a level back; and a very happy tail that is carried level with the back. The breed is distinguished by its gentle, sweet expression, produced by a combination of large, round, wide-set eyes; long spaniel ears; a full muzzle; and a black nose.

The Cesky Terrier was created by Czech breeder Frantisek Horak in 1949 with the goal of producing a terrier that was ideally suited to the terrain and hunting conditions of Bohemia. The breed was developed by mating a Sealyham Terrier male to a Scottish Terrier female, with later infusion of Sealyham blood to increase the gene pool. The Cesky Terrier was recognized by Europe's Fédération Cynologique Internationale in 1963. The first Cesky Terriers arrived in America in 1987 from the Netherlands.

The Cesky is a sturdy, agile, short-legged breed that is longer than tall. It has a muscular body; a round chest; a well-muscled, slightly arched neck; and a backline that rises over the loin  and rump. The legs are short, straight, and well boned, with large, well-arched feet. The tail is 7–8 inches long and carried down or in a saber shape. The head is shaped like a long, blunt wedge and is accentuated with a bushy beard, mustache, and eyebrows. The ears are medium sized, dropped, triangular, and set high on the head. Almond-shaped eyes give the Cesky a friendly expression.

Entered Miscellaneous Class in 2008

Size: 10–13 inches, 14–24 pounds

Coat: Long, fine hair with slightly wavy furnishings

Color: Puppies lighten as they mature to reach any shade of gray by two or three years old.

Life expectancy: 12–15 years

Activity level: Moderate. Cesky Terriers must have daily exercise and interaction with their owners, but the breed is noted to be less energetic and excitable than many other terriers. They do well in agility, earthdog, rally, and tracking.

Grooming: Adults should be brushed at least twice a week, bathed every few weeks, and trimmed every three to five weeks. Puppies should be brushed daily. Detailed grooming information and clipping instructions are available on the parent club's Web site.

Temperament: The Cesky was bred to hunt above and below ground. It has a balanced, adaptable temperament and a good hunting instinct. Ceskies are not aggressive and are less excitable than some other terriers, but they may not tolerate small pets. While keen, alert hunters, they are generally calm, well-behaved house dogs. They adapt well to a range of lifestyles, but they are intensely devoted to their owners and must have plenty of personal attention. They are somewhat independent and reserved toward strangers and can be somewhat stubborn; they need plenty of socialization and training. They respond well to food rewards and should be trained using only positive-reinforcement methods.

Parent club: American Cesky Terrier Fanciers Association (www.ceskyterrierfanciers.com); founded in 2004

Buyers' advice from parent club: Be prepared for an intelligent terrier that needs attention, exercise, and play. Also be prepared to groom your Cesky properly and to deal with terrier traits, such as strong jaws that will destroy any chew toy.

Rescue: Information on the American Cesky Terrier Fanciers Association's Rescue Team is available under "Rescue and Placement" on the club's Web site.

CHESAPEAKE BAY RETRIEVER

Year of AKC recognition: 1878

Group: Sporting

Size: Males—23–26 inches, 65–80 pounds; females—21–24 inches, 55–70 pounds

Coat: The Chessie has a protective double coat. The outer coat is harsh, wavy, and oily, up to 1½ inches in length. The undercoat is dense, fine, and woolly. The coat is shorter and straighter on the face and legs, with moderate feathering up to 1¼ inches long on the tail and hindquarters.

Color: Shades of brown, sedge (red), and deadgrass (tan). The Chesapeake's color should blend in with its working environment.

Life expectancy: 10–13 years

Activity level: High. This is a working dog with great stamina. Along with hunting and dog sports, Chessies enjoy hiking, swimming, and jogging.

Grooming: The Chessie needs weekly brushing and bathing every three or four months.

Temperament: Chessies are noted for their hardiness and water-retrieving skills. They are loyal and affectionate companions and willing workers, but they can become overly assertive and willful if training is neglected. This is a versatile breed that does well in most dog sports.

Parent club: American Chesapeake Club (amchessieclub.org); founded in 1918

Buyers' advice from parent club: Owners must be prepared to commit to the basics of training, adequate attention and interaction, and ongoing socialization with people and animals.

Rescue: Rescue information can be found on the parent club's Web site under "ACC Rescue Network."

The Chesapeake Bay Retriever is one of America's native breeds, and its development was one of history's lucky accidents. In 1807, a British ship was wrecked off the Maryland coast. Along with the crew and cargo, two Newfoundlands were rescued and ultimately presented as gifts to the crew's rescuers. Over the years, these exceptional water retrievers were bred to local stock around the Chesapeake Bay, and these matings provided the breed's foundation stock.

The Chesapeake Bay Retriever is a powerful, moderately sized dog, with the instinct, intelligence, agility, and stamina to retrieve from land or water. It is slightly rectangular in proportion with sturdy bone; a deep chest; a short, strong back; and a medium-length tail. The breed's most distinctive feature is its short, harsh, waterproof coat. The skull is broad and round, with long, powerful jaws. The eyes are widely set and range in color from yellow to amber, producing an intense, intelligent expression.

The Chihuahua came to public attention in the late nineteenth century when Americans became fascinated with tales of the Wild West. One of the earliest Chihuahua breeders was Owen Wister, author of the first western, *The Virginian*. Like other Chihuahua fanciers of the age, he acquired his dogs from undocumented sources while traveling along the borders of Mexico, Texas, and Arizona. Many believe that the breed's ancestors date back to the ancient Toltec and Mayan civilizations. Early Chihuahuas varied tremendously in size, coat length, and general appearance. In 1952, the Long Coat Chihuahua became the last AKC recognized breed to receive separate variety status.

The Chihuahua is a hardy, well-balanced dog with slightly rectangular proportions. Despite its small size, it is sturdy, with a well-developed chest, a level back, and a moderately long tail that is carried up, out, or over the back. Its round, "apple-domed" skull is balanced by a moderately short, tapered muzzle. The eyes are full, widely set, and luminous; the ears are large and erect. The expression is described as "saucy."

Year of AKC recognition: 1904

Group: Toy

Size: Not exceeding 6 pounds

Coat: There are two varieties. The Smooth Coat has a flat, smooth, and close-fitting coat, with or without undercoat. Hair on the tail is furry. The Long Coat has a flat or slightly curly coat, with longer hair on the ears, tail, feet, legs, and neck.

Color: All colors and markings

Life expectancy: 14–16 years

Activity level: Low to moderate. Running around the house generally provides sufficient exercise for Chihuahuas, but they enjoy daily walks and play.

Grooming: Weekly brushing and monthly bathing are required for Smooth Coats. Long Coats should be brushed and bathed more frequently to keep the coat clean and free of mats and tangles; trim as needed. Both varieties need regular nail clipping.

Temperament: The AKC standard describes this breed as "terrier-like," and ideally, the Chihuahua is fearless and self-assured. Chihuahuas are extremely intelligent dogs with strong natural instincts; many have a pronounced prey drive. They are also quite courageous and extremely devoted and protective, making excellent watchdogs. This can get them into trouble, though, as a Chihuahua will not hesitate to take on a possum, raccoon, bigger dog, or burglar. Owners must be prepared to step in to prevent altercations with dangerous adversaries. The small size intensifies the need for training and socialization. Because of its size, a Chihuahua can become defensive, shy, or excessively clingy if not consistently and positively socialized.

Parent club: Chihuahua Club of America (www.chihuahuaclubofamerica.com); founded in 1923

Buyers' advice from parent club: Study the breed standard. Attend dog shows to meet breeders and see their dogs. Find a reputable breeder and visit personally to see the dogs, especially the sire and dam of the puppy. The puppy should be curious, energetic, and confident.

Rescue: CCA Rescue information is available on the club's Web site under "Breed Info."

CHIHUAHUA

CHINESE CRESTED

Year of AKC recognition: 1991

Group: Toy

Size: 11–13 inches, 8–12 pounds

Coat: The Hairless variety is the only long-coated hairless breed, with soft, silky hair on the head, tail, feet, and rear hock joints. Hair may be on the face and ears. The skin is smooth and soft on the hairless parts of the body. The Powderpuff variety has a silky double coat that covers the entire body.

Color: All colors and combinations

Life expectancy: 13–18 years

Activity level: Moderately low. Cresteds need daily exercise in the form of walks, interactive play, or running in a fenced yard. Fencing must be secure, as Cresteds can easily jump a 3-foot fence and climb chain link like monkeys. They have a high tolerance for hot weather, but are extremely sensitive to cold.

Grooming: The Hairless Crested's hair should be brushed with a pin brush two or three times per week and bathed every one to two weeks. Excess body hair should be removed regularly to keep the skin clean and healthy. Powderpuffs must be brushed every two or three days to prevent matting. Shorter pet trims will minimize grooming.

Temperament: The Chinese Crested is a companion, traditionally used as a comfort dog. Cresteds bond strongly to their owners but are typically reserved with strangers. They can become shy or defensive without training and socialization. Cresteds are extremely attuned to social interaction and receptive to training. They learn quickly but are also top-class opportunists. Owners must ignore unwanted behavior.

Parent club: American Chinese Crested Club (www.chinesecrestedclub.info); founded in 1979

Buyers' advice from parent club: Find a breeder in your area and screen him or her carefully.

Regional clubs: Twelve regional clubs are listed on the parent club's Web site on the "Regional Clubs" page under "Getting a Chinese Crested."

Rescue: Information is on the club's Web site on the "Rescue" page under "Getting a Chinese Crested."

The Chinese Crested's primary trait, hairlessness, is a legacy of its Xoloitzcuintli ancestry. The trait can be traced through canine history for thousands of years, and Crested-type dogs have been documented since the nineteenth century. The breed was developed and stabilized primarily in the United States in the twentieth century.

The Crested is a small, fine-boned, elegant dog with rectangular proportions. The back is level, and the tail is long and straight, reaching the hock and carried up but never curled over the back. The legs are long and straight; the feet are oval with long toes. The head is moderately rounded and equal in length to the delicate, tapered muzzle. The ears are large, carried erect, and set low and wide on the head. The eyes are oval and wide set, giving the Crested an exotic, inscrutable, mischievous expression.

The Shar-Pei was developed in ancient China, dating back to the Han Dynasty of over 2,000 years ago, and is thought to be closely related to another ancient Chinese breed, the Chow Chow. The breed's modern history is hazy, but it was first documented by the Hong Kong Kennel Club in 1968, two years after the first Shar-Pei were imported to America. In 1973, a Hong Kong breeder, Matgo Law, asked American breeders for help to save the breed from extinction. The enthusiastic response led to the breed becoming extremely popular with rare-breed exhibitors. By the time of AKC recognition less than two decades later, almost 30,000 Shar-Pei had been registered in America.

The Shar-Pei's distinctive wrinkles and hippopotamus head make the breed unique in dogdom. This is a compact, medium-sized dog covered by a short, harsh coat and loose skin over its head and body. The head is  large, with an abundance of wrinkles framing the face. The muzzle is very broad, and the nose is large and wide. The eyes are small and almond shaped, and the small, triangular ears lie flat against the head. Overall, the dog has a regal, dignified appearance.

Year of AKC recognition: 1992

Group: Non-Sporting

Size: 18–20 inches, 45–60 pounds

Coat: Straight with a very harsh, sometimes prickly, texture (the breed's name loosely translates to "sandpaper-like coat." The coat can be very short, known as a "horse coat," to up to 1 inch long, known as a "brush coat." The coat stands off from the body; on the legs, the coat is flatter.

Color: Solid colors, with or without darker shadings in the same color, and sable

Life expectancy: 8–12 years

Activity level: Moderate

Grooming: Clean the lip folds daily, inspect the skin and coat regularly, and do not oil the skin wrinkles.

Temperament: This is a quiet, dignified, independent dog that is typically reserved with strangers. Training and socialization should begin early, and puppies should have consistent exposure to strangers and children. Puppy kindergarten classes are recommended. Shar-Pei respond well to positive-reinforcement training and food rewards.

Parent club: Chinese Shar Pei Club of America (www.cspca.com); founded in 1974

Buyers' advice from parent club: Find a reputable breeder who researches pedigrees and screens his or her dogs for inherited diseases.

Regional clubs: There are about twenty-five regional affiliates of the CSPCA; information is listed on the "Affiliate Clubs" page under "Membership."

Rescue: The Chinese Shar-Pei Club of America National Rescue Trust can be found under "Rescue" on the club's Web site.

CHINOOK

Entered Miscellaneous Class in 2010

Size: Males—24–26 inches, 55–90 pounds; females—22–24 inches, 50–65 pounds

Coat: The Chinook's thick double coat has a coarse, straight outer coat that is longer over the ruff, shoulders, withers, britches, and underside of the tail. The undercoat is short, dense, and downy.

Color: Pale honey to deep reddish gold. Darker markings on the ears and muzzle are common.

Life expectancy: 12–15 years

Activity level: Moderate. This is a working dog and must have thirty minutes to one hour of vigorous exercise daily. Secure fencing is recommended for this breed.

Grooming: Daily brushing

Temperament: Affectionate, playful, and very people oriented, this is an excellent family dog. Chinooks can tolerate inclement weather thanks to their protective coat but much prefer to be indoors with their family. They are versatile, willing workers, eager to please and highly trainable. Chinooks get along well with other dogs, but may be reserved with strangers.

Parent club: Chinook Club of America (www.chinookclubofamerica.org)

Buyers' advice from parent club: Buyers may face a long wait for a puppy because of the breed's rarity. Owners must be prepared to cope with heavy seasonal shedding. A roster of Chinook breeders is available on the parent club's Web site.

Rescue: CCA Rescue Committee information can be found on the club's Web site under "Rescue."

Developed in the United States for draft work and sled-dog racing by polar explorer Arthur Walden in the early 1900s, the Chinook has been designated as the official state dog of New Hampshire in recognition of its development in that state. Arthur Walden was primarily responsible for creating the breed at his Chinook Kennel in New Hampshire in the early 1900s. He used a combination of the Greenland Husky, German and Belgian Shepherds, and the Mastiff to produce a breed with endurance, strength, and trainability. Chinooks were used on Admiral Byrd's first Antarctic expedition in 1927. By the 1960s, only 125 dogs remained, and the *Guinness Book of World Records* classified the Chinook as the world's rarest breed. Today, there are approximately 600 Chinooks in the world.

This is an athletic, well-muscled working dog noted for its tireless gait, rectangular proportions, moderate bone, oval-shaped feet, and long, saberlike tail. The head is wedge shaped with slightly rounded cheeks and a broad, slightly arched top skull. The muzzle tapers to a blunt wedge. The Chinook's medium-sized, almond-shaped eyes are accentuated by dark eye rims and dark markings, giving the breed a kind, inquisitive expression. The Chinook's high-set, V-shaped ears have slightly rounded tips and may be erect, dropped, or anything in between.

This is one of the world's oldest breeds; its existence can be traced back to China's Han Dynasty of over 2,000 years ago or even earlier. The breed was originally used as a hunting dog in ancient China. It is thought that the breed's name was bestowed on it in the eighteenth century by Western visitors, who used the term "chow chow" as a catch-all for anything brought back from Asia. Chows became popular in Victorian England and were first shown in America in 1890.

The Chow is noted for its scowling expression and blue-black tongue. Its head is broad and large in proportion to its body. The muzzle is broad and the

nose is large. The eyes are dark, deeply set, and almond shaped; the ears are small, triangular, set wide apart, and erect. The body is compact and squarely proportioned, with good muscle and heavy bone. The chest is broad and deep, and the plumed tail is set high and carried over the back The Chow moves with a unique agile, powerful, stilted action; what it lacks in speed, it makes up for in endurance.

Year of AKC recognition: 1903

Group: Non-Sporting

Size: 17–20 inches, 45–70 pounds

Coat: There are two varieties. The rough variety has an abundant, straight, standoff outer coat that is harsh textured. The undercoat is soft, thick, and woolly. Coat length can vary, but coats are generally longer on males. The smooth variety has a double coat with a hard, dense, smooth outer coat; there is no ruff or feathering.

Color: Red, black, blue, cinnamon, and cream. All colors are solid or solid with lighter shading in the ruff, tail, and feathering.

Life expectancy: 8–12 years

Activity level: Moderate. Chows are intolerant of heat and should not be exercised in hot weather. They also have limited peripheral vision and a stilted gait but still have stamina.

Grooming: Daily brushing and frequent bathing

Temperament: The Chow Chow is noted for its regal demeanor and clean, fastidious habits. Chows are devoted to their families but typically quiet, aloof, and independent. Early socialization is recommended to offset the breed's natural reserve toward strangers. Training must be tailored to the breed's sensitive nature.

Parent club: Chow Chow Club, Inc. (www. chowclub.org); founded in 1906

Buyers' advice from parent club: Find a reliable breeder who willingly answers questions about how his or her puppies are raised, housed, fed, and cared for. Avoid puppies with watery eyes; signs of diarrhea or skin problems; or a shy, spooky temperament.

Regional clubs: There are about twenty regional Chow Chow clubs in the United States; information can be found under "Club Information" on the parent club's Web site.

Rescue: Chow Chow Welfare (www. chowwelfare.com)

CHOW CHOW

CLUMBER SPANIEL

Year of AKC recognition: 1884

Group: Sporting

Size: Males—18–20 inches, 70–85 pounds; females—17–19 inches, 55–70 pounds

Coat: Dense, straight, flat, and weather resistant with slight feathering on the ears, legs, tail, and belly and a frill on the neck

Color: White with lemon or orange markings

Life expectancy: 10–12 years

Activity level: Moderate. Clumbers are built for endurance trotting and have a surprising amount of stamina. They are content with moderate exercise, such as regular walks and interactive play. They compete successfully in agility, obedience, tracking, and hunting tests.

Grooming: Weekly brushing will help to control shedding.

Temperament: This is a typically calm and dignified breed. Clumbers are extremely devoted to their families but can be reserved with strangers. They learn quickly but can have a stubborn streak, and they respond best to positive-reinforcement training. They can be possessive with toys and food and prone to stealing food if these habits are not discouraged.

Parent club: Clumber Spaniel Club of America (www.clumbers.org); founded in 1972

Buyers' advice from parent club: Do not buy from someone who simply produces puppies for sale. Find a responsible breeder who works to improve the breed and participates in various activities with his or her dogs. Clumber puppies should be well supervised, as they can ingest chew toys, which can lead to intestinal blockage. Owners should be prepared for a breed that is prone to drooling.

Rescue: Clumber Spaniel Club of America Rescue and Placement Committee information can be found on the "Rescue & Placement" page on the club's Web site.

The Clumber was one of the first specialized spaniel breeds, developed in eighteenth-century France to hunt in heavy cover. Shortly before the French Revolution, one of the most important Clumber breeders in France relocated his dogs to Clumber Park in Britain, which became the source of the breed's name. Dogs descended from this breeding program became favorites of aristocratic sport hunters. Clumber Spaniels were imported to America in 1844, and registration records for the breed predate the formation of AKC.

This is a long, low, heavy dog noted for its dignified demeanor and slow, rolling gait. When the dog is on the move, its large, compact feet act as shock absorbers, and the docked tail is carried level with the back. Its head is large and flat with a furrow running between the eyes, up through the center of the skull; the muzzle is broad and square. Its large amber-colored eyes are deeply set, and the ears are broad, triangular, set low, and covered with light feathering.

"Spanyells" were first developed in the 1300s for different types of hunting. Over time, they evolved into water spaniels and land spaniels. Small land spaniels were eventually specialized for hunting woodcock and became known as Cocker Spaniels. Cockers have been popular hunting dogs in America since the 1700s. After being designated as a distinct breed by the AKC, the Cocker Spaniel developed into a different type than its counterpart in Britain and thus was divided into two separate breeds, the American Cocker Spaniel and the English Cocker Spaniel, in 1946.

The Cocker is famed for its cheery disposition and soft, intelligent expression. This is a sturdy, compact dog with a sloping

topline, a long neck, and a docked tail that is carried slightly higher than the back and wags merrily. The head features a rounded skull; a broad, deep muzzle; round eyes; and long ears that are well covered with feathering.

Year of AKC recognition: 1878

Group: Sporting

Size: Males—14½–15½ inches, 25–30 pounds; females—13½–14½ inches, 20–25 pounds

Coat: The Cocker has a short, fine coat on the head; medium-length body coat with some undercoat; and longer feathering on the ears, chest, legs, and abdomen. The coat is flat and silky and may range from straight to slightly wavy.

Color: Cockers are separated into three varieties by color: Black, which may include tan points; Any Solid Color Other than Black (ASCOB), which includes shades of cream, brown, and red; and Parti-color, which is white in combination with any of the solid colors. Roans also fall into the Parti-color category, and tan points may be seen on any Parti-color coloration.

Life expectancy: 10–14 years

Activity level: Moderate. A combination of long daily walks and interactive play will keep most Cockers satisfied.

Grooming: The coat needs to be brushed and combed every other day, and it should be trimmed every six weeks.

Temperament: This is a merry, sociable, affectionate breed that must have human companionship. Cockers are intelligent, willing to please, and trainable, but they can be very sensitive to reprimands. They can become clingy and may be prone to excessive barking if bored.

Parent club: American Spaniel Club (www.asc-cockerspaniel.org); founded in 1881

Buyers' advice from parent club: It is essential to seek out a responsible breeder from whom to obtain a puppy. Visit the parent club's Web site to read the "So You Want a Cocker Spaniel?" brochure online.

Regional clubs: The American Spaniel Club divides its member clubs into five zones; information is on the club's Web site on the "Member Clubs" page under "About ASC."

Rescue: American Spaniel Club Foundation (www.asc-f.org)

COLLIE

Year of AKC recognition: 1885

Group: Herding

Size: Males—24–26 inches, 60–75 pounds; females—22–24 inches, 50–65 pounds

Coat: The rough coat is a combination of short, smooth coat on the face and legs and longer coat on the body and tail. The outer coat is straight, harsh, and abundant, and the undercoat is extremely dense and soft. The smooth coat is short, hard, dense, and flat with an abundant undercoat.

Color: There are four recognized colors, including sable and white (sable with white markings); tri-color (black with white markings and tan shadings); blue merle ("marbled" blue-grey and black with white markings and usually with tan shadings); and white (white base color, usually with sable, tri-color, or blue merle markings).

Life expectancy: 12–14 years

Activity level: Moderate. Collies are working dogs, noted for their agility and stamina. As long as they have sufficient companionship and daily activity, they are wonderfully well-behaved house dogs.

Grooming: Rough Collies should be brushed and combed twice a week, with daily brushing and combing during seasonal shedding. Smooth Collies should be brushed once weekly, with daily brushing during seasonal shedding.

Temperament: Collies are sensitive, gentle, very receptive to training, and notably easy to house-train. However, they can become timid if not socialized, and they can develop bad habits, such as excessive barking, if bored or neglected.

Parent club: Collie Club of America (www. collieclubofamerica.org); founded in 1886

Buyers' advice from parent club: Educate yourself about the breed's health and temperament before choosing a Collie. Buy only from a reputable breeder who has his or her dogs health tested.

Rescue: Collie Rescue Foundation (www. collierescuefoundation.org)

Collies were indispensable to shepherds and drovers for centuries before kennel clubs came into existence. They were bred for working ability rather than for uniform appearance, and the type of dog found along the border of Scotland and England became known as the "Scotch Colly." The breed came to public attention during Victorian times as one of the Queen's favorite breeds; she owned eighty-eight Collies during her lifetime. Collies entered popular culture with the publication of Albert Payson Terhune's *Lad of Sunnybank*, and the breed achieved enduring fame thanks to the *Lassie* books, movies, and TV series.

This is a moderately sized, well-balanced, athletic dog with rectangular proportions. The Collie is muscular and sturdy but never coarse in appearance. The tail is long and is carried gaily when the dog is moving, but it is never carried high over the back. The Collie's head is shaped like a lean, elegant wedge; it is flat and tapers smoothly from the ears to the tip of the black nose. The eyes are almond shaped and placed obliquely on the skull. The ears are carried three-quarters erect with the tips folded over when the dog is alert. The Collie's expression is intelligent, capable, and sensible.

One of the oldest retriever breeds, the Curly-Coated Retriever descended from a combination of the English Water Spaniel, Irish Water Spaniel, Poodle, retrieving setters, and native water dogs of Newfoundland. CCRs were brought to Britain from Newfoundland in the early 1800s and first appeared at British shows in 1860. The breed was introduced to America in 1907.

This is a versatile hunting retriever that is sturdy, elegant, agile, muscular, and moderately built. It has slightly rectangular proportions, a level back, a deep chest, and a long tail covered with curls and carried straight. The head

is wedge shaped, with long, strong jaws and a muzzle that tapers neatly to the nose. The eyes are almond shaped, and the small ears lie close to the head.

Year of AKC recognition: 1924

Group: Sporting

Size: Males—25–27 inches; females—23–25 inches; 60–95 pounds

Coat: The Curly's unique coat is water resistant and protects it from weather and punishing cover. It is a combination of short, smooth, straight coat on the forehead, face, forelegs, and feet. The body coat is thick, crisp, and curly, with looser, more open curls on the ears.

Color: Solid black or liver

Life expectancy: 10–12 years

Activity level: High. The breed is noted for its energy and endurance. It will work and play hard in any weather, with a total disregard of inclement weather. CCRs can live in the water, so a swimming regimen will keep this charming water dog happy.

Grooming: This is an easy-care, quick-drying coat that requires only occasional brushing and bathing. The ears and tail may be trimmed slightly for neatness.

Temperament: Self confident and proud, the Curly-Coated Retriever is a determined worker and a charming, gentle family companion. The breed is responsive to training and noted to be a calm, affectionate, well-mannered house dog. However, this is a slow-maturing breed, and owners must be prepared to provide puppies with patient guidance. The breed is easy to train. These are excellent guard dogs and can be somewhat reserved with strangers.

Parent club: Curly-Coated Retriever Club of America (www.ccrca.org); founded in 1979

Buyers' advice from parent club: Be sure to purchase from a breeder who does regular health testing. A list of breeders is available on the parent club's Web site.

Regional clubs: There are four regional clubs in the US; links can be found on the parent club's Web site under "Regional Clubs."

Rescue: CCRCA Rescue and Referral information can be found under Curly-Coated Retriever Rescue on the parent club's home page.

CURLY-COATED RETRIEVER

DACHSHUND

Year of AKC recognition: 1885

Group: Hound

Size: There are two sizes. Standard—16–32 pounds, 8–9 inches; Miniature—11 pounds and under, 5–6 inches

Coat: This breed has three varieties. The Smooth variety has a short, flat, and glossy coat; the Wirehaired variety has a short, hard, wiry outer coat with a somewhat softer undercoat and possibly longer coat on the beard and eyebrows; and the Longhaired variety has a combination of glossy, slightly wavy body coat and longer coat on the neck, forechest, ears, tail, and abdomen.

Color: Dachshunds come in solid colors ranging from cream to deep red; bicolors in black, chocolate, wild boar (banded hairs that give a grizzed effect; most common in Wirehairs), and fawn with tan or cream markings; dapple (or merle); brindle; and sable.

Life expectancy: 12–16 years

Activity level: Moderate. Two daily walks will satisfy most Dachshunds, but exercise needs vary with each individual. Without more exercise, some Dachshunds will become bored and develop bad habits, such as digging or chewing; others need more activity to maintain a healthy weight. Dachshunds should be discouraged from jumping and stair-climbing, especially as puppies. Due to the breed's unique body construction— long and low with a heavy front assembly— strenuous jumping and climbing can instigate back problems. Dachshunds are extremely versatile, however, and compete successfully in obedience, agility, rally, tracking, field trials, and earthdog events.

Grooming: Weekly brushing for Smooths and Longhairs. Wirehaired coats should be handstripped to maintain the hard, protective texture. Bathe as needed, usually every couple of months.

Temperament: Dachshunds are extremely intelligent, but they are focused on their own agenda rather than worrying about pleasing everyone around them. This has earned them a reputation for being quirky or stubborn. Their vigilance and well-developed prey drive make them highly attuned to their environment and easily distracted from training. Dachshunds

The Dachshund originated in Germany and was developed to hunt game, from badgers to wild boar. Hunters sought to create a versatile, sturdy, courageous dog with the skills of both hound and terrier. By the nineteenth century, there were twelve types of Dachshunds, which were gradually refined into two sizes and three coat types. The Dachshund was first seen in the United States in the late nineteenth century, and the breed enjoyed popularity up until World War I. The Dachshund then experienced a revival after World War I with imported German stock. All six varieties have remained popular as pets, show dogs, and hunting dogs.

The Dachshund's long body and short legs give it an instantly recognizable silhouette. An equally important feature is its keel—the prominent breastbone and forechest. The back is level, and the tail is long and straight. The head is tapered to the tip of the nose, and the jaws are strong. The breed's keen, alert expression is produced by its bright, almond-shaped eyes and its rounded ears, which frame the face.

have an independent nature and excellent problem-solving skills. They are sensitive and require patience and a gentle hand to bring out their best. They easily adapt to a wide range of lifestyles and have a great sense of humor.

Parent club: Dachshund Club of America (www. dachshund-dca.org); founded in 1895

Buyers' advice from parent club: Buy from a reputable breeder who registers his or her dogs with the AKC, belongs to the DCA, and willingly answers questions. Avoid puppies that are shy or aggressive. A puppy should not leave the breeder until at least eight weeks of age. Also consider adopting from a Dachshund rescue group. Owners must ensure that fencing is reinforced to prevent Dachshunds from squeezing through small openings or digging underneath.

Regional clubs: There are over fifty regional Dachshund clubs in the United States, divided into six regions by the DCA, each with a regional chairperson. Information is available on the "Clubs" page, under "About DCA."

Rescue: Dachshund Club of America Rescue Program information can be found on the club's Web site under "Rescue."

FACING PAGE: Longhair Standard. ABOVE: Wirehair Standard. BELOW: Smooth Standard.

DACHSHUND

DALMATIAN

Year of AKC recognition: 1888

Group: Non-Sporting

Size: 19–24 inches, 45–70 pounds

Coat: Short, flat, dense, and sleek

Color: White with black or liver spots

Life expectancy: 11–13 years

Activity level: High. Dalmatians need daily vigorous exercise. These are athletic, hardy dogs built for endurance running. They must be exercised on lead or in a fenced yard. This is not an outdoor breed, as the Dalmatian's short coat makes the breed sensitive to weather extremes.

Grooming: Brush weekly; bathe three or four times per year.

Temperament: The Dalmatian is a loyal, devoted companion, but this is a working dog that needs physical activity, mental challenges, and companionship. The breed's territorial instinct makes for a good watchdog. Puppies are notably high spirited and playful, and owners should be prepared to provide supervision and consistent training to keep them out of trouble.

Parent club: Dalmatian Club of America (www.thedca.org); founded in 1905

Buyers' advice from parent club: Look at many litters, study the Dalmatian standard, attend dog shows, and talk to breeders before deciding on a puppy. Only purchase from a reputable breeder. Avoid puppies that are overly timid or domineering. Begin socialization and obedience training early. Consider adopting an adult rescue Dalmatian.

Regional clubs: There are close to forty regional Dalmatian clubs affiliated with the DCA; look for the "Regional Dalmatian Club" page under "Breeder & Club Information."

Rescue: Rescue information is available on the parent club's Web site under "Rescue Education."

The Dalmatian's early origins are uncertain. The breed may have originated around the Dalmatian coast of Croatia, but similar spotted dogs were known in many parts of Europe. Early references to Dalmatians date from the eighteenth century. Regardless of its actual ancestry, the breed unquestionably derived from a sporting heritage. It became popular as a carriage dog in the 1800s and was also used for hunting and military work. The Dalmatian is forever linked to the image of a spotted dog trotting alongside a horse-drawn carriage or a fire truck. Dalmatians rocketed to mainstream popularity after the release of the 1961 Disney film *One Hundred and One Dalmatians* based on Dodie Smith's 1956 novel.

The Dal's most notable feature is its sleek, spotted coat. It is a sturdy, athletic dog with a balanced, graceful outline; square proportions; a deep chest; a level back; a long tail; and round, compact, well-arched feet. The skull is flat, approximately equal in length and width, and the powerful muzzle equals the length of the skull. The eyes are medium sized, wide set, and round. The ears are set high and carried close to the sides of the head.

The breed originated along the border of England and Scotland in the 1700s and was used for hunting and vermin control by local farmers and landowners. The Dandie was catapulted to fame by Sir Walter Scott's popular novel *Guy Mannering* in 1814, and the breed's name was derived from the character in that book. Dandies were first shown in Britain in 1861 and were recognized by the AKC in 1886. Today, the Dandie is one of the rarest breeds, classified as a native vulnerable breed in its homeland.

This is a low-stationed dog, with its overall length being slightly less than twice its height. The Dandie's body is athletic, long, and flexible,

with good bone and muscle. The topline curves down over the shoulders and arches over the loin, creating a very distinctive silhouette. The legs are short and sturdy, and the tail is 8–10 inches long. The head is large and broad, with a strong muzzle and large black nose. The Dandie has deep-set, melancholy eyes and low-set ears; the ears hang close to the cheeks and are 3–4 inches long. The Dandie's expression reveals great determination, intelligence, and dignity.

Year of AKC recognition: 1886

Group: Terrier

Size: 8–11 inches, 18–24 pounds

Coat: A mixture of harsh and soft hair, which produces a crisp texture, the body coat is 2 inches in length; the soft, silky topknot is somewhat longer, and there is feathering on the forelegs and muzzle.

Color: Pepper (dark blue-black to silvery gray) or mustard (reddish brown to light fawn)

Life expectancy: 12–15 years

Activity level: Moderate. Dandies are athletic hunters but somewhat less energetic than other terriers.

Grooming: Brush and comb daily. The coat should be stripped twice a year to keep it neat and preserve its texture.

Temperament: Dandies possess the boldness and self-confidence typical of terriers, but they are equally noted for their gentle, dignified demeanor. They are undemanding pets and loyal, affectionate companions. A Dandie does not look for trouble but will not back down from it. Dandies are vigilant, courageous watchdogs and, like other terriers, they have a strong predatory instinct. They can also be possessive and headstrong. Owners must provide consistent benevolent leadership.

Parent club: Dandie Dinmont Terrier Club of America (http://clubs.akc.org/ddtca)

Buyers' advice from parent club: This is a very rare breed, and you may face a long wait for a puppy.

Rescue: The Dandie Dinmont Terrier Club of America's Dandies in Distress Committee can be found on the "Dandie Rescue" page under "Finding a Dandie."

DANDIE DINMONT TERRIER

DOBERMAN PINSCHER

Year of AKC recognition: 1908

Group: Working

Size: Males—26–28 inches, 75–100 pounds; females—24–26 inches, 60–90 pounds

Coat: Short, flat, and smooth

Color: Colors include black, red, blue, or fawn (called Isabella) with clearly defined rust-colored markings above each eye; on the muzzle, throat, forechest, legs, and feet; and below the tail.

Life expectancy: 10–12 years

Activity level: Moderate to high. This is a working dog developed for endurance, speed, and great intelligence. Dobermans need mental exercise just as much as physical activity. They excel at dog sports such as obedience, agility, and tracking.

Grooming: Weekly brushing is recommended, as well as regular ear cleaning and nail trimming.

Temperament: This is a breed with a purpose: to be a working partner and a devoted companion. As workers, Dobermans are vigilant, courageous, and relentless. They are also supremely trustworthy, loyal, and protective of their people, and they need to be part of the family. Dobermans learn quickly but are quite sensitive and intolerant of rough handling or inconsistent training. The breed needs plenty of social interaction and sensible leadership to achieve its full potential.

Parent club: Doberman Pinscher Club of America (www.dpca.org); founded in 1921

Buyers' advice from parent club: This is not the breed for a casual owner with limited time to devote to a dog. When looking for a puppy, work with a reliable, knowledgeable breeder and visit personally to see the puppies and their parents before making a choice.

Regional clubs: There are over fifty regional DPCA chapters in the United States; information is listed on the "Chapter Clubs" page under "The DPCA" on the club's Web site.

Rescue: Doberman Pinscher Club of America Rescue (www.dpcarescue.com)

The breed takes its name from Karl Friedrich Louis Dobermann, a tax collector who began developing the breed in Germany in the 1880s. Herr Dobermann's goal was to create an intelligent and reliable guard dog that was equally valued as a companion. The Rottweiler, Black and Tan Terrier, German Pinscher, Greyhound, and German Shepherd are thought to have played a role in the breed's development. The Doberman was recognized in Germany in 1900 and was seen in America soon after. It took a few decades for the breed to gain popularity, but since that time, it has been prized as a companion, war dog, police dog, performance dog, and one of the most competitive show dogs.

The Doberman is a compact, squarely proportioned, muscular dog with a clean, elegant outline and a look of nobility. It is powerful and agile with a long neck; a broad chest; a short, firm back; and a docked tail that is carried slightly above the back. The long, wedge-shaped head is carried high, the ears are cropped and carried erect, and the almond-shaped eyes give the breed a keen and vigilant expression.

Also known as the French Mastiff, the breed is believed to have been in existence for over 600 years, with some theories dating dogs of DDB type back to ancient Rome. Its exact origins are hazy, but the first mention of the breed name was in 1863 at a canine exhibition, when they were given the name of the French region in which they were developed. Throughout its history, the Dogue was used for guarding and hunting. Dogues were first imported to America in 1890, but the breed subsequently became extremely rare in both Europe and America. In the 1960s, French breeders began efforts to revive the breed. The general public was introduced to the Dogue de Bordeaux in the 1989 film *Turner and Hooch*.

This is a massive, powerful dog with heavy bone and loose-fitting skin. It has a broad, sturdy back; a thick

tail that reaches the hock and is carried low; and a muscular neck covered with ample skin. The head is large and broad, with a short, powerful, undershot jaw; wide-set, oval eyes; small ears that lie close to the skull; and characteristic facial wrinkles. The Dogue's expression reflects courage, candor, and purpose.

Year of AKC recognition: 2008

Group: Working

Size: Males—23½–27 inches, 110 pounds and up; females—23–26 inches, 99 pounds and up

Coat: Short and fine

Color: Dark red to light fawn with a darker colored or black mask

Life expectancy: 5–8 years

Activity level: Moderately low. Dogues should have two twenty-minute walks each day. They do not tolerate heat and should never be exercised or left outdoors in hot weather. Lack of activity will lead to weight gain and potential bad behavior. DDBs have been trained for carting, obedience, conformation, weight pulling, water rescue, tracking, search and rescue, and therapy work.

Grooming: Weekly brushing will minimize shedding. A Dogue should be bathed about every two weeks and have his facial folds cleaned during baths. Grooming also includes regular nail trimming, regular ear cleaning, and cleaning of the eye area throughout each day.

Temperament: This is a sweet, even-tempered, devoted family companion, but owners must keep the breed's heritage in mind—this is a guardian dog who is territorial, vigilant to changes in his environment, and reserved toward strangers. Dogues can be aggressive toward other dogs. This is a large and powerful but also quite sensitive breed. Early training is essential, and a consistently positive approach will yield far better results than fruitless attempts to physically dominate a Dogue.

Parent club: Dogue de Bordeaux Society of America (www.ddbs.org); founded in 1997

Buyers' advice from parent club: Owning a DDB includes serious responsibilities because of the breed's size and strength. Owners must have a serious commitment to training and ample time to devote to caring for a Dogue. Puppies should never be permitted to play-bite. Find a responsible breeder; this should be the only source from which you purchase a puppy.

Rescue: Dogue de Bordeaux Society of America Rescue (www.ddbsarescue.org)

DOGUE DE BORDEAUX

ENGLISH COCKER SPANIEL

Year of AKC recognition: 1946

Group: Sporting

Size: Males—16–17 inches, 28–34 pounds; females—15–16 inches, 26–32 pounds

Coat: Short, fine coat on the head; medium-length, flat or slightly wavy coat on the body; and feathering on the ears, chest, abdomen, and legs.

Color: Solid colors include black, liver, or shades of red. Parti-colors include white with markings in black, liver, or shades of red. Markings are in the form of solid patches, ticking, or roaning (a mixture of white hairs that makes the base color appear lighter; for example, blue roan is black with roaning). Tan points may appear on solid blacks, solid livers, parti-colored blacks, and parti-colored livers.

Life expectancy: 12–14 years

Activity level: Moderate. English Cockers need daily exercise, and long walks and interactive play will keep them content.

Grooming: Brush the coat twice weekly. The coat must be clipped or stripped regularly to keep it neat. A grooming chart and video are available from the parent club.

Temperament: English Cockers are wonderful house dogs. They are typically easy to train, adaptable, cheerful, and affectionate. Personalities vary within the breed, as some dogs are quieter and more reserved, but they are generally eager to please and very responsive to praise and rewards. English Cockers are sensitive and slow to forget mistreatment or rough handling. They enjoy most dog sports, such as obedience, agility, tracking, and flyball. They also make wonderful therapy dogs and exceptional detection dogs.

Parent club: English Cocker Spaniel Club of America (www.ecsca.org); founded in 1936

Buyers' advice from parent club: Visit the breeder to see the puppy's littermates and parents.

Regional clubs: There are over a dozen ECSCA member clubs listed on the "Member Clubs" page under "Membership" on the club's Web site.

Rescue: ECSCA Rescue can be found on the club's Web site under "Rescue."

Early spaniels in Britain were designated as either water spaniels or land spaniels. Land spaniels were later divided by size, and those under 25 pounds became known as Cockers. In 1885, a spaniel club finally documented the criteria to separate each spaniel breed. The Cocker Spaniel, the smallest variety of sporting spaniel, continued to grow in popularity in Britain and America. Over time, American Cockers became distinctly different in type, so the English Cocker Spaniel Club was formed to promote and preserve the original type, and the English Cocker was separately recognized by the AKC in 1946.

The English Cocker is famed for its soft, melting expression, created by a combination of slightly oval, wide-set eyes and long, low-set ears. The skull is described as "slightly flattened," and the muzzle length is equal to the length of the skull. The breed has strong jaws. The body is solid and compact with a deep chest, a short back, and a docked tail that is carried level with the back.

Foxhunting came into prominence in Britain as large game disappeared. Early references to Foxhounds date from the late 1500s. They were developed from heavier, slower hounds such as the St. Hubert and Talbot Hound. Stud books on Foxhound packs have been maintained in Britain since the early 1800s. Documentation on English Foxhound packs in America date to 1890, although evidence suggests that the breed existed here earlier.

The breed is heavier and slower than the American Foxhound. It has a wide skull with a pronounced brow, a long muzzle, and a sweet expression. Ears are set low and lie close to the cheeks. The neck is long and tapered, the back is level, and the long tail is carried up but never over the back. The legs are straight and sturdy; the feet are round with well-developed knuckles.

Year of AKC recognition: 1909

Group: Hound

Size: 24 inches

Coat: Short, dense, hard, and glossy

Color: Any "hound color"; often seen in black, tan, and white tricolor; red and white; tan and white; and lemon and white

Life expectancy: 10–13 years

Activity level: High. English Foxhounds are energetic dogs with the stamina to run all day, and they can become frustrated and destructive if deprived of sufficient exercise. An English Foxhound needs very regular exercise with its humans. It will run next to your horse or bike for hours, but when home will like nothing better than sleeping at your feet or in bed with you. English Foxhounds need fences (invisible or otherwise) and they get along with children, cats, other dogs, and almost anything else.

Grooming: Brush once a week.

Temperament: This is a versatile breed with a typical scenthound temperament—gentle, easygoing, friendly, tolerant of other dogs, and extremely attuned to its environment. This attention to its surroundings, coupled with the breed's prey drive, can be a distraction during training and can result in the dog's chasing small animals and wandering off to follow interesting scent trails. Teaching a Foxhound to come on command has definite advantages. However, this breed is noted for its independent nature, and owners must be prepared to approach training with patience and persistence.

Parent club: English Foxhound Club of America

Buyers' advice from parent club: Obtaining an English Foxhound puppy is not easy. This is the rarest breed registered by the AKC, and there are very few breeders, all of whom firmly believe that English Foxhounds are very special dogs with very endearing traits. The best way to find an English Foxhound puppy or adult is to get in touch with the parent club. You will be directed to a breeder or perhaps to a grown hound in need of a home.

ENGLISH SETTER

Year of AKC recognition: 1878

Group: Sporting

Size: Males—25–27 inches, 65–80 pounds; females—23–25 inches, 45–55 pounds

Coat: Flat and straight with longer, silky feathering on the ears, chest, abdomen, legs, and tail

Color: White intermixed with flecking of a darker color: orange belton (white with tan flecking), blue belton (white with black flecking), tricolor (blue belton with tan points), liver belton, lemon belton.

Life expectancy: 12 years

Activity level: Moderate to high. English Setters are energetic, but if they have adequate exercise, they are quite well-mannered house dogs. They should have daily vigorous runs in a fenced yard. English Setters make great jogging and hiking companions.

Grooming: Brush the coat two or three times per week and bathe the dog about every six weeks. The coat should be trimmed, either at home or by a groomer, every six to eight weeks.

Temperament: The English Setter is noted for its tolerant, gentle demeanor. This is a friendly, outgoing breed that thrives on companionship and gets along well with almost everyone, making it a great family dog. English Setters make great therapy dogs and do well at most dog sports, such as obedience and agility.

Parent club: English Setter Association of America (www.esaa.com); founded in 1931

Buyers' advice from parent club: Seek out a reputable breeder who is clearly interested in the welfare of each dog. Prospective owners may face a wait for a puppy. Visit breeders to meet the puppy's mother and littermates before making a final decision. Buyers seeking a field-trial dog should limit their search to field-bred lines.

Regional clubs: There are over twenty regional US English Setter clubs, information about which is given on the "Regional Clubs" page of the parent club's Web site, under "About ESAA."

Rescue: ESAA Rescue Committee information is located on the club's Web site under "Rescue."

Setters were developed from spaniel stock and were originally known as "setting spaniels." The English Setter emerged from a combination of Spanish Pointer, Water Spaniel, and Springer Spaniel stock. Two British breeders were responsible for creating the modern English Setter type: Edward Laverack in the 1800s and Richard Llewellin, who based his breeding program on Laverack dogs, which became the basis for the field-bred English Setter. The breed remains a favorite field-trial dog, and some breeders develop strains with dual potential; several English Setters have earned both field and conformation titles.

This is an elegant, well-balanced gundog that is free of extremes. The neck is long, gracefully blending into a slightly sloping topline. The tail is covered with straight feathering and carried level with the back. The head is long and lean, with a long, square muzzle and parallel planes. Its large, wide-set eyes produce a mild, intelligent expression. The low-set ears are carried close to the head and covered with silky feathering. Field-bred strains are smaller and less uniform than the type seen in the conformation ring.

In the late nineteenth century, spaniels from the same litter were divided by size into "cockers" (smaller dogs used for hunting woodcock) and "springers" (larger dogs used for flushing and retrieving game). The breed was recognized in Britain in 1902 and made its way to North America a little over a decade later. Dual-type Springers, bred for both the field and the show ring, disappeared in the 1940s, resulting in a marked divergence between working and show lines.

This is a medium-sized, compact, and sturdy sporting spaniel with slightly rectangular proportions and a deep, oval-shaped chest. Its long, muscular neck blends smoothly into a slightly sloping topline. The  docked tail is carried slightly above the level of the back, wagging merrily. The skull is medium length, fairly broad, and flat on top. The breed's characteristic kindly, trusting expression is produced by wide-set, oval-shaped eyes and long, wide ears that are set at the level of the eye and hang close to the head.

Year of AKC recognition: 1910

Group: Sporting

Size: Males—20 inches, 50 pounds; females—19 inches, 40 pounds

Coat: The medium-length outer coat is flat or wavy; the shorter undercoat is soft and dense. Moderate feathering on the ears, chest, legs, and belly, with shorter, fine coat on the head, on the front of the forelegs, and below the hocks on the front of the hind legs. Field-bred Springers typically have shorter, coarser coats and less feathering.

Color: Black and white or liver and white (black or liver can be the base color, or white can be the base color), with or without tan points; blue or liver roan.

Life expectancy: 12–14 years

Activity level: High. Springers are energetic, but not hyperactive. They possess great stamina and require daily vigorous exercise.

Grooming: Regular brushing and trimming to control shedding and keep the coat from matting.

Temperament: The breed is exceptionally intelligent and responsive to training; Springers are often trained for detection work to search for weapons, explosives, drugs, and other contraband items. Cheerful, sociable, and affectionate, the active and versatile Springer makes an excellent companion. Springers are devoted to their families and enjoy the company of people.

Parent club: English Springer Spaniel Field Trial Association (www.essfta.org); founded in 1927

Buyers' advice from parent club: Familiarize yourself with the differences between show and field dogs to find a dog that fits your expectations. Meet the parents of the litter and choose a puppy with an energy level that fits your lifestyle.

Regional clubs: There are close to 100 regional clubs—some focus on conformation and performance events, others on hunting and field events, and some offer a combination of these. They are listed under "Regional Clubs" on the ESSFTA's Web site.

Rescue: Rescue information is located under "ESS Rescue" on the parent club's Web site.

ENGLISH SPRINGER SPANIEL

ENGLISH TOY SPANIEL

Year of AKC recognition: 1886

Group: Toy

Size: 9–10 inches, 8–14 pounds

Coat: The silky-textured coat is profuse and either straight or slightly wavy. There is long fringe on the ears, body, chest, and legs.

Color: There are four varieties in the breed, divided by color: Blenheim (white with red markings), Ruby (solid red), Prince Charles (white with black markings and tan points), and King Charles (black with tan points).

Life expectancy: 10–12 years

Activity level: Low. English Toy Spaniels must be exercised on lead or in a fenced yard. They are heat intolerant and should not be left outdoors in hot weather.

Grooming: Twice-weekly brushing is recommended, along with regular ear cleaning.

Temperament: Personalities within the breed range from aloof to outgoing, but English Toy Spaniels are generally quiet, affectionate, easygoing dogs. They make excellent apartment dogs and get along well with other pets. They can be stubborn and training can require patience.

Parent club: English Toy Spaniel Club of America (www.englishtoyspanielclubofamerica.org)

Buyers' advice from parent club: A reputable breeder will keep puppies until eight to ten weeks of age before releasing them to new homes; they should not go to new homes before they are eight weeks old. The breeder will ensure that vaccinations are current on all puppies that leave for new homes.

Rescue: English Toy Spaniel Club of America Rescue information can be found on the parent club's Web site.

Toy spaniels have been a favorite of British royalty for hundreds of years and have been documented since the 1500s as "comfort spaniels." They were bred for small size but not for specific colors until the 1700s. The oldest variety of English Toy Spaniel, the black and tan variety, was named for King Charles II. This was the King's favorite breed and later became one of the most popular toy breeds in Britain (where it is called the King Charles Spaniel) and America.

The English Toy Spaniel is a small, cobby, sturdy, squarely proportioned dog with a level topline and a docked tail that is carried level with or slightly above the back. It has a cheerful demeanor and a characteristic soft, appealing expression. The head is large and domed; the muzzle is short and the jaw is broad, square, and upturned. The eyes are dark, round, and lustrous, and the low-set ears are covered with long, heavy fringe.

This is the smallest of the four Swiss Mountain Dog breeds; the others are the Appenzeller, Bernese Mountain Dog, and Greater Swiss Mountain Dog. All of these breeds trace their ancestry back to Roman molosser-type dogs. Along with the Appenzeller, the Entlebucher was used as a cattle dog, and up until 1926, the two breeds were considered as one in Switzerland. The breed has always been relatively small in number, both in its homeland and elsewhere, but enthusiasts have worked to preserve it.

This is a muscular, balanced dog with ample bone and slightly rectangular proportions. It has a sturdy, level back; a broad, deep chest; and a long tail that is carried up but never over the back. The feet are compact and slightly rounded

with well-arched toes. The head is flat and wedge shaped, the muzzle is tapered, and the nose is black. The small, dark, almond-shaped eyes give the breed an attentive, friendly expression. The ears are triangular and set high and wide; they have rounded tips and are carried close to the head.

Entered Miscellaneous Class in 2009

Size: Males—17–21 inches; females—16–20 inches

Coat: A double coat with a short, harsh, shiny, close-fitting outer coat and dense undercoat

Color: Black with tan and white markings

Life expectancy: 11–13 years

Activity level: High. This is a fast, agile working dog with plenty of drive and stamina. Entlebuchers need plenty of daily exercise, and they remain active for their entire lives. They love interactive play and dog sports such as agility and herding events. They are not well acclimated to heat and prefer cool weather for outdoor exercise. This is a heavy dog for its size and must be well conditioned to avoid injury during strenuous activity.

Grooming: Brush the coat weekly; more frequent brushing is needed during seasonal shedding.

Temperament: This is a typical working dog—high-spirited, self-confident, and tireless. Entlebuchers must have outlets for their mental and physical energy and plenty of interaction with their owners. They have well-developed protective instincts, making them great watchdogs. Intelligent and responsive, they are easy to train and enjoy most competitive dog sports. Training and socialization should begin early and should be consistent. An Entlebucher is typically good with other dogs but may not accept other pets unless socialized to them.

Parent club: National Entlebucher Mountain Dog Association (www.nemda.org); founded in 1998

Buyers' advice from parent club: Socialization should begin early with your new puppy; also enroll in training classes, beginning with puppy classes at ten weeks old, that use positive-reinforcement methods.

Rescue: Information on the National Entlebucher Mountain Dog Association Rescue Committee is located on the parent club's Web site under "Rescue/Rehome."

ENTLEBUCHER MOUNTAIN DOG

FIELD SPANIEL

Year of AKC recognition: 1894

Group: Sporting

Size: Males—18 inches; females—17 inches

Coat: The Field Spaniel's coat is designed to protect it from heavy brush, inclement weather, and icy water. It is moderately long, silky, dense, water repellent, and flat or slightly wavy, with feathering on the chest, abdomen, back of the legs, and tail. The breed carries less coat than other spaniels.

Color: This breed comes in shades of black, liver, golden liver, and roan. All colors may have tan points or a small amount of white on the chest and/or throat.

Life expectancy: 12–13 years

Activity level: High. The Field Spaniel was bred for energy and endurance in finding, flushing, and retrieving game from land and water, and it must have adequate exercise if not used in this capacity.

Grooming: The Field Spaniel requires weekly brushing, regular nail clipping, and trimming of the hair between the footpads and inside the ears as needed.

Temperament: Fields are fun-loving, docile, sensitive, and affectionate. They want to be part of the family and participate in whatever their people are doing. They are versatile dogs with potential for success in many areas of competitive dog sport, and they are valued family companions.

Parent club: Field Spaniel Society of America (www.fieldspaniels.org); founded in 1978

Buyers' advice from parent club: Before choosing a puppy, request information on the parents' health and temperament. See the litter in person and choose an outgoing, friendly puppy.

Rescue: Field Spaniel Society of America Rescue Committee information is located on the club's Web site on the "Breed Rescue" page under "About Breed."

The Field Spaniel was developed mainly from a combination of black Cocker Spaniels and Sussex Spaniel strains and emerged as a distinct breed in the second half of the nineteenth century. By the turn of the twentieth century, the Field had become quite extreme in type, and Cocker and other spaniel breeds surpassed it in popularity. The breed's numbers were very low in both Britain and America during the two World Wars, but several British breeders in the 1960s worked to restore the breed to its previous quality. The revival of the breed in the United States began in the late 1960s with the arrival of dogs from Britain. The Field Spaniel has a dedicated following today but remains one of the rarest spaniels and is classified as a native vulnerable breed in Britain.

The Field Spaniel is a well-balanced, medium-sized dog built for activity and endurance. It is slightly rectangular in proportion, with moderate bone and good muscle. The neck is long, strong, and lightly arched; the back is sturdy and level. The tail is set low and docked. The feet are large, round, and webbed. The Field's eyes are dark, medium sized, and almond shaped. The ears are wide, long enough to reach the end of the muzzle, set slightly below eye level, and hanging close to the head. The Field Spaniel's expression is grave and intelligent.

For centuries, the Sami tribes of Lapland used this breed, first as hunters and protection dogs and then as reindeer herders. As snowmobiles became more widely used, the need for the dogs decreased, but efforts to save the breed began in Finland in 1940. At first, the breed had two coat varieties, but the Finnish Lapphund was formally separated from the short-coated variety (Lapinporokoira) in l967. The Finnish Lapphund is very popular in Finland today, and real efforts to establish the breed in America began in 1987.

This is a strongly built dog—more substantial than it appears—with a thick double coat and almost square proportions. It has a medium-length neck; a broad, straight back; and a high-set tail that is covered with profuse coat and carried over the back. Its legs are heavy boned and straight, and the feet are oval shaped and well arched with thick, elastic pads. The skull is slightly domed, as broad as it is long, with a broad, straight muzzle. The ears are set wide apart and are small to medium in size, triangular in shape, and rounded at the tips. The eyes are oval and dark.

Entered Miscellaneous Class in 2009

Size: Males—18–21 inches; females—16–19 inches

Coat: Lappies have a profuse, long, straight, harsh, water-repellent outer coat with a soft, dense undercoat. The outer coat stands off from the body. The hair is shorter on the head and front of the legs, and males have a profuse mane.

Color: All colors are permitted in competition. There is usually a primary color covering the body with a secondary color on the head, neck, chest, underside of body, legs, and tail.

Life expectancy: 12–15 years

Activity level: Moderate. Finnish Lapphunds need regular exercise but are calm house dogs. They excel in obedience and agility, but they are intolerant of heat and should not be exercised in hot weather.

Grooming: Brush at least once a week to control shedding.

Temperament: The Finnish Lapphund's temperament is comparable to that of a herding dog. Lappies are good-natured, sociable, and accepting of other dogs. They make devoted companions. They are submissive toward people but should never be shy. This is not a protective breed. Lappies are alert, intelligent, and receptive to training. They make good therapy dogs.

Parent club: Finnish Lapphund Club of America (www.finnishlapphund.org); founded in 2004

Buyers' advice from parent club: A reputable breeder cares about the physical and mental well-being of every puppy produced and provides a stable environment in which to raise them. Potential owners should ask the breeder to show them health-testing documentation on the parents of the litter.

Rescue: Finnish Lapphund Club of America Rescue information can be found under "Contacts" on the club's Web site.

FINNISH LAPPHUND

FINNISH SPITZ

Year of AKC recognition: 1991

Group: Non-Sporting

Size: Males—17½–20 inches; females—15½–18 inches

Coat: This breed has a short, soft, dense undercoat and a harsh, straight outer coat that is 1–2 inches in length on the body and somewhat longer and harder textured on the neck and back. The coat is shorter on the head and legs, and it is longer and thicker on the back of the thighs and the plume of the tail. Males carry more coat than females.

Color: The coat of the Finnish Spitz is bright, clear, golden red in shades ranging from pale honey to deep auburn. A small amount of black hair or white markings is permitted in competition.

Life expectancy: 13–15 years

Activity level: High. Finnish Spitz are hunters and will take off in pursuit of birds or squirrels, so they must be exercised on lead or in a fenced yard. They are tolerant of weather extremes. Daily exercise is important to maintain healthy weight.

Grooming: This is a naturally clean, fastidious breed. Bathing is required occasionally, and brushing should be done weekly. More frequent brushing is needed during seasonal shedding in spring and fall.

Temperament: With sharp eyesight and keen hearing, the Finnish Spitz is an excellent alarm dog. However, Finnish Spitz were bred to bark while hunting, so owners must be prepared to discourage unwanted barking before it becomes a bad habit. The breed is highly intelligent and is adept at solving problems. Finnish Spitz bore easily and can develop bad habits if confined or neglected. The breed is, by nature, rather strong-willed and independent, responding best to praise and motivational training methods.

Parent club: Finnish Spitz Club of America (www.finnishspitzclub.org); founded in 1975

Buyers' advice from parent club: Contact a reputable breeder and be prepared to wait for a good-quality puppy.

Rescue: Finnish Spitz National Rescue (www.finnishspitzrescue.org)

This is a traditional hunting dog of Finland, known as the Finnish Cock-Eared Dog or the Finnish Barking Birddog. It was nearly extinct by the late nineteenth century, when efforts were made to reconstruct the breed from the remaining population of native stock. The Finnish Kennel Club recognized the breed in 1892, and Finnish Spitz were first imported to America in 1959. The Finnish Spitz continues to be used as a hunting dog in Finland, but it is primarily a companion dog in America.

The Finnish Spitz possesses the hallmark traits of Nordic breeds: square proportions that are symmetrical and not exaggerated; a strong, level back; a heavily plumed, curled tail; and a harsh, standoff double coat. The muscular body consists of a deep chest, straight legs of good bone, and rounded, compact feet. The flat skull; narrow, tapered muzzle; black nose; small, high-set, erect ears; and almond-shaped eyes give the breed a lively, foxlike expression.

The Flat-Coat was selectively bred in the nineteenth century from a combination of Newfoundlands, water spaniels, setters, and sheepdogs, the same foundation stock as the Labrador Retriever. These dogs became popular as enthusiastic workers with superlative retrieving skills. The various retrievers began to be classified by coat type at early dog shows, and the Flat-Coats were first shown in classes for Wavy- and Curly-Coated Retrievers at British dog shows in 1860. Modern Flat-Coat type was stabilized in the following decade, and S. E. Shirley, founder and first president of Britain's Kennel Club, is primarily credited with this accomplishment. The breed was recognized by the AKC in 1915 but subsequently became quite rare by the end of World War II. Breeders worked to revive the Flat-Coat, and by the 1960s, it was once again in demand.

The breed is described in its standard as "power without lumber and raciness without weediness." This is a versatile, utilitarian, athletic dog that is elegant, balanced, and

free of exaggeration. It is slightly rectangular in proportion with moderate bone, a level topline, and a long, straight tail carried slightly above the level of the back. The muzzle is approximately equal to the length of the flat skull. The eyes are almond shaped and medium sized, and the small ears lie close to the head. The expression is intelligent and kind.

Year of AKC recognition: 1915

Group: Sporting

Size: Males—23–24½ inches; females—22–23½ inches

Coat: This breed's coat is straight, flat, and glossy; its moderate density and fullness provide insulation from all types of weather. There is a longer, heavier mane on the neck and shoulders that is more pronounced in males. The ears, front, chest, backs of forelegs, thighs, and underside of the tail are well feathered.

Color: Black or liver

Life expectancy: 8–10 years

Activity level: Moderately high. Flat-Coats require regular vigorous exercise. They enjoy, hiking, jogging, and swimming, and they excel at dog sports.

Grooming: Weekly brushing and occasional bathing is recommended.

Temperament: The Flat-Coat is a family companion with well-developed hunting instincts and a good-natured, friendly, adaptable disposition. A Flat-Coat needs plenty of individual attention and interaction with its family. The breed's vigilance makes for a good alarm dog. This is a versatile breed and, in contrast to some other gundog breeds, there are no separate show and field strains.

Parent club: Flat-Coated Retriever Society of America (www.fcrsainc.org); founded in 1960

Regional clubs: There are about a dozen regional Flat-Coated Retriever clubs in the United States; information is listed under "Local Clubs" on the parent club's home page.

Rescue: Flat-Coated Retriever Society of America Rescue and Referral information is located on the parent club's Web site under "Flat-Coat Rescue."

FLAT-COATED RETRIEVER

FOX TERRIER

Year of AKC recognition: 1885

Group: Terrier

Size: Males—up to 15½ inches, 17–19 pounds; females—slightly shorter, 15–17 pounds

Coat: There are two varieties: the Smooth has a hard, dense, smooth, and flat coat; the Wire has a dense, wiry, broken-textured outer coat, comparable to the texture of coconut matting, with a fine, soft undercoat.

Color: Predominantly white with markings on the head and body.

Life expectancy: 12–15 years

Activity level: High. Fox Terriers must have plenty of exercise, either on lead or in a fenced yard, as they will chase small animals. They also excel in dog sports such as obedience and agility, which give them the opportunity to exercise their bodies and minds.

Grooming: Coats should be brushed weekly. Wires must be regularly stripped or clipped. Puppies must be taught to cooperate with grooming routines at a young age.

Temperament: This is a keen, quick, cheerful dog that makes an energetic, lively companion. Living with a Fox Terrier is never boring, but owners must be prepared for a dynamic housemate. Playful and inquisitive, Fox Terriers can get into trouble if they lack supervision and structured routines that include plenty of exercise and mental challenges. Fox Terriers have a strong hunting instinct, but they can learn to accept cats and rabbits if socialized to them as puppies.

Parent club: American Fox Terrier Club (www.aftc.org); founded in 1885

Buyers' advice from parent club: Fox Terriers from reputable breeders are generally very healthy and hardy.

Regional clubs: The American Fox Terrier Club maintains a list of close to twenty regional affiliates on its Web site.

Rescue: American Fox Terrier Club National Rescue Effort information is located under "AFTC Rescue" on the club's Web site.

Early Fox Terriers were developed by British hunt kennels, used in combination with Foxhounds for hunting and also used for general vermin control in kennels and stables. Experts can only speculate on the breed's exact origin, but the Beagle and Bull Terrier are thought to be in the Smooth's background, and the old Black and Tan Terrier is likely in the ancestry of both the Smooth and Wire. The Smooth Fox Terrier dominated the breed at first, seen in the show ring in England for almost two decades before the Wire. For almost a century, Smooths and Wires were designated as two varieties of one breed in the United States until 1984, when they were reclassified as separate breeds. Today, Fox Terriers are used as search and rescue dogs, drug-detection dogs, service dogs, circus dogs, and canine actors and are successful in various areas of the dog sport.

A small, compact, well-balanced dog, described in the standard as standing like a "cleverly made hunter." The Fox Terrier has square proportions; a short, level back; a deep chest; a high-set tail that is carried up but not over the back; straight legs; and round, compact feet. The skull is narrow and flat, and the muzzle gradually tapers. The eyes are small, round, deep set, dark, and full of fire. The ears are small and V-shaped, erect at the base with tips that fall forward, close to the cheeks.

Probably derived from the toy varieties of the English Bulldog, the Boule-dog Français, or French Bulldog, rose to popularity in the late nineteenth century and was beloved as a fashionable companion, especially for women. The breed quickly became popular in America, just as it had in France and England. Frenchies were written off as a Victorian fad in the early part of the twentieth century, cast in the shadow of the Boston Terrier. By the end of the century, Frenchies grew in popularity, and today, they continue to shine as favored companions the world over.

A compactly built, muscular dog of heavy bone, smooth coat, and of medium or small structure, the French Bulldog is prized for two distinctive features: its large and square head, flat between  the ears, and its bat ears, which must be broad at base, elongated, set high on head, not too close together, and with rounded tops. The eyes are set wide apart and are dark in color, giving the Frenchie an intelligent, alert, curious expression. The front legs are short and straight, set wide apart, and the hind legs, longer than the front, are muscular and strong.

Year of AKC recognition: 1898

Group: Non-Sporting

Size: 28 pounds or less

Coat: Moderately fine, brilliant, short, and smooth

Color: Solid brindle, fawn, white, and brindle and white are the most popular colors.

Life expectancy: 10–12 years

Activity level: Low. Frenchies are not very active, but a good daily walk is recommended. Begin lead training at an early age. Frenchies can be very willing, but they can be very stubborn, too. Turn lessons into games and this breed will want to play all the time.

Grooming: Brushing once a week will keep the coat resilient; shedding is minimal.

Temperament: Well-behaved, adaptable, and comfortable companions with an affectionate nature and even disposition, French Bulldogs are generally active, alert, and playful but not unduly boisterous. Somewhat territorial and protective, Frenchies make good watchdogs. First and foremost, they make fantastic companions and wonderful apartment dogs. They are snuggly bed mates who hog pillows and often snore. Early socialization for the puppy helps builds its confidence and character.

Parent club: French Bull Dog Club of America (www.frenchbulldogclub.org); founded in 1897

Buyers' advice from parent club: Seek out a reputable breeder, insist on AKC registration papers and a copy of the pedigree, and ask to meet the puppy's parents on the premises. Avoid "rare" colors, such as chocolate.

Regional clubs: The FBDCA's Web site lists established and developing clubs on its "Regional Clubs" page under "All About Us."

Rescue: French Bulldog Rescue Network (www.frenchbulldogrescue.org)

FRENCH BULLDOG

GERMAN PINSCHER

Year of AKC recognition: 2003

Group: Working

Size: 17–20 inches, 25–45 pounds

Coat: Short, dense, close fitting, and shiny

Color: Fawn, shades of red, stag red (red with black hairs intermixed), black with red/tan markings, blue with red/tan markings

Life expectancy: 12–14 years

Activity level: Moderately high. German Pinschers are bred for endurance and agility and must have daily exercise. They enjoy free running in a fenced yard, but they are adaptable dogs and will be happy with two long on-leash walks per day. They excel at many types of dog sports.

Grooming: The coat should be brushed weekly; the ears should be cleaned and the nails clipped as needed.

Temperament: This is a multipurpose working dog with the temperament and ability to perform a range of jobs. German Pinschers have a strong protective instinct, making them fearless and assertive watchdogs. Their heritage as vermin hunters makes them markedly determined and independent, and they have a strong prey drive. As companion dogs, they are loyal, affectionate, and playful. Most German Pinschers love playing with toys throughout their lives. Early socialization and training are essential to guide their natural instincts in a positive direction. German Pinschers are quite intelligent, and they learn quickly if trained with consistent leadership, patience, and respect.

Parent club: German Pinscher Club of America (www.german-pinscher.com); founded in 1985

Buyers' advice from parent club: This breed requires a high level of commitment from owners. When looking for a puppy, contact breeders who belong to the GPCA, and realize that it may not be easy to find a puppy. Meet the puppy's mother to gauge the puppy's eventual adult temperament.

Rescue: German Pinscher Club of America Rescue (www.germanpinschersrescue.org)

Many types of pinschers evolved in Germany, where they were used as farm dogs, ratters, and stable dogs for centuries. The German Pinscher shares a close association with the Standard Schnauzer. These various types were divided into separate breeds in the late nineteenth century based on coat and size, although several varieties, such as the Harlequin Pinscher and German Silky Pinscher, became extinct. The German Pinscher neared extinction in the wake of the two World Wars, but one breeder, Werner Jung, is credited with saving the breed. He constructed a breeding program based on four working farm dogs. The breed was first imported to America in the late 1970s and promoted at rare-breed shows.

This is an elegant, medium-sized dog. It is moderate, muscular, and agile, with square proportions and a close-fitting, smooth coat. The back is firm and level, and the body is compact and strong. The docked tail is carried above the level of the back. Feet are well arched and round. The muzzle equals the length of the flat skull. The ears are set high and carried erect if cropped or folded if uncropped. The eyes are dark and oval shaped, giving the dog a sharp, alert expression.

The German Shepherd Dog was developed in Germany in the late 1800s. Captain Max Von Stephanitz is credited with creating the breed by using several German herding breeds. The GSD became known around the world soon after its development, and it rose to popularity after World War I, thanks to a combination of the breed's wartime accomplishments and public acclaim for Rin Tin Tin and Strongheart, the first of many celebrated German Shepherd screen stars.

The German Shepherd Dog is a strong, rugged, athletic breed with an aloof, noble demeanor. It is rectangular in proportion and has a long neck, a bushy tail that  is long enough to reach the hock, and a powerful, ground-covering gait. The head features a moderately arched forehead; a long, strong, wedge-shaped muzzle; and strong jaws. The eyes are dark, medium sized, almond shaped, and set obliquely. The moderately pointed ears are carried erect, and the dog's overall expression is calm and intelligent.

Year of AKC recognition: 1908

Group: Herding

Size: Males—24–26 inches, 65–90 pounds; females—22–24 inches, 50–70 pounds

Coat: This breed has a medium-length double coat with a harsh, straight, dense outer coat. The hair on the head and legs is shorter, and the hair on the neck is longer and thicker.

Color: The GSD varies in color but is often seen in tan with a black mask and black saddle markings. White is not permitted in the show ring.

Life expectancy: 7–10 years

Activity level: High. GSDs have stamina and require daily mental and physical challenges; they will become bored and depressed if confined or neglected. As house dogs, they are well-mannered, pleasant companions.

Grooming: Frequent brushing to control shedding.

Temperament: The German Shepherd was bred to be a versatile, trainable, willing worker. It is considered to be one of the most intelligent breeds, and it has a great ability to ignore distractions and focus on work. This is a poised, confident, self-assured dog with a protective nature. GSDs make excellent watchdogs and are typically reserved with strangers. Loyal, sensitive, and reliable, German Shepherds have a strong desire to please. They have been trained to perform an incredible range of jobs. This was the first breed trained as guide dogs for the blind. The GSD also has a long and illustrious list of acting credits.

Parent club: German Shepherd Dog Club of America (www.gsdca.org); founded in 1913

Buyers' advice from parent club: There are marked differences between the sexes, which prospective owners should consider before choosing a puppy. Do not choose a shy puppy. Make sure that hips and elbows are covered in the breeder's health guarantee.

Regional clubs: Information is located under "About the GSDCA" on the club's Web site.

Rescue: American German Shepherd Rescue Association (www.agsra.org)

GERMAN SHEPHERD DOG

GERMAN SHORTHAIRED POINTER

Year of AKC recognition: 1930

Group: Sporting

Size: Males—23–25 inches, 55–70 pounds; females—21–23 inches, 45–60 pounds

Coat: Water repellent, short, hard, thick, and close-fitting

Color: Solid liver, liver and white ticked, patched, or roan (a fine mixture of white and colored hairs)

Life expectancy: 10–12 years

Activity level: High. This is an all-purpose hunting dog with exceptional mental and physical energy that must be channeled. Shorthairs require a great deal of exercise as well as interaction with their owners. They should have at least one half hour running twice a day. They also love swimming, jogging, and retrieving games.

Grooming: Weekly brushing with a grooming glove or rubber horse brush is recommended.

Temperament: Extremely intelligent and willing to please, the GSP is a versatile hunting dog for trailing, pointing, and retrieving on land or water. Shorthairs are responsive and learn quickly, but young dogs may have trouble staying focused. Obedience training is recommended for puppies to encourage self control. Puppies may appear physically mature by six months of age but do not achieve mental and emotional maturity until two years of age. GSPs also make good watchdogs.

Parent club: German Shorthaired Pointer Club of America (www.gspca.org)

Buyers' advice from parent club: Inquire about the parents' health clearances. Potential owners should be prepared for the breed's active hunting-dog temperament.

Regional clubs: Around seventy regional US GSP clubs are listed on the parent club's Web site under "Regional GSP Clubs."

Rescue: German Shorthaired Pointer Rescue (www.gsprescue.org)

The breed originated in the late nineteenth century from a combination of Pointer stock—often cited as the German Bird Dog and Old Spanish Pointer—and scenthounds selectively bred to produce an obedient, versatile gundog. The scenthounds (*Schweisshunde*, in German) were used to improve the dog's ability to track and trail. Pointers from England were later used to improve the dog's stance, style, and nose. The breed has been known in the United States since the 1920s and has since been prized as a hunting dog, show dog, and companion.

This is an aristocratic, well-balanced, medium-sized dog with notable power, endurance, and agility. It has a deep chest and a short, strong, level back. The tail is high set, docked, and carried horizontally. The skull is broad and arched; the muzzle and skull are equal in length. The GSP has dark brown, almond-shaped eyes, giving it an intelligent, good-humored expression. Its broad ears are set slightly above eye level and lie close to the head.

The German Wirehaired Pointer was developed in the late nineteenth century from a combination of Pudelpointer, Foxhound, Polish Water Dog, and German Shorthaired Pointer; it was selectively bred for ruggedness and versatility as a hunting dog. This was a highly popular sporting dog in Germany for decades before being officially recognized as a breed in 1928. The GWP was first imported to America in the 1920s. In addition to hunting, GWPs are also trained as drug-detection dogs, therapy dogs, and canine actors.

The German Wirehaired Pointer is medium sized, well balanced, and sturdy. Its hallmark traits are the hard, protective, wiry coat and the facial furnishings. The head is moderately long, with a broad skull, a long muzzle, and medium-length beard and whiskers. The jaws are strong, and the nose is dark brown. The oval-shaped eyes are overhung with bushy eyebrows. The ears are rounded and hang close to the head. The GWP's overall proportions are rectangular. The arched neck blends into a sloping backline. The chest is deep, and the docked tail is set high and carried at or above horizontal.

Year of AKC recognition: 1959

Group: Sporting

Size: Males—24–26 inches; females—smaller than males, but minimum 22 inches

Coat: The weather-resistant coat is made up of a dense undercoat and a flat, harsh, wiry outer coat of 1–2 inches in length. The coat is shorter on the head and legs, and is denser on the shoulders and tail. The breed has a wiry beard, whiskers, and eyebrows.

Color: Liver and white spotted, with or without roaning and ticking; liver roan; solid liver

Life expectancy: 14–16 years

Activity level: High. This is a high-energy, high-drive hunting dog. GWPs also compete successfully in skijoring, field trials, obedience, agility, and tracking.

Grooming: The GWP sheds minimally. Weekly brushing will maintain a coat of correct harsh texture.

Temperament: The GWP has a typical pointer personality. The breed bonds closely with people, craves human companionship, and does not do well in a kennel environment. GWPs can become possessive toward their owners. They are creative, independent, strong-willed dogs that must have a job to do. They have a high prey drive and may not get along with cats and other small pets. Like other gundogs, GWPs have a pronounced desire to please and respond readily to training.

Parent club: German Wirehaired Pointer Club of America (www.gwpca.com); founded in 1953

Buyers' advice from parent club: GWPCA member breeders provide the following paperwork to all puppy buyers: a sales or co-ownership agreement, the AKC registration papers or application, feeding and training advice, veterinary records, a three-generation pedigree, and a copy of the club's Code of Ethics.

Regional clubs: There are about a dozen regional GWP clubs in the United States, information on which can be found under "Local Clubs" on the parent club's Web site.

Rescue: Rescue information can be found on the GWPCA's Web site under "Rescue."

GERMAN WIREHAIRED POINTER

GIANT SCHNAUZER

Year of AKC recognition: 1930

Group: Working

Size: Males—25½–27½ inches; females—23½–25½ inches

Coat: This breed has a hard, dense, wiry outer coat with a soft undercoat as well as coarse hair on top of the head and a longer beard and eyebrows.

Color: Black or pepper and salt (a shade of gray created by the "peppering" of black and white hairs throughout the top coat and a gray undercoat)

Life expectancy: 12–15 years

Activity level: High. Giants are working dogs, and they must have an outlet for their mental and physical energy. They excel at most dog sports.

Grooming: The coat needs brushing two or three times per week and clipping about every six weeks.

Temperament: This is a versatile working dog that is intelligent, spirited, and alert. Giant Schnauzers learn quickly and should be introduced to basic training by eight to twelve weeks of age. They are vigilant and courageous, with strong territorial and protective instincts. Giants are excellent watchdogs but are typically reserved with strangers.

Parent club: Giant Schnauzer Club of America (www.giantschnauzerclubofamerica.com); founded in 1962

Buyers' advice from parent club: Find a reputable breeder and take your time selecting a puppy. Potential owners should be prepared for a large, high-energy working dog with an intense devotion to his owners.

Rescue: Information on Giant Schnauzer rescue can be found on the parent club's Web site.

Schnauzers and pinschers were developed in Bavaria as all-purpose farm dogs. Breeders combined the Standard Schnauzer, sheepdogs, the Great Dane, and possibly the Bouvier des Flanders to create a schnauzer breed with more size and power. The Giant quickly found favor as a livestock guardian and draft dog; by the 1890s it was also widely used to guard homes and businesses. Prior to World War I, Giants were trained as police dogs in Germany and later recruited for military work. They were imported to America after World War I, but the breed remained rare until the 1970s.

This is a robust, all-purpose, working guard dog. It is squarely proportioned and well angulated with a short, firm back and a docked, high-set tail that is carried high. The large feet are well arched and round with thick pads. The Giant Schnauzer has a strong rectangular head with its trademark coarse beard and eyebrows, contributing to a recognizable silhouette. The nose is large and black; the eyes are medium sized, oval, and dark brown; and the ears may be cropped or uncropped.

This is one of the four native Irish terrier breeds. It originated in the Glen of Imaal in County Wicklow, where it was used to hunt badger and fox and to cook dinner, the latter in its unique occupation as turn-spit dogs, turning roasting meat over open fires. Because the valley in which the breed developed has always been remote, the Glen was virtually unknown for years. Flemish and Lowland soldiers settled in the area in the sixteenth century, and their low-slung French dogs intermingled with existing terri-ers to create the breed's prototype. The Glen was recognized in Ireland in 1933 and was brought to America in the 1930s.

The Glen is a rough-and-ready worker, a short-legged terrier with a long, muscular body and great substance for his small size. The moderately short front legs are bowed,  and the feet are strong and round. The tail is strong, set high, and carried gaily; it may be docked. The Glen has a broad, slightly domed skull and a strong muzzle and jaw. The ears are rose or semi-prick.

Year of AKC recognition: 2004

Group: Terrier

Size: 12½–14 inches, 32–40 pounds.

Coat: Medium-length, harsh outer coat with a soft undercoat. The coat on head and furnishings is softer.

Color: Shades of wheaten, blue, or brindle

Life expectancy: 10–15 years

Activity level: Moderate. Glens can adapt to a city or country lifestyle. They love long walks and rambles through the woods. They should be exercised on lead or in a fenced yard, as they may chase small animals. They also dig under fencing, so it must be reinforced. Glens are not strong swimmers and should not have access to swimming pools. They make excellent agility dogs.

Grooming: The coat should be brushed thoroughly with a slicker brush once or twice a week to prevent matting and help remove dead hair. It should be stripped every six to nine months to keep it neat and to preserve its hard protective texture.

Temperament: Glens are spirited, courageous, loyal companions. They have no trouble relaxing "after hours," but they are all business when it comes to work. They are active, silent workers with strong prey drive. They should be supervised when introduced to other dogs and cats.

Parent club: Glen of Imaal Terrier Club of America (www.glens.org); founded in 1986

Buyers' advice from parent club: This is a very rare breed. There are approximately 600–700 Glens registered at any time and a limited number of puppies available.

GLEN OF IMAAL TERRIER

GOLDEN RETRIEVER

Year of AKC recognition: 1925

Group: Sporting

Size: Males—23–24 inches, 65–75 pounds; females—21½–22½ inches, 55–65 pounds

Coat: Goldens have a water-repellent double coat. The outer coat is straight or wavy; the undercoat is dense. There is longer feathering on the back of the legs, the abdomen, the neck, and the tail. The head, the feet, and the fronts of the legs have shorter coat.

Color: Rich, lustrous shades of gold

Life expectancy: 10–12 years

Activity level: High. Most Goldens do fine with thirty minutes of walking, running, or playing twice a day, and they also enjoy hiking, swimming, and sporting activities such as agility and obedience. Goldens under two years of age should not engage in overly strenuous, high-impact exercise.

Grooming: Weekly brushing and regular trimming are recommended. An online grooming tutorial is available on the national breed club's Web site.

Temperament: This is an exceptionally intelligent breed. The first three dogs to earn AKC Obedience Champion titles were Golden Retrievers. Goldens are very people-oriented, friendly, sociable, and trustworthy. They typically get along well with dogs and other pets. Individual temperaments within the breed range from mellow to challenging.

Parent club: Golden Retriever Club of America (www.grca.org); founded in 1938

Buyers' advice from parent club: Choose a serious hobby breeder from whom to obtain a puppy. Your breeder should be a member of a Golden Retriever club or all-breed dog club, be involved in some aspect of the dog sport, allow you to see the puppy's living environment and meet the puppy's dam, and show you all of the puppy's health records as well as documentation of the sire's and dam's health-testing results.

Regional clubs: There are close to seventy US regional clubs; see the "Member Clubs" page under "The GRCA" on the parent club's Web site.

Rescue: Golden Retriever Club of America National Rescue Committee (http://grca-nrc.org)

The breed was developed in Scotland in the 1800s from a combination of local retriever breeds, the Tweed Water Spaniel, the Irish Setter, and possibly the Bloodhound. The resulting combination was ideally suited to the climate, terrain, and game of the Scottish Highlands. Known first simply as "yellow retrievers," they were noted for their versatility and trainability and became immediately popular with sportsmen in the late nineteenth century. The Golden first competed in field trials in 1904 and at conformation shows in 1906, where it was classified as "Retriever—Wavy or Flat Coated." Goldens were imported to America in the 1890s and registered as a distinct breed with the AKC in 1925. By the 1930s, the Golden Retriever was widely known. Today the breed is popular as a pet, hunting dog, and field-trial dog. Goldens are trained as bomb and drug-detection dogs, service dogs, guide dogs, therapy dogs, and search and rescue dogs. They also excel at most dog sports.

The Golden is a powerful, well-balanced hunting dog with rectangular proportions; a strong, level back; and a long tail that is carried level with the back or curved slightly above and has feathering on the underside. The skull is broad and slightly arched, and the muzzle blends smoothly into the skull. The eyes are dark and wide set, and the short ears fall close to the head. The Golden's expression is friendly and intelligent.

"Setting spaniels" became popular as gundogs with sportsmen during the eighteenth century, but black-and-tan setters had been known since the sixteenth century in Britain. A strain of black and tan setting dogs owned by the Duke of Gordon in Scotland was first described in 1820; the duke is credited for establishing the breed. Gordons soon became renowned for their trainability, endurance, scenting power, and dependable working style. A pair of these dogs arrived in America in 1842, one of which went to Daniel Webster. The breed's wonderful disposition and aristocratic appearance soon made it popular as both a hunter and companion dog.

The largest of the three setter breeds, the Gordon is noted for its noble bearing, upstanding stylish gait, and sleek black and tan coat. The breed has plenty of bone and substance; a strong, short back; a deep chest; and a short tail with feathering on its underside. The neck is long, lean, and  arched; and the muzzle and skull are approximately equal in length. The eyes are dark brown and oval shaped, and the ears are large, thin, set low, and covered with feathering.

Year of AKC recognition: 1884

Group: Sporting

Size: Males—24–27 inches, 55–80 pounds; females—23–26 inches, 45–70 pounds

Coat: Straight or slightly wavy with longer hair on the ears, abdomen, chest, back of the legs, and tail

Color: Black with clearly defined markings that range from chestnut to mahogany

Life expectancy: 12–13 years

Activity level: High. This is an adaptable breed, but Gordons have stamina and energy and need plenty of daily exercise. If you don't plan to hunt with your Gordon, you can keep him active with activities such as hiking, jogging, and organized dog sports. The Gordon is equally successful as a show dog and a hunter.

Grooming: Weekly brushing is recommended. The ears should be checked frequently.

Temperament: Gordons are typically well-mannered house dogs—loyal, affectionate, and intensely devoted to their owners. They have excellent bird sense but usually work best for their owners. They were bred to be patient, methodical workers, which means that they have long memories. They don't easily forget training or mistreatment and must be taught with gentle, positive methods. Gordons can be aloof with strangers, and they have a good protective instinct. Alert and fearless, a Gordon will sound the alarm if it detects an intruder.

Parent club: Gordon Setter Club of America (www.gsca.org); founded in 1924

Buyers' advice from parent club: The Gordon Setter Club of America encourages interested parties to investigate the breed thoroughly. The club's Breeder Referral Chairperson can provide prospective owners with a list of breeders.

Regional clubs: Close to twenty US breed clubs are listed on the parent club's Web site on the "Regional Clubs" page under "The Club."

Rescue: Information on the GSCA's Rescue Program is on the "Rescue/adoption" page under "Gordon Setters" on the club's Web site.

GORDON SETTER

GREAT DANE

Year of AKC recognition: 1887

Group: Working

Size: Males—at least 30 inches, and upward of 32 inches preferred in competition; 140–175 pounds. Females—at least 28 inches, and upward of 30 inches preferred in competition; 110–140 pounds.

Coat: Short, thick, glossy, and smooth

Color: Brindle, fawn with a black mask, blue, black, harlequin (white with patches of black), and mantle (black with white markings)

Life expectancy: 7–10 years

Activity level: Moderate. Strenuous exercise is not recommended for growing Dane puppies.

Grooming: Brush weekly; coat is easy to care for.

Temperament: This is a spirited, courageous breed, noted for its sensitive, gentle nature. The Great Dane has a strong protective instinct and makes an excellent watchdog. Because of its great size, early consistent training and socialization are essential. Danes are easy to housebreak but mature slowly. Puppies may reach adult size by fifteen months of age but may not achieve mental and emotional maturity until age three. At maturity, Danes are typically adaptable, reliable dogs with the breed's famous sociable, affectionate nature and good house manners. They need human companionship but may not get along well with other pets.

Parent club: Great Dane Club of America (http://gdca.org); founded in 1889

Buyers' advice from parent club: This is an extremely large, strong dog and can be expensive to maintain. Owners should be prepared for a very large, lively puppy; obedience training is essential. Puppies can be highly destructive to landscaping. Danes require a securely fenced yard; 6-foot fencing is sufficient. Unusual colors, such as white, merle fawnequin, or merlequin, are not prized rarities.

Regional clubs: The parent club lists approximately fifty affiliates on its Web site under "Affiliation," under "Organization" on the home page.

Rescue: GDCA Rescue is on the club's Web site under "Health and Welfare," under "Great Dane" on the home page.

The Great Dane developed from an ancient combination of Mastiff and Irish Wolfhound. Since Roman times, these dogs were bred for size, strength, speed, endurance, and courage and were employed for guarding, military work, and big-game hunting. By the nineteenth century, several types of running mastiffs, known by various names, existed throughout Europe. It was designated as the national breed of Germany in 1876. Over the course of decades, breeders gradually came to a consensus regarding the breed's name and precise description. The growing popularity of dog shows attracted legions of new fanciers to the Great Dane in the late nineteenth century. It remains popular as a show dog and companion.

The Great Dane is known as the "Apollo of Dogs," legendary for its size and power. This giant breed is equally noted for its elegance and regal appearance. It is squarely proportioned with a long, well-arched neck; a short, level back; a deep chest; and a gracefully tucked-up underline. The long, straight tail may curve but is not carried above the level of the back. The feet are round and compact with well-arched toes. The head is long and rectangular with a full, square jaw. The eyes are deep set, medium sized, and almond shaped. The ears are set high and medium sized—folded forward close to the cheek if natural or held erect if cropped.

This ancient livestock guardian may have originated in Central Asia or Siberia. It was used for centuries to protect flocks in the Pyrenees Mountains. Great Pyrenees were brought to Newfoundland by early settlers as guards and companions, and the breed is believed to have contributed to the development of the Newfoundland breed. General Lafayette imported a pair of Great Pyrenees to America in 1824. Although Pyrs proved their merit as effective livestock guardians, there were no serious efforts to establish the breed in America until the 1930s. Great Pyrenees were used as military dogs during both World Wars.

The Great Pyrenees is distinguished by its size, majesty, and thick white coat. It is designed for strenuous work in any type of weather or terrain. It has moderate  bone, good muscle, rectangular proportions, a moderately broad chest, and a broad back. The plumed tail is carried over the back in a wheel when aroused. The Pyr's expression is contemplative, kindly, and regal. The head is wedge shaped, and the muzzle equals the length of back skull. The dog has strong jaws and a black nose. It has a slight furrow between its dark brown, almond-shaped eyes, and it has small ears with rounded tips, set at eye level and carried flat and close to the head.

Year of AKC recognition: 1933

Group: Working

Size: Males—27–32 inches, 100 pounds and up; females—25–29 inches, 85 pounds and up

Coat: The weather-resistant double coat consists of a long, flat, thick coarse outer coat and a dense, fine, woolly undercoat. The coat is shorter and finer on the face and ears and longer and more profuse on the neck and shoulders, with feathering on the back of the legs and tail. Males carry more coat.

Color: White or white with gray, badger, reddish brown, or tan markings

Life expectancy: 10–12 years

Activity level: Moderate. The Great Pyrenees is not typically a good off-leash companion and requires sturdy fencing. This is an excellent breed for carting and sled work.

Grooming: Weekly brushing is recommended. The Pyr's coat should never be clipped in summer because the coat provides protection from the sun.

Temperament: A gentle, affectionate dog famed for its quiet, patient demeanor, the Great Pyrenees is a loyal and loving companion with its family but is typically reserved with strangers. The breed is confident and fearless, with strong territorial and protective instincts; naturally vigilant, they make excellent watchdogs (though they can be barkers, especially at night). Males may not tolerate other dogs in the home. Strong-willed and independent, they need patient, consistent leadership.

Parent club: Great Pyrenees Club of America (http://clubs.akc.org/gpca); founded in 1934

Buyers' advice from parent club: Look for a strong, sturdy, healthy puppy from a reputable breeder. Ask to see both parents of the puppy. Owners who are not ready for the demands of a puppy should consider a mature dog.

Regional clubs: The GPCA has close to twenty-five US clubs, divided into five regions. Information is found on the club's Web site under "Affiliated Clubs."

Rescue: The GPCA Rescue Program can be found under "Rescue Information" on the club's Web site.

GREATER SWISS MOUNTAIN DOG

Year of AKC recognition: 1995

Group: Working

Size: Males—25½–28½ inches, 115–140 pounds; females—23½–27 inches, 85–110 pounds

Coat: Dense and protective, 1¼–2 inches in length, with a thick undercoat

Color: Black with symmetrical rust and white markings

Life expectancy: 8–11 years

Activity level: Moderate. This is an agile, robust working breed. Swissies enjoy hiking, carting, obedience work, herding, weight pulling, backpacking and more. They require daily exercise but should not be exercised in hot weather. Strenuous high-impact exercise is not recommended for growing puppies.

Grooming: Brush twice a week and more frequently during seasonal shedding in spring and fall.

Temperament: Noted for their sociable nature, Swissies are faithful, willing workers and excellent watchdogs. They are typically slow to mature and need consistent positive training and owners.

Parent club: Greater Swiss Mountain Dog Club of America (www.gsmdca.org); founded in 1968

Buyer's advice from parent club: A very powerful breed, a Swissie can pull 3,000 pounds of freight. They grow large at a young age, but are not fully mature until four or five years. They must have extensive early socialization and training to encourage good manners and self control. Owners must be prepared to establish fair, consistent leadership to prevent bad habits such as pulling on the leash, jumping, or refusing to cooperate for grooming.

Regional clubs: Thirteen regional clubs are listed on the parent club's Web site under "Recognized Clubs."

Rescue: Greater Swiss Mountain Dog Rescue Foundation (www.gsmdrescue.org)

This is one of four breeds developed from local mastiff stock and widely used in Switzerland for draft work, herding, and guarding. This oldest and largest of Swiss breeds contributed to the early development of both the Saint Bernard and the Rottweiler. The breed was nearly extinct by the end of the nineteenth century, when Zurich dog expert Dr. Albert Heim fostered the breed's revival. The Greater Swiss Mountain Dog was first shown in 1908, and recognized by the Swiss Kennel Club in 1909. The breed was first imported to America in 1968, and the first American litter was born in 1970.

This is a large, powerful, heavy-boned, well-muscled dog. It has slightly rectangular proportions; a level back; a broad chest; and a long, thick tail that reaches to the hock. The flat, broad skull equals the length of the large, blunt muzzle. The nose is black; the brown eyes are almond shaped; and the ears are medium sized, triangular with rounded tips, and lay close to the head. The expression is animated and gentle.

Possibly the oldest type of hunting dog, Greyhound-type dogs have been documented by ancient civilizations for 5,000 years. In medieval times, Greyhounds were used to chase large game, ranging from stag to boar. As large game disappeared in Britain, coursing became popular as an organized sport. By the nineteenth century, winning Greyhounds were treated as national sports heroes. They were among the first breeds brought to the New World by European explorers in the 1500s. In America, game abounded and Greyhounds were widely used for their traditional purpose. They were recognized by AKC in 1885. A few decades later, Greyhound racing debuted in the 1920s. Both racing and coursing remain popular amateur sports, and Greyhound racing and coursing clubs can be found throughout the United States.

The Greyhound is the fastest breed of dog, clocked at over 40 mph. It is built for speed, a perfect combination of utility and beauty. The breed remains consistent with ancient descriptions. It has a long, flat, narrow head; a long, tapered muzzle; and strong jaws. The ears are small, thin, and folded back or raised in semi-pricked carriage when the dog is alert. It has a long, muscular neck; a deep chest; a broad, muscular back; long, strong, straight legs; and long, oval-shaped feet to provide extra leverage when running. The long, fine tail is carried with a slight upward curve.

Year of AKC recognition: 1885

Group: Hound

Size: Males—28–30 inches, 65–70 pounds; females—27–28 inches, 60–65 pounds

Coat: Short, smooth, and fine

Color: All colors

Life expectancy: 10–13 years

Activity level: Moderate. Greyhounds need regular opportunities to run. They will take off in pursuit of anything they perceive as prey, so they must be exercised on lead or in a fenced yard. Greyhounds are intolerant of cold and should not be left outdoors in cold weather.

Grooming: Weekly brushing is recommended.

Temperament: Greyhounds are friendly and sociable with people and very tolerant of other dogs. Some Greyhounds have a very strong prey drive and are not recommended for homes with small pets. They are very affectionate with their owners and are well-mannered, quiet house dogs. Although Greyhounds are sensitive and intelligent, it can be challenging to maintain their attention for formal training because they instinctively prioritize hunting.

Parent club: Greyhound Club of America (www.greyhoundclubofamerica.org); founded in 1907

Buyer's advice from parent club: Find a good breeder, and ask questions about longevity, temperament, and health. Begin looking at puppies well in advance of your purchase, as relatively few litters are bred each year. Consider rescuing a retired racer—many organizations specialize in these adoptions.

Rescue: The Greyhound Club of America lists rescue information on its Web site on the "GCA Rescue" page under "Club." Resources for rescuing a retired racer are also referenced on this page.

GREYHOUND

HARRIER

Year of AKC recognition: 1885

Group: Hound

Size: 19–21 inches, 45–60 pounds

Coat: Short, dense, hard and glossy

Color: Any color but most often tricolored (black, tan, white in saddle or open markings or red and white from pale tan to deep red)

Life expectancy: 12–15 years

Activity level: High. Bred to work tirelessly under all conditions, Harriers must be exercised on lead or in a fenced yard.

Grooming: Weekly brushing is recommended.

Temperament: An even-tempered, outgoing, friendly, and tolerant hound, the Harrier gets along well with other animals. Harriers are people-oriented and need regular social interaction. If neglected or bored, a Harrier can become destructive or overly vocal. A Harrier in the habit of howling won't please an owner's neighbors. Although quick to alert owners of intruders, Harriers do not make good guard dogs. Harriers were traditionally bred for hunting and also do well in agility and tracking. They have excellent problem-solving skills and are easier to train than most other hounds.

Parent club: Harrier Club of America (www. harrierclubofamerica.com); founded in 1992

Buyer's advice from parent club: Most Harriers come from working lines. Owners should be prepared for a dog with strong scenthound instincts. They will wander if not fenced or leashed, and they can dig under fences. Training should start early to channel their instincts in the right direction. Food portions must be controlled to prevent a Harrier from overeating.

Rescue: Harrier Club of America Rescue can be found on the club's Web site under "Harrier Rescue."

Many theories have been advanced concerning the breed's beginnings. Scenthounds developed in Europe were brought to England during the Norman Conquest and were used to hunt hare. Information on Harrier packs in England can be traced back to the Penistone Pack established in 1250. Early records show that Foxhounds, Harriers, and Beagles were interbred and classified by size and of hunting specialization rather than lineage. Harriers were developed by selectively breeding from this basic stock to create a slow, sturdy scenthound with exceptional stamina.

The Harrier is a large-boned, sturdy hound. It is well balanced with slightly rectangular proportions; a long, strong neck; a level back; and a deep chest. The feet are strong and round. Its long tail tapers to a point with a brush of hair, carried high but not over the back. The skull and muzzle are approximately equal length and the nose is wide with well-opened nostrils. The Harrier has a characteristic gentle expression with medium-sized brown or hazel eyes and low-set ears held close to the head.

The national dog of Cuba descended from small breeds brought to the island from Europe via the port of Tenerife over the centuries. It was bred as a family companion dog and became very popular both in Cuba and in Europe. Known variously as the Havana Silk Dog, Spanish Silk Poodle, and Bichon Havanese, the breed neared extinction in Cuba in the 1950s, as people and their dogs left the country during the Cuban Revolution, but a few dogs that ended up in the United States were used to establish breeding programs. Most of today's Havanese trace their ancestry back to these bloodlines.

This is a small, sturdy dog with rectangular proportions and a profuse coat. It has a neck of moderate length, a back that rises from shoulder to hips, and a high-set tail covered with a plume of  silky hair and carried loosely over the rump. The skull is broad and slightly rounded, with a rectangular muzzle. The medium-length ears are set high, and the dark eyes give the breed a soft, intelligent expression.

Year of AKC recognition: 1996

Group: Toy

Size: 8½–11½ inches

Coat: Havanese have a long, abundant double coat that is soft and light in texture. The outer coat is slightly heavier than the undercoat.

Color: All colors or color combinations

Life expectancy: 14–16

Activity level: Moderate. Havanese enjoy activities such as obedience, rally, agility, and even flyball.

Grooming: The coat sheds minimally and should be brushed or combed daily to prevent matting.

Temperament: The Havanese is known for its friendly disposition. Havanese are wonderful companions—playful, affectionate, and entertaining. They are sociable and typically get along well with other pets. As they are attentive and responsive to training, they can do well in dog sports and make wonderful therapy dogs.

Parent club: Havanese Club of America (www.havanese.org); founded in 1979

Buyers' advice from parent club: Buyers may face a wait for a puppy, as the interest in puppies far exceeds their availability from good breeders who do all necessary health testing. Buyers may have to travel to obtain a puppy, as there are not Havanese breeders in every state.

Regional clubs: There are about twenty local Havanese clubs, whose information can be found on the parent club's Web site under "Local Clubs."

Rescue: Havanese Rescue, Inc. (www.havaneserescue.com)

HAVANESE

IBIZAN HOUND

Year of AKC recognition: 1978

Group: Hound

Size: Males—23½–27½ inches, 50 pounds; females—22½–26 inches, 45 pounds

Coat: There are two coat types in the breed: short and wire. The short coat is hard, short, and flat, and the wirehaired coat is hard, wiry, and 1–3 inches in length.

Color: White, red, or any combination of the two

Life expectancy: 11–14 years

Activity level: Moderate to high. This is a strong, resilient hunting dog, bred to track fast game over challenging terrain. Ibizans possess unequalled jumping ability and can easily clear a 5-foot fence. Noted for their versatility and trainability, they can be superior performers in obedience, tracking, lure coursing, and open field coursing. Puppies are slow to mature and owners should be prepared to supervise adolescents closely.

Grooming: Weekly brushing is all that's needed for both coat types, along with occasional bathing and ear cleaning.

Temperament: Affectionate and loyal, Ibizans make excellent family companions. They have a strong hunting instinct but can be trained to accept cats and other small pets. They can be quite vocal and therefore make good watchdogs, as they are quick to sound the alarm. In general, Ibizans are aloof with strangers. They are quick to learn, and their remarkable problem-solving skills include an amazing ability to open gates and cupboards. They are quite sensitive and intolerant of rough handling or punishment.

Parent club: Ibizan Hound Club of the United States (www.ihcus.org); founded in 1975

Buyers' advice from parent club: Find a reputable breeder. Ask about the puppy's pedigree, hereditary problems, and any health testing done on the parents.

Rescue: Information on IHCUS Rescue can be found on the parent club's Web site under "Rescue."

Prick-eared sighthounds are believed to have been prevalent in ancient Egypt. However, breed historians can only speculate on a possible connection between dogs of Northern Africa and the Balearic Islands. For centuries, the Ibizan Hound was primarily used to hunt rabbits on the island of Ibiza. Today the breed remains true to its original purpose in Spain. The Ibizan was first brought to the United States in 1956 and has never become a popular companion dog.

This is an elegant, athletic dog noted for its graceful outline, light pigment and eye color, and large, pointed ears. It has a long, narrow head; a flat skull; a long, tapered muzzle with a slightly Roman profile; and a light, flesh-colored nose. Its small eyes range in color from amber to caramel. The Ibizan is moderately built, with a long, slender, arched neck; a level back; long, light-boned legs; and oval-shaped hare feet. Its low-set tail reaches to the hock and is carried in the sickle, ring, or saber position.

Iceland's only native breed, the Icelandic Sheepdog derives from ancestors who are thought to have arrived with Vikings in the ninth and tenth centuries. Over the centuries, the Icelandic Sheepdog became perfectly adapted to the terrain and farming methods of the island and was widely used as a general-purpose farm dog. The breed became rare in the late nineteenth and early to mid-twentieth centuries. Efforts to revive the breed began in the late 1960s, when some were imported to California to start a breeding program. Today the breed is primarily a companion but is still used for herding in Iceland. Icelandic Sheep-dogs are also trained for search and rescue.

This is a typical Nordic spitz breed, rectangular in proportion with a confident, lively bearing and an abundant coat. It has a moderately long, muscular, slightly arched neck; a level, sturdy back; a deep chest; and a

high-set tail that is curled over and touching the back. The head is triangular with flat cheeks and a tapered muzzle. The eyes are medium sized and almond shaped, contributing to a gentle, happy expression. The ears are erect, medium sized, and triangular, with rounded tips.

Year of AKC recognition: 2010

Group: Herding

Size: Males—18 inches, 30 pounds; females—16½ inches, 25 pounds

Coat: A thick, waterproof, protective double coat in which the outer coat is coarse and the undercoat is thick and soft. The shorthaired coat type has a medium-length outer coat, and the longhaired coat type has a slightly longer outer coat. Both have bushy hair on the tail; shorter hair on the face, top of the head, ears, and fronts of the legs; and longer hair on the neck, chest, and back of the thighs.

Color: The predominant color should be chocolate brown, gray, black, or a shade of tan. The most common markings are white, tricolor (white with tan points) on a black dog, and a black mask and some black in the body coat on a tan or gray dog.

Life expectancy: 12–14 years

Activity level: Moderate. This is a hardy, agile working dog, but it does not have the high drive of some other herding breeds. Versatile and playful, Icelandic Sheepdogs do well in dog sports such as agility, herding, and tracking. They also love long walks, hiking, and swimming. Some will climb or jump over fences.

Grooming: Brush at least weekly.

Temperament: Cheerful, friendly, inquisitive, and playful, this is an excellent family dog, famed for its wide smile. Icelandic Sheepdogs are very sociable and need plenty of interaction with their owners; they can suffer from separation anxiety without adequate attention. They are responsive and eager to please but naturally soft tempered. Training must be gentle and positive; rough handling or harsh training can cause stress barking. This is an outgoing breed that will get along well with people and other animals if socialized properly.

Parent club: Icelandic Sheepdog Association of America (www.icelanddogs.com); founded in 1997

Buyers' advice from parent club: This breed must be treated as a member of the family.

Rescue: The National Icelandic Sheepdog Rescue Alliance (www.nationalicelandicsheepdog rescuealliance.org)

ICELANDIC SHEEPDOG

IRISH RED AND WHITE SETTER

Year of AKC recognition: 2009

Group: Sporting

Size: Males—24½–26 inches; females—22½–24 inches

Coat: Long, silky feathering is present on the ears, flank, chest, throat, tail, and backs of legs. On the head, fronts of the legs, and body, the hair is short, flat, and straight or slightly wavy.

Color: White with solid red patches

Life expectancy: 11–15 years

Activity level: Irish Red and Whites are high-energy dogs who need daily running time. If you don't plan to use your dog for hunting, he will enjoy performance events such as rally, tracking, and agility.

Grooming: Brush your dog once or twice weekly.

Temperament: Courageous, spirited, and determined, Irish Red and White Setters make great companions for active families. They are sociable and typically good with other pets. They are friendly, good-natured, and eager to please, and they respond readily to training. However, the breed tends to have a soft temperament, meaning that it is sensitive to reprimands and harsh treatment. They must be trained using gentle positive-reinforcement methods.

Parent club: Irish Red and White Setter Association of America (www.irwsa.com); founded in 1997

Buyers' advice from parent club: Be certain that you are dealing with a breeder who is a member of the IRWSA. Always meet the breeder in person and ask many questions. The parent club recommends that owners find responsible breeders who will provide them with the AKC registration application and papers and a three-generation pedigree.

Rescue: The Irish Red and White Setter Association Rescue page is located under "Rescue" on the parent club's Web site.

The Irish Red and White Setter has been known in Ireland since the seventeenth century. By the nineteenth century, the breed was eclipsed by the flashy, solid-red Irish Setter and its growing popularity. Efforts to revive the nearly extinct IRWS began in 1920s. It became reestablished in Ireland in the 1940s, and a club was formed in Ireland to promote the breed in 1944. A few dogs were imported to America in the 1960s, but the breed did not develop a serious following until two decades later. A club was formed to promote the breed in the late 1990s, and today, these dogs are prized as gundogs and also trained as therapy dogs.

The IRWS is primarily a field dog. Powerful and athletic, the breed is squarely proportioned and has moderate bone. It has a moderately long, strong, slightly arched neck; strong, level back; deep chest; and tapered tail that is carried level or below the back. The skull is broad and domed, with a clean, square muzzle. The ears are set level with the eyes and carried close to the head. The eyes are round, ranging from hazel to dark brown in color, giving the dog a gentle expression.

Although no clear evidence exists, the breeds purported to be in the Irish Setter's background include the Irish Water Spaniel, Irish Terrier, English Setter, Gordon Setter, Pointer, and spaniels. Self-colored dogs were much less common than the red and white dogs, though certain Irish nobles preferred the red setters. Solid-red setters became popular in Ireland during the early nineteenth century and were first imported to America in the 1870s, when they were called Irish Red Setters.

The Irish Setter is a stylish, athletic gundog, famed for its glossy red coat. It is slightly longer than tall, is sturdy, and has plenty of bone. It has a long,

graceful, arched neck; a firm, slightly sloping topline; a deep chest; and a long, tapered tail that is carried nearly level with the back. The long, lean head is slightly domed, with a moderately deep muzzle and a black or brown nose. The medium-sized, almond-shaped eyes give a soft, alert expression. The long, thin ears are set low and hang in neat folds close to the head.

Year of AKC recognition: 1878

Group: Sporting

Size: Males—27 inches, 70 pounds; females—25 inches tall, 60 pounds

Coat: The coat is moderately long and flat on the body and short and fine on the head and front of the forelegs. Long, silky feathering is present on the ears, back of the forelegs, thighs, belly, and brisket, and there is moderately long fringe on the tail.

Color: Mahogany or chestnut red

Life expectancy: 12–15 years

Activity level: High. Adult Irish Setters need daily time to run either on lead or in a safely fenced yard.

Grooming: Brushing and combing two or three times per week is advised. A grooming DVD can be ordered from the parent club.

Temperament: This is an outgoing, affectionate, sensitive breed. Irish Setters were bred to work closely with human partners, and they need plenty of companionship. Their strong hunting instinct is matched by their desire to please. They are very trainable and easy to house-train. Puppies mature slowly and can be rambunctious and sometimes stubborn until around three years of age. Training must be consistent, patient, firm, and gentle.

Parent club: Irish Setter Club of America, Inc. (www.irishsetterclub.org); founded in 1891.

Buyer's advice from parent club: Potential owners should be prepared for an energetic dog that requires training and space to run. You should attend dog shows to meet breeders and see their dogs. Make sure that the breeder you choose is reputable, and see the dam and puppies before making a decision. Confirm that the litter is AKC registered and the parents have been screened for health disorders.

Regional clubs: Regional clubs are divided into four regions and are listed on the "Local Clubs" page under "ISCA" on the parent club's Web site.

Rescue: The ISCA's Irish Setter Rescue is located under "Rescue" on the parent club's Web site.

IRISH TERRIER

Year of AKC recognition: 1885

Group: Terrier

Size: Males—18 inches, 27 pounds; females—18 inches, 25 pounds

Coat: The breed has a harsh, dense, wiry outer coat with a finer, softer undercoat.

Color: Irish Terriers are whole-colored in bright red, golden red, red wheaten, or wheaten.

Life expectancy: 13–15 years

Activity level: High. The Irish Terrier is built for speed and endurance. These dogs should be exercised in fenced areas; fencing should be at least 6 feet high and secured at both the top and bottom. Irish Terriers do well in obedience, agility, tracking, and flyball.

Grooming: The coat should be hand-stripped two or three times per year, beginning at about five months of age. Clipping is not advised, as it will dull the color and soften the texture.

Temperament: Versatile, intelligent, and adaptable, Irish Terriers easily fit into a range of lifestyles. Irish Terriers are typically loyal, devoted, and affectionate with their owners, and sociable with people, but they are completely serious about their work. The breed's nickname of "daredevil" befits its spirit and courage to the point of recklessness. Irish have a strong prey drive and make excellent watchdogs. Early consistent socialization and training will channel their instincts in the right direction. They have an independent nature and can be stubborn, but they are also very sensitive and should never be subjected to harsh training. They make great therapy dogs.

Parent club: Irish Terrier Club of America (www. itca.info); founded in 1897

Buyers' advice from parent club: Contact many breeders and be prepared to wait for a puppy to be available, or consider an older dog.

Regional clubs: There are four regional ITCA affiliates; information can be found on the parent club's Web site under "About the ITCA."

Rescue: The ITCA Rescue Committee can be found on the club's Web site under "Rescue."

This is one of the oldest terrier breeds, a descendant of Britain's ancient rough-coated Black and Tan Terrier. The Irish Terrier first appeared at dog shows in 1875, and within a decade was one of the most popular breeds in Britain. In the 1880s, Irish Terriers arrived in America, where they became equally popular. During World War I, they were trained as messenger dogs.

The Irish Terrier is sturdy, strong, and stylish. It differs from other terriers in its rectangular proportions. This is an animated, wiry dog with moderately long legs and small, arched feet. It is covered in a crisp red coat. The head is long with a flat skull, flat cheeks, strong jaws, and a black nose. Small, dark eyes create an intense expression. The small, V-shaped ears fold forward. The docked tail is set high but not curled.

Rat-tailed or whip-tailed spaniels were described in southern Ireland as early as the 1100s. The Irish Water Spaniel was developed from two strains of working water retrievers, the South Country Water Spaniel and the North Country Water Spaniel. It was first described as a distinct breed in 1841 and was exhibited at the earliest dog shows. The IWS was the third most-popular breed in America by 1875.

This is the tallest spaniel breed, ruggedly built and covered in a liver-colored, curly coat. Well balanced and slightly rectangular, the IWS has a strong, arched neck; a strong level back; and a deep chest. The legs are straight and sturdy; the feet are large and webbed. The long tail is covered with curly coat at the base and short, smooth hair to the tip. The skull is large with a high dome, crowned by a topknot of loose curls. The muzzle is long and square; the eyes are medium sized, almond shaped, and hazel. The ears are long, set low, and covered by long curls.

Year of AKC recognition: 1884

Group: Sporting

Size: Males—22–24 inches, 55–68 pounds; females—21–23 inches, 45–58 pounds

Coat: The body coat of dense, crisp curls is a combination of a short, undercoat and a longer, water-resistant outer coat. A characteristic topknot of curls sits on the head. The coat is short and smooth on the face, and the ears are covered with long, loose curls.

Color: Shades of liver (deep reddish brown)

Life expectancy: 12–13 years

Activity level: Moderate. This is a dual-purpose hunting dog used for upland game and waterfowl. The IWS has great endurance and tolerance for cold weather. It is a powerful swimmer. Its versatility makes it well suited to a number of dog sports.

Grooming: Brush every two weeks; trim every two months.

Temperament: This is a companion hunting dog, and there is no distinction between field and show lines. The IWS is creative, inquisitive, and quick to learn. This breed has a strong working drive and an instinctive desire to please—a combination of traits that makes for a very trainable breed. Irish Water Spaniels are good watchdogs, but can be reserved with strangers.

Parent club: Irish Water Spaniel Club of America (www.iwsca.webs.com); founded in 1937

Buyers' advice from parent club: Finding a puppy may require some effort, as this is a rare breed.

Rescue: The IWSCA lists rescue information on its "Rescue Contact Information" page under "The IWS" on the club's Web site.

IRISH WATER SPANIEL

IRISH WOLFHOUND

Year of AKC recognition: 1897

Group: Hound

Size: Males—minimum of 32 inches, 120 pounds; females—minimum of 30 inches, 105 pounds. This is the tallest breed of dog in the world, and 32–34 inches is preferable in competition.

Coat: Harsh, rough, wiry outer coat and softer undercoat

Color: Gray, brindle, red, black, white, or fawn

Life expectancy: 6–8 years

Activity level: Moderate. Wolfhounds have plenty of endurance and must have a fenced yard to run. Puppies should avoid strenuous exercise before one year of age.

Grooming: Weekly brushing is recommended.

Temperament: The Irish Wolfhound is traditionally described as "gentle when stroked, fierce when provoked." Mature Wolfhounds are noted for their calm, affectionate, gentle nature. They are exceptionally easy to housetrain and accepting of most other dogs. Some Wolfhounds get along well with cats, but not all. They have the typical prey drive of sighthounds and may chase small animals.

Parent club: Irish Wolfhound Club of America (www.iwclubofamerica.org); founded in 1926

Buyers' advice from parent club: Irish Wolfhounds need plenty of food, space, and companionship. This is an expensive breed to maintain. Contact the parent club to learn about the breed and locate responsible breeders.

Regional clubs: Links to fifteen breed clubs are listed on the IWCA's Web site under "US Local Clubs."

Rescue: The IWCA provides rescue information under "National Rescue Directory" on its Web site.

Gigantic Wolfhounds have been prized since ancient times. For centuries, ownership was restricted to nobility. Wolfhounds were sent as gifts to royal kennels in India, Persia, Russia, and Eastern Europe. But by the nineteenth century, the breed was considered extinct. Major H.D. Richardson was responsible for rekindling interest in the breed in Britain. Captain George Graham is cited as the breeder responsible for reconstructing the breed, developing sustained interest, and getting it recognized.

The Irish Wolfhound is built for speed and power. This is the tallest sighthound, athletic and powerful, with a commanding presence, covered by a rough shaggy coat. It has a long, sturdy back with an arched loin; a very deep, wide chest; long, strong straight legs; and a long tail carried with an upward sweep. The long head is carried high, the muzzle is slightly tapered, and the small ears are folded back.

References to miniature sighthounds date back over 2,000 years. Historians debate whether the Italian Greyhound was originally bred as a companion or a hunting dog, but by the 1600s, the breed was seen throughout Europe and became popular in Italy, hence the breed's name. IGs were prized pets of nobility, and the favorite of European royals such as Frederick the Great, Catherine the Great, and Queen Victoria. Peter the Great carried his beloved Italian Greyhound Lisette into battle, hidden inside his coat.

Although much smaller, the Italian Greyhound is similar in proportion and outline to a lighter, more elegant Greyhound. It has a long, graceful neck; a deep, narrow chest; long, fine-boned legs; and long, oval-shaped hare feet. The long, slender tail is carried low. The head is long with a flat skull; a long, tapered

muzzle; and a dark nose. The eyes are dark and bright, and the ears are small and fine textured, either folded back or carried at right angles to the head when the dog is alert.

Year of AKC recognition: 1886

Group: Toy

Size: 13–15 inches, 7–14 pounds

Coat: Short, fine, satiny

Color: Any color except brindle or black and tan

Life expectancy: 14–15 years

Activity level: Moderate. IGs are sighthounds and love to run, but they also are adaptable companions. Daily walks and interactive play will satisfy their exercise needs.

Grooming: Regular care of the teeth and nails and occasional brushing are recommended.

Temperament: Despite its small size, the IG is a true sighthound. IGs get along well with other dogs and bond strongly with their owners, but they can be aloof with strangers. They have a well-developed prey drive and will chase small animals. They do not always care to prioritize training, but a positive, patient approach will get results. IGs do well in obedience and agility. House-training can be a challenge because this is a comfort-loving breed that may be reluctant to go outside in cold or wet weather. Loyal, gentle, and affectionate, an IG loves nothing better than curling up with his owner. The breed is a great choice for urban dog lovers.

Parent club: Italian Greyhound Club of America (www.italiangreyhound.org); founded in 1954

Buyers' advice from parent club: Contact a responsible breeder who researches pedigrees, screens his or her dogs for health problems, and works to match potential owners with suitable puppies. Visit breeders to see their dogs, and get a health guarantee from the breeder when purchasing a puppy.

Regional clubs: Five US regional breed clubs are listed on the parent club's Web site under "Links & Resources."

Rescue: Italian Greyhound Club of America Rescue information is available on the club's Web site under "IGCA Rescue."

ITALIAN GREYHOUND

JAPANESE CHIN

Year of AKC recognition: 1888 (registered as the Japanese Spaniel until 1977)

Group: Toy

Size: 8–11 inches

Coat: This breed's coat is long, silky, soft, and straight with a combination of shorter hair on the head, muzzle, and forelegs, and longer, more profuse coat on the neck, shoulders, and rump, as well as a heavily plumed tail. Chin puppies carry much less coat. They undergo a dramatic coat change between seven and nine months of age but may not attain full adult coat until three years of age.

Color: Black and white, red and white, black and white with tan points

Life expectancy: 10–12 years

Activity level: Low. Chin compete successfully in most dog sports, but short walks and interactive play will keep them fit and happy. This is a heat-sensitive breed and it should not be exercised in hot weather.

Grooming: Brush once or twice per week; the face must be cleaned daily.

Temperament: The Chin's fascinating temperament is paradoxical. Its regal ancestry is revealed in its dignified, aloof, haughty demeanor. At the same time, it's easy to appreciate why the Chin has been a cherished companion for centuries. It is gentle, affectionate, and sensitive, celebrated for its wry sense of humor and fastidious habits. Chin are quite intelligent, but can be stubborn.

Parent club: Japanese Chin Club of America (www.japanesechinonline.org); founded in 1912

Regional clubs: There are three regional clubs: one in western Pennsylvania, one in the Houston area, and one in the Carolinas. Links to each can be found on the "Breeder Directory" page under "Breeders" on the parent club's Web site.

Rescue: Japanese Chin Care and Rescue Effort (www.japanesechinrescue.org)

One of several short-faced toy breeds developed in ancient China, the Chin was introduced to the Western world by Commodore Matthew Perry upon the opening of Japan in 1854. The breed became very popular during Victorian times and was prized by Queen Alexandra and many European royals. It's unknown how the Chin came to Japan, and the breed is likely to be a relative of the Pekingese. The breed was known as the Japanese Spaniel until the name was changed to Japanese Chin in 1977.

This is a small, compact, fine-boned, squarely proportioned dog with a luxuriant coat and a well-plumed tail carried over the back. Its demeanor is regal and stylish, and its most notable feature is its aristocratic, inquisitive expression. It has a large, broad head; a prominent forehead; a short, broad muzzle; and a black nose. The small, dropped ears are well feathered and frame the face to accentuate the dog's large, round, wide-set eyes. A small flash of white showing in the eye creates the Chin's characteristic look of astonishment.

The Keeshond shares its heritage with other European spitz breeds, such as the Pomeranian and the Finnish Spitz. The breed evolved in Holland, where it was known as a barge dog and used to patrol barges, riverboats, and farms. In the 1700s it became the mascot of the Dutch Patriot party, which did not help the breed's image after this party met resounding defeat. It also lost its traditional working niche when ships gradually became larger, and bigger breeds were needed to guard them. The Keeshond began to regain its former popularity after it was officially recognized by the Dutch Kennel Club in 1933.

This is a balanced, medium-sized dog with typical Nordic breed traits. Sturdy and short coupled with a deep chest; a straight back; and a long, high-set, plumed tail that is curled closely over the back, the Keeshond is noted for its alert carriage and intelligent, foxlike expression. The head is wedge shaped, with dark, almond-shaped eyes and small, high-set, triangular, erect ears. The feet are compact and round.

Year of AKC recognition: 1930

Group: Non-Sporting

Size: Male—18 inches; female—17 inches

Coat: The abundant, stand-off coat is a combination of a long, harsh outer coat and a thick, downy undercoat. There's shorter, softer hair on the head. Males typically carry more coat than females.

Color: The Keeshond is a mixture of gray, black, and cream, varying from light to dark. Hairs of the outer coat are black tipped and the undercoat is pale gray or cream. Dark markings around the eyes produce the breed's distinctive spectacles.

Life expectancy: 12–15 years

Activity level: Moderate. Daily walks, runs in a fenced yard, and interactive play will satisfy the breed's exercise needs. Keeshonden are noted for quick reflexes, jumping ability, and aptitude for dog sports such as agility and obedience.

Grooming: Brush thirty minutes per week with a pin brush; bathe every six to eight weeks. Shaving or clipping is not recommended.

Temperament: This is a lively, intelligent, affectionate breed. Bred to be vigilant and alert, Keeshonden make great watchdogs. They are noted for their loud bark, a vocal trait that must be properly channeled to prevent excessive barking. Intuitive and eager to please, they are quick learners. Keeshonden are noted for their sociable nature; they get along well with other dogs and must have daily interaction with their owners. Don't spoil the Keeshond or else it can become quite clingy. Keeshonden are excellent therapy dogs.

Parent club: Keeshond Club of America (www.keeshond.org); founded in 1935

Buyers' advice from parent club: Find a reputable hobby breeder. Never purchase on impulse.

Regional clubs: Thirteen affiliated and three non-affiliated clubs are listed on the KCA's Web site on the "Local Keeshond Clubs" page under "Organizations."

Rescue: The KCA lists information on its Web site on the "Keeshond Rescue" page under "Organizations."

KEESHOND

KERRY BLUE TERRIER

Year of AKC recognition: 1922

Group: Terrier

Size: Males—18–19½ inches, 33–40 pounds; females —17½–19 inches, weighing slightly less than males

Coat: Soft, dense, wavy, nonshedding

Color: Deep slate gray to light blue gray. Puppies are born black and slowly fade to blue by eighteen months of age.

Life expectancy: 12–15 years

Activity level: High. This is an energetic dog, bred to hunt and retrieve. Kerries excel at obedience, agility, herding, earthdog, and flyball events.

Grooming: Daily brushing and monthly trimming are recommended. Professional groomers may not know how to trim a Kerry, so find grooming information on the parent club's Web site prior to visiting your chosen groomer.

Temperament: This is a fun-loving, quick-witted, adaptable breed. Kerry Blues are outgoing, playful, and very sociable with people, but they may not get along with other dogs. Likewise, their instinctive prey drive may not make this the best choice for homes with small pets. They can learn to get along with cats, but should be supervised. Kerries are quick learners and problem-solvers. They house-train easily and make excellent watchdogs. A firm, patient approach is essential for training the Kerry Blue. This breed is not a good choice for overly indulgent or submissive owners.

Parent club: United States Kerry Blue Terrier Club (www.uskbtc.com); founded in 1926

Buyers' advice from parent club: Find a reputable breeder by contacting the AKC or the USKBTC. Research the breed carefully and do not be in a hurry to acquire a dog. Visit breeders to meet their dogs. Be prepared to wait for a puppy. Consider an adult or rescue Kerry.

Regional clubs: Information on twelve clubs can be accessed on the "Chapter Club Roster" page under "About Us" on the USKBTC's Web site.

Rescue: USKBTC Rescue can be found on the club's Web site under "Rescue."

Closely related to the Irish Terrier and Soft Coated Wheaten, the Kerry Blue was developed in Ireland, around County Kerry for which it's named. For at least 150 years, it was used as a versatile all-purpose worker to hunt small game, to go to ground after vermin, to herd sheep and cattle, to guard the homestead, and to provide companionship. The breed was first exhibited at dog shows in Ireland in 1916 and was imported to America in the 1920s. Today, versatile as ever, Kerries are trained as assistance dogs, therapy dogs, and search and rescue dogs.

A well-balanced, stylish terrier, athletic and upstanding, the Kerry Blue has a short, level back; a deep chest; a moderately long neck; and moderately long legs with plenty of bone and muscle. The tail is docked, moderate length, set high, and carried up. The head is long, with strong jaws and a black nose. Ears are small, V-shaped, folded over, and carried close to the cheeks. Small, dark eyes give this terrier breed a keen expression.

The Komondor descended from flock guardians used in Eastern Europe and Russia for thousands of years. A direct descendant of the Russian Ovtcharkas, the Komondor by name can be traced to Hungarian documents from the sixteenth century. The breed has been known in Hungary for at least 1,000 years and was first imported to America in the 1930s. It is considered a rare breed, with approximately 1,000–1,500 Komondorok registered in the United States annually.

This is a large, rugged, athletic dog with plenty of bone and substance and slightly rectangular proportions. It has a level back; a deep,

powerful chest; and sturdy, well-muscled legs. The feet are large with well-arched toes. The long tail reaches the hock; it is slightly curved upward but never raised higher than the back. The skull is broad, with a wide, coarse muzzle; strong jaws; and a black nose. The eyes are medium sized and almond shaped. The elongated, triangular ears hang close to the head. The entire dog is covered from head to tail in long, ropelike cords of white hair.

Year of AKC recognition: 1937

Group: Working

Size: Males—minimum 27½ inches, approximately 100 or more pounds; females—minimum 25½ inches, approximately 80 or more pounds

Coat: The Komondor's corded coat is its most distinctive trait. It protects the dog from weather and predator attacks. The coarse outer coat and the dense, woolly undercoat naturally form into heavy, tassel-like cords that cover the entire dog and eventually grow to floor length.

Color: White

Life expectancy: 10–12 years

Activity level: Moderate. Komondor puppies are quite energetic. This is a slow-maturing breed, and puppies may not settle down until two or three years of age. A mature Komondor is surprisingly fast, agile, and athletic but typically calm and dignified in the house. Two or three daily walks will keep an adult Komondor happy.

Grooming: Cords must be tended to weekly to keep them clean and neat. The coat and skin must be checked carefully for fleas and ticks, and the ear canals must be kept free of hair.

Temperament: The Kom has a typical working-dog temperament—calm, steady, and completely devoted to its owner. Training must be tailored to the breed's sensitive, independent nature. Forceful methods will backfire. The breed has strong protective, territorial instincts, and owners must channel this behavior appropriately. Puppies need consistent early socialization and training to become tolerant of strangers in their territory.

Parent club: Komondor Club of America (http://clubs.akc.org/kca); founded in 1967

Buyer's advice from parent club: Do not buy a Komondor if you are unprepared for the responsibilities of living with a guard dog. Be sure to visit breeders to see adult Komondors before deciding that this is the breed for you. Before purchasing a puppy, confirm that the parents have been health screened.

Rescue: KCA Rescue is located on the club's Web site under "Rescue."

KUVASZ

Year of AKC recognition: 1931

Group: Working

Size: Males—28–30 inches, 100–115 pounds; females—26–28 inches, 70–90 pounds

Coat: The double coat combines coarse, straight or wavy guard hair and a short, fine undercoat. The coat is shorter on the head, muzzle, ears, feet, front of forelegs, and hind legs below the thighs. There is feathering on the backs of the forelegs, a mane on the neck, and 4–6 inches of hair on the tail.

Color: White

Life expectancy: 10–12 years

Activity level: Kuvaszok were bred to tirelessly patrol rough terrain and are nearly impervious to inclement weather. They need daily hard running in an enclosed area. Fencing must be 5 to 6 feet high. Growing puppies should avoid strenuous exercise.

Grooming: Brush weekly with a pin brush, bathe frequently, and trim the feet as needed.

Temperament: Centuries of livestock guarding has instilled the Kuvasz with courage, boldness, and independence. With proper socialization, Kuvaszok are polite and tolerant of strangers, and they are completely devoted to protecting their territory and pack. This is a determined, assertive breed, noted for its loyalty. A Kuvasz needs an equally strong, consistent leader. Kuvaszok grow quickly but mature slowly. They are extremely sensitive to praise and do not easily forget mistreatment. They respond well to positive reinforcement, and early socialization and obedience training are essential. Forceful training can lead to aggressive reactions.

Parent club: Kuvasz Club of America (www.kuvasz.com); founded in 1966

Buyers' advice from parent club: Meet the parents to gauge the puppy's temperament. A reputable breeder is the only source from which you should obtain a puppy. Also consider an adult or rescue Kuvasz.

Rescue: The KCA lists rescue contacts under "Rescue Information" on its Web site.

This ancient breed originated in Tibet and was developed in the region of modern-day Hungary as a livestock guardian. The name comes from *kawasz*, a Turkish word that means "armed guard of nobility." Kuvaszok were first shown in Europe in 1883 at a show in Vienna. The breed neared extinction following World War II; less than thirty members of the breed could be found for a factory owner who wanted to own the breed as guard dogs. This owner and some dedicated breeders worked together to revive the breed in its homeland.

This is a large, rugged dog with slightly rectangular proportions and moderate bone covered in an abundant coat of white. It has a muscular neck; a straight, broad back; and a well-developed forechest. The tail reaches to the hock and is carried low. It has a long, wedge-shaped head; flat cheeks; a well-developed underjaw; and a black nose. The eyes are wide set, dark, and almond shaped. The ears are V-shaped, are slightly rounded, and hang close to the head.

Forerunners of the Labrador Retriever developed in Newfoundland between the sixteenth and eighteenth centuries. This was an international trade hub, and sailors and fisherman from all over Europe arrived with a variety of setters, spaniels, and retrievers, which were bred with local dogs. These dogs, variously known as Lesser Newfoundlands or St. John's Dogs, were used for a wide range of jobs in Newfoundland. They were brought to England in the early nineteenth century and further refined into a sporting dog for waterfowl and upland game. The breed quickly became popular with sport hunters and was recognized in Britain in 1903. It became a popular hunting breed in America after World War II. The Labrador has been the most popular breed in America since 1992.

This is a medium-sized, short-coupled breed that is noted for its sleek, waterproof coat, webbed feet, and otterlike tail. It is a sturdy, athletic, well-balanced gundog with a broad head, a medium-length muzzle, and strong jaws. The ears hang close to the head, and the expression is kind and friendly.

Year of AKC recognition: 1917

Group: Sporting

Size: Males—22½–24½ inches, 65–80 pounds; females—21½–23½ inches, 55–70 pounds

Coat: The Labrador has a short, straight, dense, weather-resistant outer coat with a soft undercoat.

Color: Black, yellow, or chocolate

Life expectancy: 10–12 years

Activity level: Moderate to high. This is an athletic breed with the energy and stamina for a long day of hunting. Labradors need plenty of daily exercise. They love swimming, agility, flyball, and, of course, retrieving.

Grooming: Brush the coat three times per week; Labradors need more frequent brushing during heavy shedding periods in the spring and fall.

Temperament: Labs are versatile, easygoing, and friendly. True to their heritage, they usually love water and retrieving. They are intelligent and willing to please, and they respond well to positive-training techniques. This is a very sociable breed, and Labs must have plenty of interaction with their families. They are slow to mature and can retain puppylike exuberance until age three. Like other retrievers, they love to mouth and chew things. Puppies should be supervised to prevent chewing damage and accidental ingestion of foreign objects.

Parent club: The Labrador Retriever Club, Inc. (www.thelabradorclub.com); founded in 1931

Buyers' advice from parent club: Visit the breeder to meet the puppy's parents and evaluate their temperaments. Confirm that the parents have been health screened.

Regional clubs: Over forty US regional breed clubs are listed on the "Regional Clubs" page of the parent club's Web site under "About LRC."

Rescue: Information on the LRC's Rescue Program is given on the club's Web site under "Rescue."

LABRADOR RETRIEVER

LAKELAND TERRIER

Year of AKC recognition: 1934

Group: Terrier

Size: Males—14–15 inches, 17 pounds; females—slightly smaller

Coat: The double coat comprises a hard, wiry outer coat with a close-fitting, soft undercoat. Furnishings are present on the muzzle and legs.

Color: Solid blue, black, liver, red, and wheaten. Saddle-marked dogs have a blue, black, liver, or grizzle (red or wheaten mixed with blue, black, or liver) saddle over a wheaten or golden tan body.

Life expectancy: 12–15 years

Activity level: Moderate to high. This is an energetic working terrier. A Lakeland should have three of four walks or outdoor exercise periods each day. Lakelands are generally quiet house dogs that are adaptable to a range of lifestyles, making the breed a good choice for urban dog owners.

Grooming: The coat should be brushed and combed weekly. Periodic hand-stripping will preserve color and texture. Information on how to groom and different grooming options is on the parent club's Web site. Keep in mind that not all professional groomers are familiar with Lakeland trimming patterns.

Temperament: Bold, friendly, and confident, the Lakeland is a gentle, loving, and entertaining companion. The Lakeland is quite intelligent and a quick learner, but he also possesses the typical independent, inquisitive terrier nature. The breed is noted for its sense of humor. Obedience-training a Lakeland takes patience and determination.

Parent club: United States Lakeland Terrier Club (http://uslakelandterrier.org); founded in 1954

Buyers' advice from parent club: Select a breeder from the parent club membership. A responsible breeder will discuss the breed's characteristics and needs as well as the owner's expectations. Visit the breeder to see the parents and the litter. A typical Lakeland puppy is happy and self-assured.

Rescue: The USLTC's Rescue page is available on the club's Web site under "Our Club."

This is one of the oldest terriers, developed by farmers to hunt and control vermin around the Lake District of Cumberland, England. It shares an ancestry with the Dandie Dinmont, Bedlington, and Border Terriers. Efforts to promote the Lakeland as a recognized breed began in 1912, but did not gain momentum until after World War I. The breed's name was chosen by a group of fanciers in 1921, and the breed began entering British dog shows in 1928. The breed has never been overly popular as a pet in America, though many dogs have stood out in US show rings.

This is a balanced, squarely built, long-legged terrier with a slightly arched neck; a short, level back; and a high-set, docked tail that is carried up and slightly curved. The head is rectangular with a flat skull and a strong, straight muzzle that is approximately equal to the length of the skull. The nose is black, and the eyes are oval shaped and moderately small, producing an alert, intense, determined expression. The small, V-shaped ears are folded over just above the top of the skull.

Heinrich Essig, alderman of the town of Leonberg in southwestern Germany, is credited with creating the Leonberger. Widely known as a dealer in exotic animals, he had a special fondness for giant dog breeds. For several decades, he experimented with crossbreeding to create a giant breed that resembled a lion. It's believed that he incorporated Saint Bernard, Newfoundland, Great Pyrenees, and local mastiff-type dogs into a breed he eventually named for his hometown. Herr Essig died in 1889, but enthusiasm for the Leonberger led to the formation of clubs to promote the breed beginning in 1891, and a breed standard was established. The two World Wars took a toll on the breed, and efforts to establish breeding programs in Germany were revived in the late 1940s. The breed was re-established in the United States starting in 1975 through the efforts of five individual families who had brought in dogs from Germany.

Year of AKC Recognition: 2010

Group: Working

Size: Males—28–31½ inches; females—25½–29½ inches

Coat: A medium to long, water-resistant double coat on the body; the outer coat is flat and straight and can be soft to coarse, and the undercoat is soft and dense. Males have a well-defined mane.

Color: Yellow, shades of golden to red, red-brown, cream, and pale yellow, either alone or in combination. All colors have a black mask.

Life expectancy: 7 years

Activity level: Moderately high. Leonbergers are more active and energetic than most breeds of this size. They must have daily exercise, but they generally do not have too much enthusiasm for organized sports. They love swimming and play.

Grooming: Brush daily during seasonal shedding and at least once a week at other times of the year.

Temperament: This is a confident, self-assured, vigilant dog with a well-developed protective instinct. Leonbergers are devoted pets, and they thrive on spending time with their people. They are typically calm, stable, and sociable companions. However, this is a slow-maturing, fast-growing breed. Leonberger puppies must have daily training and socialization until age two; owners must be prepared to provide leadership. Leos are willing to please but are very sensitive; training sessions must be short, positive, and consistent.

Parent club: Leonberger Club of America (www.leonbergerclubofamerica.com); founded in 1985

Buyers' advice from parent club: Find a breeder who is a member of a breed club. This is an expensive breed to maintain and is not a breed for fastidious housekeepers, among other considerations.

Regional clubs: There are nine regional US breed clubs; a link to the "Regional LCA Clubs" page appears under "The LCA" on the club's Web site.

Rescue: Leonberger Rescue (www.leonberger-rescue.org) and Leos in Need Rescue (www.leosinneedrescue.org)

This is a large, rugged dog with an abundant double coat and a black mask. It has moderate to heavy bone; slightly rectangular proportions; a muscular neck; a firm, level back; a broad chest; and a long tail that is carried no higher than the back. The legs are straight and parallel, and the feet are round with black pads. The head is rectangular with a broad jaw. The eyes are medium sized and oval shaped, giving the breed a soft, good-natured expression, and the ears are triangular, hanging close to the head.

LEONBERGER

LHASA APSO

Year of AKC recognition: 1935

Group: Non-Sporting

Size: Males—10–11 inches; females—slightly smaller

Coat: Dense, straight, hard textured, and long

Color: All colors. Beard and ears may or may not have dark tips.

Life expectancy: 12–15 years

Activity level: Moderate. A Lhasa Apso should have two fifteen- to twenty-minute walks each day.

Grooming: Brush at least once a week to prevent matting, and bathe about every two weeks. Pets can have their coats clipped short for easier maintenance.

Temperament: Don't be misled by the Lhasa's glamorous looks—this is a strong-willed dog in a small package. For centuries, this was a guardian dog, bred for stoicism, courage, and independence. Lhasas are excellent watchdogs. Intelligent and resourceful, they can also be manipulative, but they are extremely loyal. Lhasas are noted for their sensitivity to human emotions, and they form strong attachments to their owners. They are incomparable companions for owners who are prepared for a dog with character. Lhasas need plenty of training, socialization, and, most importantly, a confident leader. Puppies are mischievous and surprisingly energetic for their size. As this is a slow-maturing breed, a Lhasa may not become polite and dignified until age three or four. Coercive training methods will never work with this breed; they respond well to positive, reward-based training methods.

Parent club: American Lhasa Apso Club (www.lhasaapso.org); founded in 1959

Buyers' advice from parent club: Buy from a reputable breeder and ask for references.

Regional clubs: There are over a dozen regional Lhasa Apso clubs in the United States; information is listed on the parent club's Web site on the "Member Clubs" page under "The Club."

Rescue: American Lhasa Apso Club Rescue (www.lhasaapsorescue.org)

This is an ancient Tibetan breed, closely related to the Tibetan Terrier and Tibetan Spaniel. Known as the *Apso Seng Kye* ("bark lion sentinel dog"), the breed was used as a guardian. It was once the tradition for the Dalai Lama to send Lhasa Apsos as gifts to each emperor of China, showing how valued the breed was. In 1933, a pair of Lhasas were given to an American naturalist by the 13th Dalai Lama, and these dogs were used to establish the breed in the United States.

This is a rectangular dog covered with a long, heavy coat. The coat falls over the head, hiding the dark brown eyes. The ears are dropped and heavily feathered. The legs are straight and well covered with coat, the feet are round, and the tail is well feathered and carried over the back in a screw.

Also known as the "Little Lion Dog" since the mid-fifteenth century because of its distinctive lion clip, the Löwchen has been bred for over four centuries as a companion. It originated in the Mediterranean and was a favorite breed of Florentine aristocracy. Madame Bennert and Dr. Hans Rickert of Belgium are credited for rescuing the breed from devastation after World War II. The first Löwchens in America arrived from Britain in 1971. The name *Löwchen* (German for "little lion dog") came about soon thereafter. In Europe, the breed is called *Petit Chien Lion*.

This is a small, sturdy dog with round bone and moderate bone density. He has slightly rectangular proportions, high head carriage, and an arched neck. The back is level and the tail is set high, carried like a cup handle over the back. The Löwchen

has a short, broad skull and muzzle; a dark nose; and a bright, lively expression. Its eyes are large, dark, round, and wide set. The ears are set at eye level, of moderate length, and covered with fringe.

Year of AKC recognition: 1996

Group: Non-Sporting

Size: 12–14 inches, around 15 pounds

Coat: The Löwchen has a dense, long, soft, and slightly wavy single coat. The breed is kept in a traditional "lion trim" in which the forequarters are left fully coated and the hindquarters are clipped close to the skin to the hock joint. The tail is clipped, leaving a plume at the tip.

Color: All colors and color combinations

Life expectancy: 13–15 years

Activity level: Moderate

Grooming: Weekly brushing is recommended, along with professional trimming every two months.

Temperament: Bred for centuries to be an ideal companion, the Löwchen is alert, lively, affectionate, and outgoing. This is an adaptable breed and a good candidate for obedience and agility. Puppies should be discouraged from excessive barking to prevent them from forming bad habits.

Parent club: Löwchen Club of America (www.thelowchenclubofamerica.org); founded in 1971

Buyer's advice from parent club: Purchase your puppy from a reputable breeder; the LCA's Web site lists breeders by region under "Breeder Referral."

Rescue: Löwchen Club of America Rescue information is on the club's Web site under "Breed Rescue."

LÖWCHEN

MALTESE

Year of AKC recognition: 1888

Group: Toy

Size: Under 7 pounds

Coat: The breed has a long, silky single coat that hangs flat against the body and may reach floor-length. The Maltese coat is not weather-protective, so they should not be left outdoors in hot or cold weather.

Color: White

Life expectancy: 12–15 years

Activity level: Low. Daily walks will satisfy the breed's exercise requirements. They love interactive play and can do well in obedience, agility, and rally. If exercising the breed in a fenced area, the fencing must be checked carefully for small gaps that can permit a Maltese to escape.

Grooming: The Maltese's coat must be thoroughly brushed and combed daily. The coat can be clipped every six to eight weeks to keep it at a more manageable length.

Temperament: Throughout its history, the Maltese has been strictly a companion breed. Gentle, affectionate, and sociable, Maltese are spirited, entertaining companions. They are quite intelligent and they learn quickly, giving them the aptitude to excel in competitive events. Maltese are sensitive, and training must be positive and gentle. On the other hand, owners must resist the urge to be overly indulgent. Most bad habits result from owners' overlooking unwanted behavior.

Parent club: American Maltese Association (www.americanmaltese.org); founded in 1961

Buyers' advice from parent club: Buy a puppy only from a reputable breeder. Visit personally to ascertain the puppy's living conditions and the temperament of the parents.

Regional clubs: The American Maltese Association has four regional member clubs; information can be accessed under "Member Clubs" on the parent club's Web site.

Rescue: The American Maltese Association's National Rescue Program can be found on the parent club's Web site under "Maltese Rescue."

Small, silky-coated white dogs have been prized companions since Roman times. The Maltese may have originated on the island of Malta, but many historians believe that the breed's name became a catch-all description for various types of small, fluffy white dogs found in the Mediterranean. They remained popular as aristocratic lapdogs for centuries and were among the first breeds exhibited at dog shows in Britain the 1860s. Despite their long-standing popularity in Europe, they were very rare in America until the 1950s.

This is a compact, fine-boned dog, completely covered with a silky white coat. The Maltese is squarely proportioned with a level back; a deep chest; sturdy, straight legs; and small, round feet with black pads. The long tail is covered with long hair and carried over the back. The skull is slightly rounded, the muzzle is tapered, and the nose is black. The eyes are dark and round, and the ears are low set and heavily feathered, hanging close to the head.

This is the oldest documented terrier breed, originally developed as the premier rat hunter. The breed was extremely popular as a pet and working dog in Victorian times. A Toy Manchester named Tiny reportedly killed 300 rats in fifty-four minutes, fifty seconds. Today, it is a rare breed in America.

The Manchester is a stylish, eye-catching, black-and-tan dog. It is sleek and slightly rectangular with a graceful neck; a slightly arched back; a narrow, deep chest; and a tucked-up abdomen. The tapered whip tail is carried slightly curved

but never over the back. The breed has a long, wedge-shaped head and a bright, keen expression with small, sparkling eyes. The ears on Standard Manchesters can be naturally erect, cropped, or button (erect at the base and folded over at the tip). For competition, Toy Manchesters must have naturally erect ears, wide at the base and tapered to pointed tips.

Year of AKC recognition: 1886

Group: Toy variety: Toy; Standard variety: Terrier

Size: There are two varieties: Toy—not over 12 pounds; Standard—12–22 pounds

Coat: Short, sleek, close fitting, and dense

Color: Black and tan

Life expectancy: 15–17 years

Activity level: Moderate. Manchesters are athletic and energetic but equally enjoy comfort. They require daily walks or play in a fenced yard and will contentedly curl up for a snooze afterwards. Noted for their fastidious habits, they are a good choice for urban dog owners.

Grooming: Weekly brushing is recommended.

Temperament: This is a quick-witted, extremely loyal breed with a strong prey drive. Manchesters are therefore observant, alert, and always on the lookout. They make excellent watchdogs. Owners must be prepared to step in if a Manchester's courage oversteps its good sense. Manchesters should have consistent socialization and training.

Parent club: American Manchester Terrier Club (clubs.akc.org/amtc); founded in 1923

Buyer's advice from parent club: This is a rare breed; approximately 450 Manchesters are registered each year. Join a discussion forum to learn more about the breed.

Rescue: AMTC Purebred Rescue (www. amtcrescue.com)

MANCHESTER TERRIER

MASTIFF

Year of AKC recognition: 1885

Group: Working

Size: Males—30 inches and up, 160–230 pounds; females—27½ inches and up, 120–170 pounds

Coat: Short, coarse, straight outer coat and a dense undercoat

Color: Fawn, apricot, or brindle with a black mask and black ears

Life expectancy: 6–10 years

Activity level: Low to moderate. Mastiffs under age two should not have strenuous exercise. They enjoy carting, tracking, obedience, search and rescue, and weight pulling.

Grooming: The coat requires daily brushing, with seasonal shedding in spring and fall. Mastiffs drool and can be messy when drinking.

Temperament: Personalities range from outgoing to reserved. This is a gentle, calm, self-assured, courageous breed that bonds strongly to its family. Mastiffs must have human companionship and are typically clean, quiet housedogs. They are intelligent, eager to please, and house-train easily. Obedience training is essential for this large, strong breed. The Mastiff can be stubborn but responds well to positive reinforcement and short, upbeat training sessions.

Parent club: Mastiff Club of America (www.mastiff.org); founded in 1929

Buyer's advice from parent club: Purchase a puppy from a reputable breeder or consider adopting through the MCOA rescue service. Be aware that poorly bred Mastiffs can inherit aggressive tendencies. Meet the puppy's parents to evaluate their disposition and choose a puppy temperamentally suited to your family and lifestyle. This is an expensive breed to maintain.

Regional clubs: Information on ten US breed clubs can be found on the MCOA's Web site under "Regional Mastiff Clubs."

Rescue: Information about MCOA Rescue and MCOA-approved regional rescue groups can be found on the club's Web site under "Mastiff Rescue."

Mastiffs are one of the oldest breeds, used since ancient times as guardians, hunters, and war dogs. In 55 B.C., Julius Caesar wrote about Mastiffs in his account of invading Britain, as did Geoffrey Chaucer in the fourteenth century. They were known as bandogs, butcher's dogs, and holding dogs. The breed we know today as the Mastiff was developed in England. Mastiffs were among the first breeds brought to America by early explorers.

A massive canine athlete, the Mastiff is rectangular and heavy boned, with great muscle. It has a powerful neck; a straight, firm back; and a strong, wide chest. The tail is set high, reaches to the hock, and is carried slightly curved but never over the back. The head is large and broad, somewhat flattened between the ears, and showing distinctive brow wrinkles when alert. The ears are small, V shaped, and lie close to the cheeks. The muzzle is dark, short, and broad, with a strong under jaw. The Mastiff's typical expression is alert and kindly.

Bull Terriers were developed by crossing various terriers with Bulldogs. The resulting progeny came in a wide variety of sizes. Bull Terriers were evidently divided by size for show classification. Toy Bull Terriers were exhibited until 1914 but never developed a strong following. Slightly larger Bull Terriers tended to be better in overall quality and were eventually stabilized as the Miniature Bull Terrier. The breed was accepted into the AKC's Miscellaneous Class in 1963.

This is a strongly built, squarely proportioned, active dog, distinguished by its long, oval-shaped head. The Mini Bull has small, thin, erect ears; a black nose; and dark eyes with a piercing glint. It

has a muscular neck; a short, strong back; and a broad chest. The short tail is set low, fine, and tapered, and carried horizontally. The legs are moderate in length, sturdy, and straight, and the feet are round and compact.

Year of AKC recognition: 1991

Group: Terrier

Size: 10–14 inches

Coat: Short, hard, flat, and glossy

Color: White or colored

Life expectancy: 11–13 years

Activity level: High. This is an exuberant, fun-loving breed that usually remains quite lively until five to six years of age. Miniature Bull Terriers need plenty of daily activity and personal attention, especially interactive play. Puppies should not engage in strenuous exercise. If confined or neglected, a Miniature Bull Terrier is apt to become bored and resort to bad habits such as barking, chewing, or excavating the yard.

Grooming: Weekly brushing is recommended. Brush more often during seasonal shedding in spring and fall.

Temperament: The standard describes the Miniature Bull Terrier as full of fire, courageous, even tempered, and amenable to discipline. This is a quintessential terrier—inquisitive, playful, good natured, and completely devoted to its family. Tenacious and bold, they have a well-developed guardian instinct and make excellent watchdogs. They require consistent, firm discipline, and puppies must be closely supervised. Male Miniature Bull Terriers may not get along well with other male dogs.

Parent club: Miniature Bull Terrier Club of America (www.minibull.org); founded in 1966

Buyer's advice from parent club: Before purchasing a dog, learn about the breed through careful research, attending dog shows, talking to breeders, and joining the MBTCA. Do not purchase a puppy without a health guarantee.

Rescue: Information on MBTCA Rescue can be found under "Rescue" on the club's Web site.

MINIATURE BULL TERRIER

MINIATURE PINSCHER

Year of AKC recognition: 1925

Group: Toy

Size: 10–12½ inches

Coat: Short, smooth, straight, close fitting, and satiny

Color: Red, stag red (red with black hairs), black with rust markings, chocolate with tan markings

Life expectancy: 12–16 years

Activity level: High. This is an energetic, inquisitive breed. The Min Pin needs a structured routine, regular exercise, and secure fencing. Without supervision, Min Pins may chew on or ingest objects found lying around the house, squeeze through spaces in fencing, or jump through open windows.

Grooming: Brush briskly twice a week.

Temperament: Although it is now a companion breed, the Min Pin is descended from self-reliant, independent, versatile working dogs. It well deserves its nickname, "The King of Toys." Min Pins are perceptive, tough, fearless, and protective toward their pack. They have excellent watchdog instincts. They are also entertaining, affectionate, comfort-loving, fastidious house dogs. This is a great choice for urban dog owner.

Parent club: Miniature Pinscher Club of America (www.minpin.org); founded in 1930

Buyers' advice from parent club: The Min Pin is a creative, high-energy breed. They are much more entertaining than TV, but can be challenging for novice owners. Do sufficient research to confirm that this is the right breed for you, and find a serious hobby breeder who can provide ongoing advice. Attend dog shows to meet breeders and see their dogs firsthand.

Regional clubs: There are fourteen local clubs listed on the parent club's Web site on the "Local Clubs" page under "Club Information."

Rescue: Rescue information is listed on the parent club's Web site under "MPCA Rescue."

Pinschers and schnauzers were developed in Germany as multipurpose hunters, ratters, watchdogs, and companions. The Min Pin is one of several breeds that trace back to the Old German Pinscher or Reh Pinscher, named for a type of small red deer found in Germany. Other ancestors of the Min Pin may include the Italian Greyhound and Dachshund. Although the Min Pin resembles a miniature Doberman Pinscher, the breeds are not related. The breed was first exhibited in Germany in 1900 and was imported to America in 1919. Upon AKC recognition, it was shown in the Terrier Group; it moved to the Toy Group in 1930, but its name was not officially changed from Pinscher (Miniature) to Miniature Pinscher until 1972.

This is a spirited, stylish, compact, smooth-coated Toy dog known for its high-stepping gait. It has a well-developed chest and a slightly arched neck. The back is level or slightly sloping to the rear. The docked tail is set and carried high. The head is tapered, narrow, and flat with a strong muzzle. The eyes are dark, bright, and slightly oval shaped. The ears are set high, carried erect, and cropped or uncropped.

The Miniature Schnauzer was the result of a committed effort in the 1800s to produce a small schnauzer, primarily through crossing Standard Schnauzers with Affenpinschers and Poodles. The breed was exhibited in Europe as early as 1889 and has been bred in America since 1925. The Mini was intended to be a small vermin hunter that could be more easily kept as a pet. It was established as a breed by the end of the nineteenth century and has enjoyed popularity around the world since its development.

This is a small, sturdy, muscular dog with square proportions and a hard, wiry, protective coat. It has a strong, well-arched neck; a short, straight back; straight legs; round feet with thick, black pads; and a high-set, docked tail that is carried high. A long, rect-

angular head and a strong muzzle are accentuated by a bushy beard and mustache. The small, dark, deep-set, oval-shaped eyes are accentuated by bushy eyebrows, giving the Miniature Schnauzer a keen expression. The ears are set high on the head—erect and pointed if cropped, or small, V shaped, and folded close to the head if uncropped.

Year of AKC recognition: 1926

Group: Terrier

Size: 12–14 inches, 11–20 pounds

Coat: This breed has a double coat consisting of a wiry top coat and a soft undercoat. Furnishings on the legs and face are longer than the body coat.

Color: Black, salt and pepper, and black and silver

Life expectancy: 12–15 years

Activity level: Moderate. Spirited, playful, and athletic, this is an adaptable breed and a good choice for urban dog owners. Mini Schnauzers need daily exercise, but it can come in many forms.

Grooming: Brush and wash the furnishings weekly. The coat will need clipping or stripping every five to eight weeks. The coat will become soft and curly if clipped instead of hand-stripped.

Temperament: Mini Schnauzers were bred to be versatile, independent workers. They are often described as spunky and fearless, and they are lively, entertaining companions. The breed is extremely affectionate, sweet, and sociable toward people. Quick learners, Mini Schnauzers are well mannered and obedient as long as their owners invest some time into training. They are protective of their territory and make good watchdogs. Mini Schnauzers have well-developed hunting instincts, and some may not get along with cats or other pets.

Parent club: American Miniature Schnauzer Club (www.amsc.us); founded in 1933

Buyers' advice from parent club: A responsible breeder breeds for temperament, good health, and soundness, and ensures that the puppy he or she offers to you is suitable for you, your family, and your living situation. When dealing with a breeder, be sure to secure all warranties and representations in writing. The AMSC Web site provides a list of breeders, kennels, and phone numbers.

Regional clubs: There are twenty regional Miniature Schnauzer clubs listed on the parent club's Web site under "AMSC Local Clubs."

Rescue: Information on AMSC Rescue is available on the parent club's Web site under "Rescue."

MINIATURE SCHNAUZER

NEAPOLITAN MASTIFF

Year of AKC recognition: 2004

Group: Working

Size: Males—26–31 inches, 150 pounds; females—24–29 inches, 110 pounds

Coat: Dense, no more than 1 inch long

Color: Blue, black, mahogany, tawny, and brindle; may have white markings.

Life expectancy: 7–9 years

Activity level: Moderate. Neos enjoy daily walks and play in a sturdily fenced yard, but they are intolerant of heat and should not be exercised in hot weather. Growing puppies should not be subjected to strenuous exercise.

Grooming: Weekly brushing is recommended.

Temperament: This is a peaceful, steady, quiet dog with a somewhat independent nature. Neos are extremely loving and loyal toward their family and are typically tolerant of other animals in the household. They tend to be reserved with strangers and should be socialized toward a wide variety of people. Neos learn quickly but can be stubborn at times. They must have steady, consistent, positive training beginning no later than four months of age. They respond best to daily ten- to twenty-minute training sessions.

Parent club: United States Neapolitan Mastiff Club (www.neapolitan.org); founded in 1993

Buyers' advice from parent club: See the breed in person and talk to other owners before deciding on a Neapolitan Mastiff. Join the parent club to learn more about care and training. Neos are messy when eating and drinking. They also drool.

Rescue: NeoRescue, Inc. (www.neorescueinc.com)

A giant breed developed in northern Italy, the Neapolitan Mastiff can trace its origins to the dogs of war used by the Roman armies in ancient Egypt, Persia, Mesopotamia and Asia. It's believed that Alexander the Great in the fourth century B.C. had a hand in the creation of the Neo, by crossing Macedonian and Epirian war dogs with shorthaired Indian dogs to create the ancient molosser. In Italy, the Neo was later used on large estates and farms as a guard of both owner and property. After World War II, a small group of Italian dog fanciers, led by Dr. Piero Scanziani, set out to revitalize the neglected Italian mastiff. The breed was recognized by the Fédération Cynologique Internationale in 1949, and by the 1970s had gained a new following in the United States.

This is a massive, powerful, heavy-boned dog noted for its loose skin, abundant wrinkles, and massive head. It has slightly rectangular proportions; a muscular neck; a broad chest; and a wide, strong back. The feet are large and round. The tail is wide, thick, and tapered. Docked by one third, it hangs in a slight S shape and is carried up or curved over the back. The head is large, wide, and flat, covered with extensive folds and wrinkles. It has a well-developed brow and pendulous lips. The squared muzzle is one third the length of the head. The eyes are deep set and amber or brown in color. The ears may be cropped or uncropped. The expression ranges from wistful to intimidating.

The Newfoundland's ancestors were developed from a combination of working and hunting dogs brought to Newfoundland by European sailors and indigenous breeds of the region. Over the centuries, these dogs were selected for hardiness, swimming ability, and versatility. They were bred as all-purpose working dogs. After arriving in Britain in the nineteenth century, the breed was refined to the type we are familiar with today. The breed has had a rich history in America as mascots during the Civil War, search and rescue dogs during World War II, and as prized companions to President Grant and Robert Kennedy.

This is a large, strong working dog with a heavy, protective coat; slightly rectangular proportions; and a dignified demeanor.

Heavy boned and muscular, the Newf has a broad, sturdy, level back, a deep chest and a broad tail reaching to the hock and carried out but not over the back. The feet are large, round, and webbed. The head is massive, with a broad skull; small, deep, wide-set eyes; and small, triangular ears with rounded tips that lie close to the head. The expression is soft and benevolent.

Year of AKC recognition: 1886

Group: Working

Size: Male—28 inches, 130–150 pounds; females—26 inches, 100–120 pounds

Coat: The waterproof coat is an oily double coat consisting of an outer coat that is coarse, moderately long, straight or wavy and a dense undercoat. The coat is shorter on the face and muzzle, and there's feathering on the back of legs and tail.

Color: Black, brown, gray, or Landseer (white with black markings)

Life expectancy: 9–10 years

Activity level: Moderate. Newfs must have daily exercise such as swimming and walks. They enjoy tracking, carting, sledding, and backpacking but cannot tolerate hot weather. Puppies should not engage in strenuous exercise before eighteen months of age.

Grooming: Brush twice a week using a long-toothed steel comb and a slicker brush.

Temperament: This is a sweet, good-natured dog that is gentle and willing to please. Puppies should be introduced to basic obedience by eight weeks of age. They respond well to positive training and praise.

Parent club: Newfoundland Club of America (www.ncanewfs.org); founded in 1930

Buyers' advice from parent club: Champagne, white and brown, white and gray, and black and tan are not rare or desirable colors. Reputable breeders do not breed for size at the expense of health, temperament, or soundness, and will not let a puppy go to a new home before eight weeks of age. Newfs cannot be guaranteed not to drool. Visit breeders to see the puppies and meet the dam, and always confirm that the parents have been screened for health disorders.

Regional clubs: There are about twenty-five regional breed clubs listed on the "Regional Clubs" page of the parent club's Web site.

Rescue: NCA Rescue Network (www.ncarescue.org)

NORFOLK TERRIER

Year of AKC recognition: 1979

Group: Terrier

Size: 9–10 inches, 11–12 pounds

Coat: The protective outer coat is hard, wiry, and straight, with a mane about 1½–2 inches long on the neck and shoulders. There's a definite weather-resistant, downy undercoat. The outer coat is slightly longer and harsher on the legs. The coat on the head and ears is short and smooth, and the eyebrows and whiskers are slightly longer.

Color: Red, wheaten, black and tan, grizzle

Life expectancy: 12–16 years

Activity level: High. Norfolks should have long walks or interactive play thirty minutes per day. They are natural hunters with a strong prey drive and will chase if given the chance. They must be exercised on lead or in a safely fenced area. They also enjoy participating in tracking, earthdog, and agility events.

Grooming: Be sure to brush and comb weekly; strip the coat twice a year. Clipping the coat is not recommended.

Temperament: Adaptable, loyal, and affectionate, the Norfolk is famed for its great charm. The breed has a strong prey drive and is known as "a perfect demon in the field." Norfolks get along well with dogs and cats but are not recommended for homes with small pets.

Parent club: Norfolk Terrier Club (www.norfolkterrierclub.org); Norwich and Norfolk Terrier Club of America founded in 1979; new name established in 2007

Rescue: NTC Rescue and Rehoming can be found under "Rescue/Rehoming" on the parent club's Web site.

The ancestors of both the Norwich and Norfolk Terries were developed from an eclectic mixture of terrier stock in the nineteenth century. These little rough-coated dogs soon earned a widespread reputation for gameness as well as for being a great companion breed. An ongoing demand led to breeding programs in Britain and America long before fanciers sought official recognition for their breed, which was variously known as the Trumpington, Jones, or Cantab Terrier. These dogs were bred for terrier spirit and working ability rather than for uniform appearance. This led to two distinct types within the breed: the erect-eared strain, which is now known as the Norwich Terrier, and the drop eared type, which was separately classified as the Norfolk Terrier in 1979.

This is a game, hardy, short-legged terrier with a weather-resistant coat. It is compact, with good bone and substance; a level back; a docked tail set high; short, powerful legs; and round feet with  thick pads. Its small, dark, sparkling, oval-shaped eyes are wide set, and the small, dropped, V-shaped ears are carried close to the cheeks. The Norfolk has a slightly rounded skull, a strong, wedge-shaped muzzle, and strong jaws.

The Norwegian Buhund was traditionally used as an all-purpose farm and herding dog. Six dogs of Buhund type were found in a Viking grave dating back to 900 AD; these dogs accompanied Vikings on their journeys and were also commonly buried with their Viking owners. Buhunds were first shown in Norway in 1920. They still fulfill their original role today but are primarily companion dogs. They are also trained as hearing-assistance dogs and police dogs.

This is a spitz-type dog with square proportions and a protective double coat. It has a medium-length neck; a level back; a deep chest; and a high-set tail that is tightly curled and carried over the back. The head is  flat and wedge shaped. The muzzle is equal in length to the skull, with a black nose. The eyes are dark and oval shaped, and the ears are medium sized and erect with pointed tips.

Year of AKC recognition: 2009

Group: Herding

Size: Males—17–18½ inches, 31–40 pounds; females—16–17½ inches, 26–35 pounds

Coat: This breed's coat is a combination of a hard, thick, smooth outer coat and a soft, dense undercoat. The coat is shorter on the head and front of the legs and longer on the neck, chest, and back of the thighs.

Color: Wheaten (cream to bright orange) or black

Life expectancy: 12–15 years

Activity level: High. This is an energetic breed with a strong motivation to work. They must have daily mental and physical activity. Buhunds make great jogging and hiking companions, and they enjoy interactive play such as Frisbee and retrieving, hiking, and dog sports such as agility and rally.

Grooming: Brush at least weekly; more frequent brushing is needed during seasonal shedding.

Temperament: Buhunds want to be part of the action. They are affectionate and sociable, and they need plenty of companionship and attention from their owners. They are also gentle, typically getting along well with other animals, and they make great family dogs. Norwegian Buhunds are self-confident and alert, making excellent watchdogs. Many Buhunds have a strong herding instinct and will try to herd children and other pets.

Parent club: Norwegian Buhund Club of America (www.buhund.org); founded in 1983

Buyers' advice from parent club: Talk to many Buhund owners and breeders before deciding that this is the right breed for you.

Rescue: Norwegian Buhund Rescue (www.buhundrescue.org)

NORWEGIAN BUHUND

NORWEGIAN ELKHOUND

Year of AKC recognition: 1913

Group: Hound

Size: Males—20½ inches, 55 pounds; females—19½ inches, 48 pounds

Coat: The coat is thick, hard, and weather resistant. The smooth double coat consists of a combination of coarse straight guard hairs and a soft, dense, woolly undercoat. The coat is shorter on the head, ears, and front of the legs and is longer on the back of the neck, back of the hind legs, and the tail.

Color: Gray. The undercoat is light silver, as are the legs, stomach, buttocks, and underside of tail. The body coat is of varying shades and is darkest on the saddle. The muzzle, ears, and tail tip are black.

Life expectancy: 12–15 years

Activity level: High. This is a breed with energy and stamina. Elkhounds can hunt all day in the harshest terrain and most inclement weather. They should have at least twenty to thirty minutes of exercise twice a day. They do well in obedience, agility, and tracking.

Grooming: Brush twice a week, except during seasonal shedding in spring and fall when a good daily brushing is required.

Temperament: This is a bold, energetic hunter with keen senses and a somewhat independent nature. Elkhounds are friendly and sociable, loyal and affectionate with their family, and can be protective and possessive. They are very intelligent and responsive to praise but also sensitive to criticism and correction. They have extremely keen senses and well-honed problem-solving skills. Training requires consistency, persistence, and a creative approach.

Parent club: Norwegian Elkhound Association of America (www.neaa.net); founded in 1934

Regional clubs: There are fourteen regional clubs, listed under "Regional Clubs" on the NEAA's Web site.

Rescue: Rescue information can be found on the NEAA's Web site under "Rescue."

This Nordic breed has been used in Scandinavia to guard homesteads and hunt moose and bear since ancient times. The Elkhound can be traced back 6,000 years and is believed to have been the esteemed canine comrade of the Vikings. It was first imported to America in early 1900s. This adaptable breed is still used as a hunting dog in Scandinavia, in addition to its role as a companion and a show dog. The first known dog show to include an Elkhound took place in 1877 and was held by the Norwegian Hunters Association. The breed gained a following in England in the 1920s and in America a decade later.

Dignified, confident, and rugged, the Norwegian Elkhound is a hardy, gray, Nordic type of hunting dog. It is medium sized and close coupled with square proportions and moderate substance. It has a slightly arched, muscular neck; a straight back; a deep chest; small, oval-shaped paws; and a high-set tail covered with thick fur carried over the back. It has a broad, slightly arched skull; a tapered muzzle; and high-set prick ears, sensitive to sounds undetectable by humans. The eyes are oval-shaped, dark brown, and medium in size, giving the face a keen, courageous expression.

The Norwegian Lundehund, or Puffin Dog, originated north of the Arctic Circle on the Lofoten Islands in the 1600s. Puffin hunting was essential to survival, and the breed was perfected for the physical challenges of finding these pelagic seabirds in rocky crevices on steep cliffs. Puffin dogs became heavily taxed and puffin hunting was eventually banned, nearly leading to the breed's extinction. By 1900, only a few dogs remained in isolated villages. Most Lundehunds were wiped out by distemper epidemics; by 1960, only five or six remained. Conservation breeding programs were founded with the help of geneticists. The first pair of Lundehunds arrived in Canada in 1960; in 1987, the first one was imported to America.

This is a small, agile, spitz-type breed with rectangular proportions. It has a level back and a long tail carried trailing or over the back. The head is wedge shaped and slightly rounded with a prominent brow and a tapered muzzle. The almond-shaped eyes should be light in color. Several amazing anatomical traits enhance the breed's ability to climb and squeeze into tiny spaces. Its flexible neck can bend backward, allowing its head to touch its back. Its forelegs can rotate almost 90 degrees. Its ears are very mobile, and the ear leathers can be turned and folded to close over the ear openings. The breed's feet are its most unique feature: its oval-shaped feet have at least six toes; the front feet have eight pads, with a three-jointed toe and a two-jointed toe; and the back feet have seven pads.

Entered Miscellaneous Class in 2008

Size: Males—13–15 inches; females—12–14 inches

Coat: This breed has a double coat made up of a harsh outer coat and a dense soft undercoat. The coat is shorter on the head and front of legs and longer on the neck and back of thighs.

Color: Fallow to reddish brown, to tan with black tipping, white with red or dark markings

Life expectancy: 12–15 years

Activity level: Moderate. Daily walks, romps in a fenced yard, and one-on-one play with its owner will keep the Lundehund happy and out of mischief.

Grooming: Weekly brushing is recommended.

Temperament: Gentle, affectionate, and playful, a Lundehund is devoted to its family. This breed has well-developed instincts and keen senses, which translates to an alert, energetic dog that is highly attuned to its environment. Lundehunds are protective of their families and wary of strangers. Bred to be a persistent worker with a somewhat independent nature, the Lundehund is a proficient problem-solver. It learns quickly but does not respond well to repetitious training. Owners must provide short, positive lessons to train a Lundehund.

Parent club: Norwegian Lundehund Association of America (www.nlaainc.com); founded in 2004

Buyers' advice from parent club: Purchase a puppy from a responsible breeder who is actively doing health tests.

Rescue: NLAA Rescue Referral information is located under "Rescue" on the club's Web site.

NORWEGIAN LUNDEHUND

NORWICH TERRIER

Year of AKC recognition: 1936

Group: Terrier

Size: 10 inches, 12 pounds

Coat: A hard, wiry, straight outer coat and a soft, downy undercoat. The eyebrows and whiskers are slightly longer.

Color: All shades of red, wheaten, black and tan, or grizzle

Life expectancy: 12–15 years

Activity level: High. Norwich require vigorous play for a minimum of twenty to thirty minutes a day. They have a strong prey drive and will chase small animals. They cannot be trusted off-leash at any time and must have secure fencing that is reinforced at the bottom to prevent digging. Norwich enjoy chasing and retrieving games and excel at agility, earthdog, tracking, and obedience events.

Grooming: Brush and comb weekly. The coat should be stripped twice a year to maintain the desired texture. Avoid clipping because it will alter the coat's texture and fade the natural color.

Temperament: This is an inquisitive, independent-minded breed with strong hunting instincts. Norwich generally get along well with cats and other dogs, but they are not recommended for homes with small pets. They respond best to positive-reinforcement training techniques.

Parent club: Norwich Terrier Club of America (www.norwichterrierclub.org); founded in 1938, renamed the Norwich and Norfolk Terrier Club of America in 1979; original name restored in 2009

Buyers' advice from parent club: Prospective owners should locate a responsible breeder through the club or by attending dog shows.

Regional clubs: Information on three clubs can be found on the parent club's Web site on the "Other Norwich Clubs" page under "The Club."

Rescue: NTCA Rescue and Rehoming is located under "Rescue" on the club's Web site.

Little, rough-coated red terriers were widely used as stable dogs and vermin hunters in East Anglia before becoming popular as a companion dog for students at Cambridge in the 1880s; they were known as Cantab or Trumpington Terriers. They were first imported to America prior to World War I and quickly gained a following among horse lovers and fox hunters. The Norwich remained a well-kept secret for decades. Bred for working ability rather than uniformity, the Norwich evolved into two distinct types. The breed was officially divided into Norwich (prick-eared) and Norfolk (drop-eared) in 1979.

One of the smallest working terriers, the Norwich is a stocky, short-legged, rough-coated dog with a slightly foxy expression. It is squarely proportioned, with good bone and substance. The back is level and the body is short and compact. The medium-length tail is docked. The Norwich has a broad, slightly rounded skull; a wedge-shaped muzzle; small, dark, oval-shaped eyes; and medium-sized, erect ears with pointed tips.

The Nova Scotia Duck Tolling Retriever originated from a variety of setters, retrievers, spaniels, and collies brought to Nova Scotia by early settlers. The breed, used as a toller and retriever, was developed in the nineteenth century and was originally known as the Little River Duck Dog. The dogs worked as decoys to lure waterfowl. Their playful behavior and fluttering tails would arouse the curiosity of ducks and entice them to come near the shoreline, slowly luring them into range. The breed was recognized in its homeland of Canada in 1945 and was introduced to America in the 1960s.

The smallest retriever breed, this compact, medium-sized dog is athletic and powerful. It has a medium-length neck;

a level back; a deep chest; and oval-shaped, webbed feet. The tail is long and broad at the base, well feathered, and held high in a curve when the dog is alert. The skull is wedge shaped, broad, and slightly rounded with a tapered muzzle. The eyes are almond shaped and wide set. The ears, which are covered with feathering and frame the face, are triangular with rounded tips, set high, and long enough to reach the inside corner of the eye. The breed's expression is friendly, intelligent, and alert.

Year of AKC Recognition: 2003

Group: Sporting

Size: Males—18–21 inches; females—17–20 inches

Coat: This breed has a water-repellent double coat and a soft, dense undercoat. The desired medium-length coat may have a slight wave. The coat on the muzzle is shorter, and there is feathering on the tail and ears.

Color: Any shade of red, possibly with white markings

Life Expectancy: 12–14 years

Activity level: High. In addition to hunting, these dogs enjoy tracking, agility, and obedience.

Grooming: Brush twice a week to keep the coat lustrous and healthy. Check the ears regularly for foreign objects and parasites.

Temperament: This is an alert, determined hunter with a strong desire to work and please, but it can be reserved with strangers. Breeders place great emphasis on hunting ability in this breed.

Parent club: Nova Scotia Duck Tolling Retriever Club (www.nsdtrc-usa.org); founded in 1984

Buyers' advice from parent club: Owners must begin puppy socialization early and must learn to channel their puppy's energy into suitable activities. Consider enrolling in puppy training classes.

Rescue: The parent club's Toller Rescue Program can be found under "Rescue" on the club's Web site.

OLD ENGLISH SHEEPDOG

Year of AKC recognition: 1888

Group: Herding

Size: Males—22 inches and up; females—21 inches and up, 60–100 pounds

Coat: A profuse double coat with a hard-textured, shaggy outer coat and a water-resistant undercoat.

Color: Any shade of gray, grizzle, blue, or blue merle, with or without white markings. Puppies are born black and white and gradually lighten.

Life expectancy: 10–12 years

Activity level: Moderate. This is a strong, energetic breed that should have three or four thirty-minute exercise sessions daily.

Grooming: Three to four hours of grooming per week is necessary to keep the coat clean and mat-free. New owners should ask for a demonstration on how to properly brush through the thick undercoat. The coat can be trimmed, but short coats also require time and work to brush thoroughly.

Temperament: This is a playful, clownish, sociable breed. "Bobtails" can be boisterous, and discipline and training must commence at a young age. These dogs can be quite demanding of attention, and the breed is noted for its booming bark. They are agile, adaptable, and intelligent, still possessing strong herding instincts that qualify them to work as drovers' or shepherds' dogs.

Parent club: Old English Sheepdog Club of America (www.oldenglishsheepdogclubofamerica. org); founded in 1905

Buyers' advice from parent club: Prospective owners must have time for the challenges of grooming and the willingness to cope with a very large dog. Purchase from a reputable breeder. Confirm that the puppy's parents have been screened for health concerns.

Regional clubs: Links to thirteen clubs are given under "OES Clubs" under "Club Information" on the OESCA's home page.

Rescue: Information on the OESCA's rescue chairperson and links to other rescue groups are found on the "Contacts and Organizations" page under "Rescue" on the club's Web site.

The Old English Sheepdog was developed in the nineteenth century from the Scotch Bearded Collie and the Russian Ovtcharka. The breed was also known as the Bobtail because a dog's docked tail signified a working dog that was exempt from Britain's onerous dog tax. It was first shown in 1873 and swiftly became a popular show dog. It became popular in America in the late nineteenth century, bred and shown at early dog shows by prominent society figures such as the Vanderbilt, Morgan, and Guggenheim families.

This is a strong, compact, balanced, and athletic dog covered with a profuse coat that provides insulation. Noted for its trademark shuffling gait, the OES has a short, compact body and a back that is lower at the shoulder than the hips. The feet are round, with tough, thick pads, and the tail is docked short. The head is large and squarely formed, with long, square jaws; a large, black nose; and medium-sized ears carried close to the head. The eyes can be brown or blue, or one of each.

This ancient hound breed was developed from a combination of French hunting Griffons and Bloodhounds in the twelfth century. Otterhounds were used to hunt otters that preyed on fish. In the glory days of the breed in Britain, during the second half of the nineteenth century, there were as many as twenty packs actively hunting. The breed lost its purpose when otter hunting was banned in Britain. It is now classified as a native vulnerable breed in Britain, and it is one of the world's rarest breeds; the Otterhound population is estimated to be less than 1,000 worldwide.

This is a large, rugged, rough-coated hound with good substance and strong bone. It is well balanced with a level back; a deep chest; and a long, high-set tail covered with a fringe of hair and carried in saber fashion. Its broad, compact, webbed feet have arched toes and thick pads. The head is large and narrow, and the skull and muzzle are equal in length. The muzzle is square, with powerful jaws and a large, dark nose. The eyes are dark and the long, pendulous ears are well covered with hair and hang close to the head.

Year of AKC recognition: 1909

Group: Hound

Size: Males—27 inches, 115 pounds; females—24 inches, 80 pounds

Coat: The rough double coat is made up of an outer coat that is dense, coarse, and crisp and an undercoat that is water resistant, short, woolly, and slightly oily.

Color: Any color or combination of colors

Life expectancy: 10–13 years

Activity level: High. Otterhounds have the stamina to work all day and can be boisterous. They must be exercised on lead or in a fenced yard, as they will roam and follow interesting scent trails and are natural escape artists. Otterhounds enjoy long walks, jogging, and hiking, and, because of their superb noses, excel at tracking.

Grooming: Weekly brushing is the general rule, but coats with soft textures may need to be brushed two or three times per week. Trimming the feet will cut down on the amount of dirt tracked into the house. The beard and other facial furnishings may need frequent washing.

Temperament: The Otterhound is beloved for its friendly nature and its fine sense of humor. While sociable and willing to please, Otterhounds can be stubborn and somewhat independent. Their size and strength (of mind and body) make training a priority. Short, upbeat training sessions are recommended. Although they are not guard dogs, they make wonderful watchdogs, endowed with a deep, melodious voice. Breeders share that, in addition to baying, Otterhounds also groan, grunt, sigh, and mutter.

Parent club: Otterhound Club of America (clubs. akc.org/ohca); founded in 1960

Buyers' advice from parent club: Only four to seven Otterhound litters are born annually in the United States. Visit the parent club's Web site for a list of breeders, and check with Rescue or Breeder Referral to find someone in your area so you can meet Otterhounds before deciding on this breed.

Rescue: OHCA Rescue Information can be found under "Otterhound Rescue" on the club's Web site.

OTTERHOUND

PAPILLON

Year of AKC recognition: 1915

Group: Toy

Size: 8–11 inches

Coat: The Papillon coat is abundant, long, straight, fine, and silky with no undercoat. It is flat on the back and sides and shorter on the head, the front of the forelegs, and on the back legs from foot to hock. There is a longer frill on the chest; feathering on the back of the legs; a long, flowing plume on tail, and long fringing on the ears.

Color: This breed is always parti-color or white with patches of any other color, which must extend over ears and eyes. Symmetrical markings on the head are preferred in competition. The nose, eye rims, and lips should be black.

Life expectancy: 14–16 years

Activity level: Moderate. Papillons should have at least thirty minutes of exercise daily. Despite their small size, this is a very athletic breed and one of the most competitive contenders at agility trials.

Grooming: Brush and comb twice a week.

Temperament: Happy, outgoing, and alert, the Papillon is considered one of the most intelligent breeds. Paps excel at most dog sports and make excellent therapy and service dogs. They are very empathetic to their owner's moods.

Parent club: Papillon Club of America (www. papillonclub.org); founded in 1930

Buyers' advice from parent club: Visit the PCA's Web site to find breeders in your area. Some breeders may also have older puppies and adult dogs available; these can be good choices for busy households.

Regional clubs: There are fifteen regional clubs listed under "Independent Papillon Clubs" on the parent club's Web site.

Rescue: Papillon Club of America Rescue Trust (www.pcarescuetrust.org)

Continental toy spaniels have been depicted in artwork since the sixteenth century. They were favorite lapdogs of royals such as Marie Antoinette and Madame Pompadour. Until the late nineteenth century, the breed had dropped ears, known today as the Phalene, meaning "night moth." The erect-eared variety became known as the Papillon (French for butterfly), named for its large ears, which resembled the wings of a butterfly. The breed was first imported to America in 1907. It has been consistently popular as a companion, show dog, and canine athlete.

This is an elegant fine-boned dog with slightly rectangular proportions. The back is level and the tail is set high, covered with a voluminous plume of hair and carried up over the back. The feet are long and oval shaped. The head is small and slightly rounded, with a fine, tapered muzzle, one third the length of the head. The eyes are dark and round, with an alert expression. The ears are large with rounded tips. Erect ears are carried like the spread wings of a butterfly. Dropped ears are completely down, framing the face.

The breed traces its ancestry to a strain of fox terrier, developed by Rev. John Russell (1795–1883) in the south of England, that was renowned for working ability and hunting instinct. The Parson Russell Terrier was introduced into America in the 1930s. It was admitted to the AKC Miscellaneous Class in 1998 and was originally recognized as the Jack Russell Terrier. In 2003, the parent club requested that the name be changed to Parson Russell Terrier.

This is a sturdy, rugged, compact terrier designed to hunt fox above and below ground. It is well balanced and squarely proportioned, with moderate bone and a slight arch over the loin. The protective coat can be smooth or

rough. The feet are round and the tail is docked. The Parson has a flat skull, a strong rectangular muzzle, small V-shaped ears held close to the head, and almond-shaped eyes.

Year of AKC recognition: 1997

Group: Terrier

Size: Males—14 inches; females—13 inches

Coat: The breed's harsh, weatherproof double coat can be broken or smooth; both coat types are dense, straight, and protective. The broken coat is wiry and crisp.

Color: White with black or tan markings, tricolor

Life expectancy: 13–15 years

Activity level: High. This breed has exceptional strength and endurance and a strong hunting drive. A fenced yard is essential. Parsons excel at agility, flyball, lure coursing, and earthdog events.

Grooming: Smooth coats should be brushed weekly. The broken coat should be hand stripped, which may take two to three hours per week.

Temperament: This is a working fox hunter—bold, alert, confident, fearless, and tenacious. Intelligent and quick to learn, Parsons possess great problem-solving ability and single-minded determination. Without supervision and an outlet for their energy, they can get into trouble. They are extremely affectionate, loyal companions but may not always get along well with other dogs. Due to their strong hunting instincts, they are not recommended for homes with small pets.

Parent club: Parson Russell Terrier Association of America (www.prtaa.org); founded in 1985. The club changed its name from "Jack" to "Parson" in 2003.

Buyers' advice from parent club: Owners should be prepared for a smart, high-energy hunting dog. Parson Russell Terriers need consistent leadership, a structured routine, and an outlet for their prodigious energy. A "Puppy Buyer's Guide" is available on the parent club's Web site under "Breed Education."

Rescue: The Parson Russell Terrier Rescue Network can be accessed under "Rescue" on the parent club's Web site.

PARSON RUSSELL TERRIER

PEKINGESE

Year of AKC recognition: 1906

Group: Toy

Size: Up to 14 pounds

Coat: The Peke's double coat is composed of a long, coarse, stand-off outer coat with a soft, thick undercoat. There's a longer mane on the neck and shoulders with long feathering on the back of the legs, the ears, the tail, and the feet.

Color: All colors and markings are seen. The muzzle, nose, lips, and eye rims must be black. The face may be solid black or the same color as the coat.

Life expectancy: 12–14 years

Activity level: Low. Pekes should have daily walks or play sessions, but they always must be kept cool and should not be exercised in hot weather.

Grooming: Brush the Pekingese's full coat daily and be sure to keep the face wrinkles clean.

Temperament: Bold, courageous, and dignified well defines this noble toy breed. The Peke is a loyal, steadfast companion. Typically aloof with strangers, Pekes are devoted to their owners, and because of their well-developed protective instinct, they make excellent watchdogs. This same instinct can make them possessive of their food, toys, and favorite humans. They are noted for their stubbornness, and training must combine creativity and good dog psychology.

Parent club: Pekingese Club of America (www. thepekingeseclubofamerica.com); founded in 1909

Buyers' advice from parent club: Select a Pekingese pup from a dedicated, responsible breeder who breeds for the best traits and raises his or her pups with ideal care and attention. Also consider adopting an adult Peke from a breeder or through the parent club's rescue program.

Regional clubs: Close to twenty breed clubs are listed on the parent club's Web site under "Local Pekingese Clubs."

Rescue: The PCA Rescue and Rehoming Committee can be found on the club's Web site under "Rescue & Rehoming."

DNA studies have confirmed the antiquity of the Pekingese: it has existed for over 2,000 years as a distinct breed. Early documentation of the breed traces back to China's Tang dynasty in the eighth century. Pekes were bred in the Imperial kennels to resemble a miniature lion, and breeding and ownership were strictly controlled by Chinese royalty until Britain invaded China in 1860. Several Pekes were taken from the Imperial Palace and made their debut at European dog shows shortly afterward. The breed arrived on American soil in the early twentieth century and remains a popular toy breed.

The Pekingese is a well-balanced, compact dog with rectangular proportions. Although it appears aristocratic and exotic, this is not a delicate, dainty dog. The forelegs are short, heavy boned, and slightly bowed, with large feet. The hindquarters are lighter, giving the breed its distinctive rolling gait. The head is large, broad, and flat with a broad lower jaw, wide chin, and flat muzzle. The eyes are large, round, wide set, dark, and lustrous. The heart-shaped ears are covered with feathering, framing the face. The Peke has a regal, Oriental expression.

The Pembroke Welsh Corgi is an ancient breed descended from cattle dogs and brought to Wales by European settlers in the tenth century. This type of Corgi was developed in the region of Pembrokeshire, where it was used as a general purpose farm dog. Cardigans and Pembrokes were recognized as one breed for several decades before being divided in 1934. Many people are familiar with Pembrokes as cherished pets of Queen Elizabeth II.

Compared to the Cardigan Welsh Corgi, the Pembroke is shorter backed with lighter bone, straighter legs, smaller pointed ears, and a short tail. The Pembroke is a moderately long and low-set dog, well balanced, sturdy, and agile, with plenty of stamina. It has  a long neck; a firm, level back; a deep chest; short legs; oval feet with strong pads; and a tail docked as short as possible. The head is foxy in shape and expression, with a wide, flat skull; a tapered muzzle; a black nose; and oval-shaped, medium-sized eyes. The ears are tapered to rounded points and held erect.

Year of AKC recognition: 1934

Group: Herding

Size: 10–12 inches; males—up to 30 pounds, females—up to 28 pounds

Coat: Medium-length double coat, consisting of a coarse, longer outer coat and a short, thick, protective undercoat

Color: Red, fawn, sable, or black and tan; any of these with or without white markings

Life expectancy: 12–13 years

Activity level: Moderate. Pembrokes must be exercised in a fenced yard or walked on a lead. They enjoy long walks, hiking, and jogging, but in moderation, as this is a short-legged dog. They do well in many dog sports, including herding and obedience trials.

Grooming: Brush two to three times per week.

Temperament: This is a great family dog—bold, friendly, and adaptable. This is a good breed for urban dog owners. Pembrokes are sensitive, intelligent, and responsive to training: basic obedience training is strongly recommended. They have a strong herding instinct and may turn their attention to herding children and other pets.

Parent club: Pembroke Welsh Corgi Club of America (www.pembrokecorgi.org); founded in 1936

Buyers' advice from parent club: Before acquiring a Pembroke, you should be prepared to make a long-term commitment to caring for a dog. Visit breeders and ask questions about health, care, and temperament. Always buy from a reputable breeder who consistently evaluates the health and temperament of his or her dogs. Always get a sales contract and a health guarantee.

Regional clubs: Sixteen breed clubs are listed on the parent club's Web site on the "Regional Clubs" page under "About the Club."

Rescue: Breed rescue information is found on the parent club's Web site under "Rescue/Lost and Found."

PEMBROKE WELSH CORGI

PETIT BASSET GRIFFON VENDÉEN

Year of AKC recognition: 1990

Group: Hound

Size: 13–15 inches

Coat: This breed's coat is long, rough, and harsh with a soft, thick undercoat. In French, the word "griffon" means rough or wirecoated. The eyebrows, beard, mustache, ears, and tail all have longer coat.

Color: PBGVs are white with any combination of lemon, orange, black, sable, tricolor, or grizzle markings. They are marked for high visibility in the field.

Life expectancy: 14–16 years

Activity level: Moderate. This is a hound with prodigious mental and physical stamina. It must be exercised on lead or in a securely fenced yard. Some dogs will dig under fencing, which must be reinforced at the bottom.

Grooming: Brush weekly.

Temperament: Bold and vivacious in character, this is a busy, happy, extroverted dog with a strong desire to please. PBGVs must have personal attention and generally get along well with other pets.

Parent club: Petit Basset Griffon Vendéen Club of America (www.pbgv.org); founded in 1984

Buyer's advice from parent club: To find a puppy, visit the PBGVCA member breeders list and/or contact the parent club's public education committee, rescue committee, or a regional PBGV club in your area.

Regional clubs: There are three regional clubs. Contact information can be accessed on the parent club's Web site.

Rescue: Rescue information can be found under "Breed Info" on the parent club's Web site.

Developed in the sixteenth century in the Vendéen region of France, the PBGV descended from the larger Griffon Vendéen. The Petit is the smallest of the four Vendéen hounds recognized in Europe. For centuries it was used to hunt small quarry such as rabbit and hare over harsh terrain. The first PBGVs were brought to America in the early 1970s and gained a loyal following during their stint at rare-breed shows in the 1980s. They entered the AKC Miscellaneous Class in 1989.

This long, low, rough-coated scenthound has good bone and substance. The breed is prized for its rough, unrefined outline. It is an unexaggerated hunter that is compact, tough, and robust. The back is level, with a slight arch over the loin, and the chest is deep. The PBGV has a strong, tapered tail, set high and carried like the blade of a saber. The head is oval shaped and carried proudly. The breed's large, dark eyes are accentuated by bushy eyebrows, giving the dog a friendly, intelligent expression. The ears are long, set low, and covered with long hair.

The Pharaoh Hound is identical to hunting dogs depicted in Egyptian art over 5,000 years ago. It has existed as a hunting dog in the Mediterranean for 2,000 years, although there is no consensus on precisely how and when it arrived there. Also known as the Kelb tal-Fenek ("dog of the rabbit") on Malta, it was designated as the national dog of Malta in 1977. Pharaoh Hounds were introduced to Britain in the 1930s and imported to America in 1967. The first litter was born in America in 1970, and the breed entered the AKC Miscellaneous Class in 1979.

This is an elegant, graceful, medium-sized sighthound with a distinctly noble bearing. Athletic and well balanced, it is slightly rectangular, with a long, muscular neck with a slight

arch; a deep brisket; a slightly sloping back; and long, sturdy, straight legs. The long tail is carried curved. The Pharaoh Hound has a long, lean head; a flesh-colored nose; powerful jaws; and oval-shaped, amber-colored eyes. The erect ears are large, fine, broad at the base, high set, and very mobile. When the Pharaoh Hound is happy or excited, its nose and ears will blush deep red.

Year of AKC recognition: 1984

Group: Hound

Size: Males—23–25 inches; females—21–24 inches

Coat: Short and glossy, texture varying from fine to slightly harsh

Color: Shades ranging from tan to chestnut with white markings and white tail tip preferred in competition

Life expectancy: 12–14 years

Activity level: Moderate to high. The Pharaoh Hound is described in the standard as very fast with a marked keenness for hunting both by sight and scent. The dog should have daily running time in a securely fenced area and should be on leash at other times. Pharaoh Hounds also enjoy hunting, lure coursing, agility, and racing.

Grooming: Very little grooming is needed, but a good weekly brushing will keep the coat shiny and healthy.

Temperament: Friendly and affectionate, this is a typical, easygoing hound. Pharaoh Hounds are alert, playful, and accepting of other dogs (they can usually learn to live amicably with cats). Intelligent and adaptable, they are eager-to-please companions but can be quite sensitive to disapproval. Training must be positive, patient, and consistent.

Parent club: Pharaoh Hound Club of America (www.ph-club.org); founded in 1970

Rescue: The PHCA Rescue Program is found under "PHCA Rescue" on the club's Web site.

PHARAOH HOUND

PLOTT

Year of AKC recognition: 2006

Group: Hound

Size: Males—20–25 inches, 50–60 pounds; females—20–23 inches, 40–55 pounds

Coat: This breed's coat is smooth, glossy, fine, and protective. Very rarely are double-coated Plotts seen.

Color: Any shade of brindle, with or without black saddle; solid black; black with brindle trim

Life expectancy: 12–14 years

Activity level: High. This breed is famed for its energy and stamina. A Plott must have daily running on lead or in a fenced areas.

Grooming: Brush this low-maintenance coat weekly.

Temperament: For hundreds of years, the Plott has been bred for vigor, determination, and courage; this is a bold, fearless hunter. As a companion, the breed is loyal, intelligent, and eager to please. Owners should be ready to hear the Plott's voice in the home! The breed standard notes, "Disposition generally even, but varies among strains, with a distinction between those dogs bred for big game and those bred as coonhounds."

Rescue: Buckeye Plott Hound Rescue (coonk9@yahoo.com)

In 1750, the Plott brothers emigrated from Germany with five Hanoverian Hounds to settle in America. Only one of the brothers survived the journey; he settled in North Carolina and established a breeding program with his dogs. The dogs were bred by successive generations of the Plott family and came to be known by the family name as their popularity spread due to their hunting ability; they were used mainly on bear. Outcrosses to other local strains of hunting hound were done to revitalize the gene pool after generations of breeding. While the original function of the breed is to trail big game, it has treeing instinct, as well, and is thus classified as a coonhound.

This is a power-ful, well-muscled hound capable of great speed and stamina. It has moderate bone, a muscular neck, a gently slop-ing back, and a deep chest. Its long tail is carried like a saber. The skull is moderately flat, and the muzzle is of moderate length with flews. The eye rims, lips, and nose have black pigmentation. Eye color ranges from hazel to brown, and the Plott's expression is confident and inquisitive. The medium-length, soft-textured ears are rather broad and high set; they may lift when the dog is attentive.

Pointing dogs came into prominence in the 1600s in Europe, first used in combination with Greyhounds for hare coursing and hawking. Historical data is scarce, but most likely pointing dogs were the result of mixing Greyhounds, Foxhounds, Bloodhounds and spaniels. As hunting with firearms became more common, a dog that could point became the preferred hunting companion. The Pointer (sometimes called the English Pointer) was developed in Britain through various crosses to setters to create a faster version of the pointing breeds then popular in France, Spain, and Germany. By the mid-1800s, Pointers were a popular gundog, and their fame intensified with the introduction of dog shows and field trials. A Pointer known as Sensation was imported from Britain in 1876 by a group of sportsmen who founded the Westminster Kennel Club, and he is immortalized on the club's logo.

This is a lithe, muscular, balanced dog instantly recognizable from its smooth outline; long, slightly arched neck; deep chest; and long, tapered tail. The Pointer has a strong back with a slight slope from  shoulder to croup; the tail reaches to the hock and is carried only slightly above the level of the back. The legs are straight and sturdy, and the feet are oval shaped with well-arched toes. The Pointer has a long muzzle; a slight furrow between the eyes; round, dark eyes; and an intelligent, alert expression. The ears are soft and thin, with somewhat pointed tips set at eye level, and hang close to the head.

Year of AKC recognition: 1884

Group: Sporting

Size: Males—25–28 inches, 55–75 pounds; females—23–26 inches, 45–65 pounds

Coat: Short, dense, smooth, and glossy

Color: Liver, lemon, black, or orange, either solid color or in combination with white

Life expectancy: 12–17 years

Activity level: High. Pointers need daily running time in a securely fenced area. As long as their exercise needs are met, they are well-mannered, quiet house dogs.

Grooming: Weekly brushing is recommended.

Temperament: This is a congenial, affectionate, fun-loving dog that needs to be treated as a member of the family. Pointers are sociable and get along well with other dogs and cats. Although they are not aggressive or territorial, they are excellent watchdogs. Puppies are energetic and inquisitive and must have training and careful supervision to keep them out of trouble. Pointers are responsive to consistent, positive training.

Parent club: American Pointer Club (www.americanpointerclub.org); founded in 1938

Buyers' advice from parent club: Obedience training is strongly recommended; enrolling in a class with your puppy when he is around six months old offers both training and socialization opportunities.

Regional clubs: Fifteen breed clubs are listed on the APC's Web site on the "Regional Pointer Clubs" page under "Club Info."

Rescue: Pointer Rescue (www.pointerrescue.org)

POLISH LOWLAND SHEEPDOG

Year of AKC recognition: 2001

Group: Herding

Size: Males—18–20 inches; females—17–19 inches

Coat: This breed's double coat is long, thick, shaggy, and straight. The outer coat is crisp and water-resistant, and the undercoat is soft and dense. Protective coat covers the forehead, cheeks, and chin.

Color: Most commonly, white with black, gray, or sand patches; gray with white; or chocolate. Puppies are born darker than their adult colors, unless they are born white.

Life expectancy: 12–14 years

Activity level: Moderate. This is a versatile working dog that must have daily mental and physical exercise to remain calm and stable.

Grooming: Daily brushing is recommended to maintain this heavily coated dog. The feet and face must be cleaned frequently.

Temperament: The PON is a self-confident, adaptable, and spirited working dog. With its family, it is loyal and affectionate, but it can be suspicious and reserved toward strangers. Due to its high degree of intelligence and independence—sometimes called cleverness—the PON can be somewhat stubborn as well as pushy and dominant if not trained consistently with positive methods. The PON has an intense desire to please, which owners can use to their best advantage in training and teaching manners. Like many other herding dogs, PONs are vigilant watchdogs. The breed is noted for its excellent memory.

Parent club: American Polish Lowland Sheepdog Club (www.aponc.org); founded in 1987

Buyers' advice from parent club: The parent club's Web site includes contact information of breeders, though none is officially endorsed. The club encourages perspective buyers to do breed research, talk to breeders, and always ask a lot of questions.

Rescue: Information on PON Rescue and Adoption Services can be found on the parent club's Web site on the "PON Rescue" page under "About PONs."

The Polski Owczarek Nizinny (or PON for short) is also known as the Nizinny in its native Poland. Developed in Central Asia, PONs share an ancestry with the Tibetan Terrier and Lhasa Apso. The breed has been used in Poland for herding and guarding since the sixteenth century. A resurgence of interest in the breed occurred after Poland regained independence after World War I. The horrors of World War II, however, virtually wiped out the breed. Thanks are due, in part, to Dr. Danuta Hryniewicz for rescuing the breed from virtual oblivion. The breed's popularity grew during the 1970s on the Continent, and the first PON entered the United States in 1979. Breeders Betty and Kaz Augustowski established the first major PON kennel in the country in 1982 and helped to usher the breed toward AKC recognition two decades later.

This is a moderate, rugged working dog with slightly rectangular proportions and a profuse coat. It has a medium-length, muscular neck; a level back; and a deep chest. The short, low-set tail is docked or naturally short. The breed has a moderately broad skull with a slightly domed forehead and a noticeable furrow and strong jaws. The eyes are medium sized and oval shaped, and the heart-shaped dropped ears are set moderately high.

The Pomeranian descended from spitz-type dogs used for general farm work throughout Europe. Many came from Pomerania, a region of Germany, but the breed's ancestry also traces to dogs from other parts of Europe. These were much larger dogs, some weighing over 30 pounds. Breeders in Britain were responsible for developing the type we are familiar with today. The breed was known in Britain for almost a century, but it remained very obscure until Queen Victoria acquired a Pom named Marco during a trip to Italy. This sparked tremendous interest in the breed, and it soon become one of the most popular pets of the Victorian era.

The Pomeranian is a compact, short-backed, well-balanced, and sturdy dog. It is essentially a miniature type of Nordic dog, with all the hallmark traits of that group. It has a heavy, stand-off double coat; a short neck; high head carriage; a short,  level back; and a voluminously plumed tail, set high and laid flat over the top of the back. It has a slightly rounded skull; a short, straight, tapered muzzle; small, high-set, erect ears; and dark, bright, almond-shaped eyes. The Pom's expression is described as foxlike.

Year of AKC recognition: 1888

Group: Toy

Size: 3–7 pounds

Coat: The Pomeranian has a heavy, stand-off double coat consisting of a long, straight, harsh outer coat and a soft, dense undercoat. The coat is heavier over the neck, shoulders, and chest, with shorter coat on the head and legs. The tail is profusely covered with long, harsh, straight hair.

Color: This breed has a great variety of colors, including black and tan, brindle, parti-color, red, orange, cream, sable, black, brown, and blue.

Life expectancy: 12–16 years

Activity level: Moderate. Pomeranians must be exercised on lead or in a fenced yard. Poms should not be left outdoors during hot weather, as they can overheat quickly.

Grooming: Brush twice a week; trim occasionally for neatness.

Temperament: Although classified as a toy companion breed, the Pom retains the bold, fiery disposition of its working-dog ancestors. This is a vivacious, inquisitive little dog. Fearless and extroverted, it has keen senses and strong instincts to guard its territory. Poms are extremely loyal and make excellent watchdogs.

Parent club: American Pomeranian Club (www.americanpomeranianclub.org); founded in 1900

Buyers' advice from parent club: Choose a puppy from a reputable hobby breeder, and don't buy a puppy impulsively. Always insist upon a written contract and health guarantee.

Regional clubs: Twenty regional clubs are listed on the APC's Web site on the "Regional Clubs" page under "APC Info."

Rescue: Contact information for the APC's Rescue Coordinator and regional rescue groups can be found on the "Rescue" page under "APC Info" on the club's Web site.

POMERANIAN

POODLE

Year of AKC recognition: 1887

Group: Standard and Miniature varieties: Non-Sporting; Toy variety: Toy

Size: There are three varieties. Toy—10 inches and under, 4–6 pounds; Miniature—10 to 15 inches, 12–20 pounds; Standard—over 15 inches; males—60–70 pounds, females—40–50 pounds

Coat: The coat is shiny, harsh-textured, uniformly curly, and dense throughout.

Color: Solid colors in shades of blue, gray, silver, brown, café au lait, apricot, cream, black, and white

Life expectancy: Toy and Miniature—15–18 years; Standard—10–13 years

Activity level: Moderate. Standards are high-energy dogs and should have at least two thirty-minute periods of exercise daily. Toys and Miniatures should have two or three short walks or play sessions daily. Poodles excel at competitive dog sports, earning top scores in obedience, agility, and rally; training for these activities keeps the Poodle mentally and physically active.

Grooming: Poodles don't shed, but they must be brushed daily to keep their coats free of mats. They should be trimmed every six to eight weeks. The puppy clip, English saddle clip, continental clip, and sporting clip are the only allowable show trims for Poodles. For pet Poodles, there are countless popular trims; however, these pet trims or cuts are not standardized styles, and professional groomers will interpret them differently.

Poodles were originally bred as water dogs and were popular as pets, performing dogs, hunters, and truffle finders long before they gained acclaim as show dogs. The breed's type was developed in eighteenth-century France and further refined by breeders in nineteenth-century Britain. Today's Poodle retains the retrieving and swimming abilities of its water-dog ancestors. The custom of shaving the Poodle's hindquarters and tying its hair in a topknot traces back to the traditional grooming of working water retrievers. Poodles were first imported to America in late 1800s, and they have been one of the most popular breeds for decades. Prized for their companion qualities, they also work as therapy dogs, service dogs, and hunting dogs.

This is an elegant breed, noted for its glamorous coat and dignified bearing. Each variety is sturdy and athletic. Squarely built, the Poodle has a level back; a deep chest; and a high-set, docked tail that is carried up. The small, oval-shaped feet are well arched with thick pads. The Poodle has a moderately rounded skull and a long, straight, tapered muzzle. Its ears are set at approximately eye level, and they hang close to the head. The eyes are dark and oval shaped.

Temperament: Poodles are considered one of the most intelligent breeds. They learn quickly and are easy to train. They are also quite sensitive and have long memories. Rough handling or harsh training methods will have a long-lasting negative effect on a Poodle. Although sociable by nature, puppies need consistent socialization to build their confidence and to discourage them from becoming overly clingy and dependent on their owners. They are wonderfully well-mannered house dogs and typically friendly and accepting of other pets.

Parent club: Poodle Club of America (www. poodleclubofamerica.org); founded in 1931

Buyers' advice from parent club: Purchase only from a reputable breeder. Visit the PCA's website for breed information.

Regional clubs: The Poodle Club of America has an interactive map on its Web site for locating regional clubs. Go to the "Affiliate Clubs" page under "About PCA."

Rescue: Poodle Club of America Rescue Foundation information is available on the club's Web site under "PCA Rescue Foundation."

FACING PAGE, LEFT: Silver Miniature. FACING PAGE, RIGHT: White Standard. ABOVE, TOP: White Toy. ABOVE, BOTTOM: Brown Miniature. RIGHT: Black Miniature with corded coat.

POODLE

PORTUGUESE WATER DOG

Year of AKC recognition: 1983

Group: Working

Size: Males—20–23 inches, 42–60 pounds; females—17–21 inches, 35–50 pounds

Coat: Thick, curly or wavy

Color: Black, white, brown, or combinations of these colors

Life expectancy: 11–13 years

Activity level: High. PWDs should have thirty minutes of exercise twice a day. In addition to running, hiking, swimming, and interactive play, PWDs have a natural aptitude for many dog sports. They enjoy agility, obedience, rally, tracking, water work, herding, draft work, fly ball, hunting, and carting. Puppies are very active and inquisitive and must be carefully supervised. They should not have strenuous exercise until one year of age.

Grooming: Brush the dog's complete coat two to three times per week and bathe every two to three weeks. The coat must be clipped regularly or it will become unmanageable. The customary clips for this breed are the lion clip and the retriever clip.

Temperament: A loyal, spirited, versatile working dog with plenty of stamina, the PWD needs interaction and attention and can be quite demanding. The breed must have a regular routine to channel its mental and physical energy. Puppies should be introduced to basic training at a young age. Like other water retrievers, PWDs love to chew and carry things in their mouths. Training and supervision are essential to prevent habits such as nipping and destructive chewing.

Parent club: Portuguese Water Dog Club of America (www.pwdca.org); founded in 1972

Buyers' advice from parent club: PWDs require a commitment to regular grooming, daily exercise, and plenty of social interaction. A puppy information packet for prospective owners can be accessed through parent club's Web site. Always find a responsible breeder.

Rescue: Information on PWDCA Rescue and Relocation can be found on the "Rescue" page under "Breed" on the club's Web site.

Known as the Caõ de Agua, the Portuguese Water Dog was developed as a versatile water retriever by fishermen along Portugal's coast. According to one theory, the breed shares a common ancestry with the Poodle. It nearly disappeared by the early twentieth century when a Portuguese dog fancier took steps to save it from extinction. A few dogs were subsequently sent to England, and a pair of these arrived in America in 1958. By the early 1970s, there was enough interest to form an American club to promote the breed, and it was recognized by AKC in 1983. The Portuguese Water Dog made headline news in 2009 when Senator Ted Kennedy gave "Bo" to the Obama family to fill the role of White House "First Dog."

This is a medium-sized, rugged, sturdy working dog with slightly rectangular proportions, covered in a protective wavy or curly coat. It has a broad chest; a muscular back; and a long, tapered tail  held in a ring. The skull is broad with a prominent forehead and a substantial muzzle. The eyes are medium size and wide set, and the ears are carried against the head. The PWD's expression is penetrating and attentive.

The Pug originated in China, bred in the Imperial kennels, and it bears similarities to the Pekingese. The breed became a favorite aristocratic pet when Dutch traders introduced it to Europe in the sixteenth century. It became so popular at the Dutch court that it was known as the Dutch Pug. By the advent of dog shows in the mid-1800s, the Pug had a secure niche as one of the most celebrated companion breeds and easily transitioned to become an equally popular show dog. Pugs remain popular today.

A compact, square, cobby dog, which the breed standard describes as *multum in parvo* (a lot in a small package). The Pug has a slightly arched neck; a short, level back; a wide chest; and a tightly curled tail lying over the hip. The head is large and round with a short, blunt, square muzzle and a deep wrinkle over the nose. Large, dark, round, prominent eyes give the Pug a fiery expression. Its small, soft, thin, velvety ears can be carried folded back or tipped toward the cheeks.

Year of AKC recognition: 1885

Group: Toy

Size: 10–13 inches, 14–18 pounds. This is the largest Toy breed.

Coat: Short, fine, smooth, glossy

Color: Silver, apricot-fawn, and black. The muzzle, ears, moles and cheeks, the thumb mark on the forehead, and the trace on the back should be as black as possible.

Life expectancy: 13–15 years

Activity level: Moderate. Pugs love daily running and tend to be quite animated and playful. After a workout, they are content to take a nap on your bed or the best chair. Pugs should never be exercised in hot weather. They are not strong swimmers and should not be allowed near pools or hot tubs. Pugs excel in several dog sports and make excellent therapy dogs.

Grooming: Brush once or twice a week to control shedding, and clean the face wrinkles frequently. Black Pugs generally shed less.

Temperament: This is an easygoing, playful, affectionate breed. Pugs are totally devoted to their owners. They are generally sociable and accepting toward other animals. Quite perceptive but sometimes stubborn and willful, Pugs can respond well to training when it suits them.

Parent club: Pug Dog Club of America (www. pugs.org); founded in 1931

Buyers' advice from parent club: Find a reputable breeder, consider your selection carefully, and ask many questions before choosing a puppy. You may need to place your name on a waiting list for a puppy.

Regional clubs: Over twenty breed clubs are listed on the "Chapter Clubs" page under "All about the PDCA."

Rescue: Contact information for PDCA Chapter Club Rescue Coordinators can be found on the PDCA's Web site under "Rescue: Pugs for Adoption."

PULI

Year of AKC recognition: 1936

Group: Herding

Size: Males—17 inches; females—16 inches; 25–35 pounds

Coat: The Puli is completely covered with a profuse, dense, weather-resistant coat. The outer coat is wavy or curly, and the undercoat is soft, dense, and woolly. The coat will begin to clump together and form woolly cords around nine months of age. The cords can reach floor length by maturity at four or five years of age.

Color: Black, rusty black, gray, and white in solid colors. Traditionally, light-colored dogs were used to guard livestock at night, and darker dogs were used to drive and herd sheep during the day.

Life expectancy: 10–15 years

Activity level: High. This is a tough, energetic dog, built to work in any terrain or weather. Pulik do well in herding, obedience, agility, and tracking events. The Puli's coat is tied up out of its eyes when competing in obedience and agility.

Grooming: The coat will not cord if it is brushed regularly to prevent hair from tangling or fusing. Corded coats must be checked regularly for debris, parasites, and skin irritations. In addition, it must be completely dried after bathing, which can take several hours.

Temperament: This is an energetic, bouncy, affectionate breed that is playful and fun-loving. Very affectionate with its owner, a Puli is typically suspicious of strangers and makes an excellent watchdog. These dogs are highly intelligent and must have regular interaction and mental challenges.

Parent club: Puli Club of America (www.puliclub. org); founded in 1951

Buyers' advice from parent club: Find a puppy from a breeding program that is focused on health, structure, and temperament. The puppy's parents and grandparents should be health-screened.

Rescue: Puli Club of America Rescue Trust (www.pulirescue.org)

This ancient breed of Hungarian sheepdog has been a part of rural life in its homeland for over a thousand years. In the seventeenth century, the Puli was bred with newly introduced herding breeds from France and Germany. At that point, it nearly disappeared as a distinct breed. In 1912, breeding programs were founded to reconstruct the ancestral working Puli, and the first standard was written in 1915. The breed was first imported to the United States in 1935 for sheepdog tests sponsored by the United States Department of Agriculture.

This is a small to medium-sized, compact, square dog covered with a profuse, shaggy coat. The Puli has moderate bone; a muscular neck; a sturdy, level back; a moderately broad chest; and a tail carried over the back. It moves with a unique, light-footed, springy, acrobatic gait.

The Puli has a slightly domed skull; a strong, straight muzzle; and a black nose. The eyes are large and almond shaped. The dog's V-shaped, medium-sized hanging ears are set higher than eye level.

This is a traditional herding dog of the Pyrenees Mountains in southern France, dating back to medieval times or even earlier. The breed was used during World War I by French troops as messenger dogs, search and rescue dogs, and sentinels. Some Pyrenean Shepherds came to America in the nineteenth century and were used to develop the Australian Shepherd, but it wasn't until the 1970s, when a breeder in Washington imported a pair from France, that the breed gained attention in the United States. More dogs were imported in the 1980s to establish American breeding programs.

This is a medium-sized, compact, athletic dog with a distinctive flowing gait and vibrant expression. The head is small and triangular shaped with a flat skull and a straight muzzle. The eyes are almond shaped, giving the breed an alert, mischievous expression. The ears are high set and moderately wide at the  base and may be cropped or uncropped. The Rough-Faced variety has a unique windswept face, produced by coat that gradually lengthens from the muzzle and chin to the sides of the head. The Pyrenean Shepherd has a level back and a low-set tail that may be docked, natural bobtail, or long. The Rough-Faced variety has more rectangular proportions and a plume on the tail, while the Smooth-Faced variety is more squarely proportioned.

Year of AKC recognition: 2009

Group: Herding

Size: There are two varieties. Rough-Faced: Males—15½–18½ inches; females 15–18 inches. Smooth-Faced: Males—15½–21 inches; females 15½–20½ inches. Average weight—15–30 pounds.

Coat: The Rough-Faced variety has a demi-long or long coat that is flat to slightly wavy, is harsh textured, and has minimal undercoat. The Smooth-Faced variety has a body coat that is fine and soft, up to 2 inches long on the body and up to 3 inches long on the ruff and culottes. The muzzle is covered with short hair that becomes longer on the sides.

Color: Shades of fawn, shades of gray, merle, brindle, black, black with white markings

Life expectancy: Can live into the late teens

Activity level: Moderate. The breed has stamina and enjoys exercise but is adaptable to urban lifestyle as long as it has adequate activity. Pyrenean Shepherds should have regular on-lead walks as well as opportunities for free running and play in a fenced area. These are athletic dogs that do well in flyball, tracking, agility, and obedience.

Grooming: Coats of correct texture do not require much maintenance. Demi-long coats and coats on Smooth-Faced dogs need brushing once a month; long coats require brushing twice a month. You can let the long coat cord naturally, in which case you'll need to separate the cords by hand and brush the rest of the body every few weeks. The double dewclaws must be trimmed regularly.

Temperament: This is a lively, cheerful companion that is especially sensitive to its owner's moods. Pyrenean Shepherds have strong working drive and powerful herding instincts. They typically get along well with other animals but may become a bit bossy and try to herd them. Naturally alert and distrustful of strangers, they are proficient watchdogs. Puppies must have extensive early socialization.

Parent club: Pyrenean Shepherd Club of America (www.pyrshep.com); founded in 1987

Buyers' advice from parent club: This is a rare breed, and most Pyrenean Shepherd breeders have a waiting list for puppies.

Entered Miscellaneous Class in 2010

Size: Miniature—10–13 inches; Standard—13–18 inches

Coat: Short, close, smooth, and shiny

Color: White with large patches of one or more colors, most often black, chocolate, red, apricot, blue, fawn, tan, or lemon

Life expectancy: 12–18 years

Activity level: Moderate. An energetic and athletic little breed, the Rat Terrier must have daily activity in the form of long walks, interactive play, or running in a safely fenced area. Rat Terriers may take off in pursuit of perceived prey and should not be exercised off lead. They are powerful jumpers, and perimeter fencing must be 5 to 6 feet tall.

Grooming: Brush once or twice per week using a grooming glove or soft brush to control shedding.

Temperament: As the parent club describes this full-blooded Yankee Doodle breed, it is "known for intelligence, athletic ability, loyalty, and just plain fun!" Rat Terriers are vigilant, quick to react, and highly observant of their environment. This makes for a very playful dog, and they typically remain very playful throughout their lives. Likewise, they may not be reliable with small animals. The Rat Terrier also shares its ancestry with hounds, which makes it much more pack-oriented. They are notably loyal and affectionate with their owners and generally friendly toward other dogs. Rat Terriers are sensitive and quite responsive to training and are known to be easy to house-train. They may be reserved or submissive toward strangers. They can be territorial and protective toward their family pack. Puppies should have an early introduction to obedience training and ongoing socialization to ensure a balanced temperament.

Parent club: Rat Terrier Club of America (www.ratterrierclub.com); founded in 1993

Buyers' advice from parent club: Educate yourself about the breed before acquiring a Rat Terrier. Find a reputable breeder through the parent club and ask plenty of questions prior to purchase. Consider adopting a rescued Rat Terrier.

Rescue: The RTCA lists breed rescue information under "Rescues" on its Web site.

The Rat Terrier is a traditional farm dog used as a watchdog, ratter, and hunting dog. It was developed in the nineteenth century by crossing Fox Terriers with other terrier breeds, including the Manchester Terrier, the Bull Terrier, and the now-extinct White English Terrier. Rat Terriers were also crossed to hounds, including Beagles, Whippets, and Italian Greyhounds, to improve speed and hunting ability. Though the breed is new to the AKC ranks, it has been around for decades as a working dog and companion.

A sturdy, athletic dog, the Rat Terrier is hard muscled with rectangular proportions. The breed is found in two sizes: miniature and standard. Both sizes are well balanced and compactly built, with a smooth, level back; a strong, arched neck; moderate bone; and oval-shaped feet. The tail is docked and carried slightly below or above the back, never over the back or curled. The head is shaped like a smooth, blunt wedge, with a flat skull and strong, smoothly tapered muzzle. It has wide-set, oval-shaped eyes and a keen, intelligent expression. The ears are V-shaped and can be carried erect, semi-erect, tipped, or button.

Grands Bleus de Gascogne, Welsh Hounds, English Foxhounds, and Bloodhounds were brought to America before the Revolutionary War. These breeds were unable to cope with the challenges of American climate and terrain as well as quarry that climbed trees or jumped into swamps to evade pursuers. Over the centuries, these breeds were combined and selectively bred for added stamina and courage plus the ability to tree, climb, and swim, and this provided the basis for the coonhound breeds. Years later, red foxhounds imported from Ireland and Scotland were added to the mix, and this resulted in the Redbone Coonhound.

This is a lean, muscular, well-balanced dog with a flashy red coat and a confident demeanor. The head is moderately broad and flat, with a square muzzle. This breed has a medium-length neck; straight legs; round

feet with well-arched, stout toes; a deep chest; and a back that slopes slightly from shoulder to hip. The medium-length tail has a slight brush of hair at the tip and is carried like a saber. The eyes are dark brown to hazel in color, wide set, and round. The ears are set low, fine textured, and long enough to reach the end of the black nose when pulled forward.

Year of AKC recognition: 2009

Group: Hound

Size: Males—22–27 inches; females—21–26 inches

Coat: Short, smooth, coarse, and protective

Color: Solid red

Life expectancy: 12–15 years

Activity level: High. This is a versatile, fast, agile hunting dog built to work over varied terrain from swampland to mountains. Surefooted and swift, they are also excellent swimmers. They will chase small animals and will roam to follow interesting scents if bored, and may not come back when called. They are also great climbers and jumpers and must be exercised either on lead or in areas with secure, high fencing.

Grooming: Brush weekly.

Temperament: This is an undemanding, even-tempered hound. Redbones are trainable and willing to please, but they are too sensitive to tolerate heavy-handed treatment. They are affectionate and love to be with their family; this is a great pet for owners who can ensure that their dog's exercise needs are met. They also have great problem-solving ability. The Redbone is a slow-maturing breed; puppies are energetic and rambunctious and must have plenty of exercise and supervision. Redbones are determined hunters, selectively bred to vocalize as they follow tracks. Noted for a booming bark, they also howl, and they make vigilant watchdogs.

Parent club: Redbone Coonhound Association of America (www.redbonecaa.com)

RHODESIAN RIDGEBACK

Year of AKC recognition: 1955

Group: Hound

Size: Males—25–27 inches, 85 pounds; females—24–26 inches, 70 pounds

Coat: Short, dense, sleek, and glossy

Color: Light wheaten to red wheaten

Life expectancy: 10–12 years

Activity level: Moderate. The athletic Ridgeback must have daily exercise, running, long walks, or vigorous interactive play. Ridgebacks are also excellent swimmers. They can jump high fences, and if bored, they may resort to escaping to roam the neighborhood for entertainment. Puppies are very energetic and must be carefully supervised. With proper care and training, Ridgebacks mature into calm, well-behaved, and thoroughly enjoyable house dogs. They excel at lure coursing and agility.

Grooming: Weekly brushing is recommended.

Temperament: This is a dignified, even-tempered breed with a strong protective instinct and the hunting instincts of their ancestors. Ridgebacks are extremely affectionate and must have daily personal attention and time with their family. They are reserved with strangers but generally tolerant of other dogs and will get along with cats if they have been socialized with them. Ridgeback puppies should have consistent, firm, positive training to learn basic obedience and house manners. This will go a long way to prevent bad habits such as hogging the couch or stealing food from the kitchen table.

Parent club: Rhodesian Ridgeback Club of the United States (www.rrcus.org); founded in 1959

Buyers' advice from parent club: Potential owners must have a clear idea of the breed's background and temperament before making a commitment to this breed. Always find a reputable, knowledgeable breeder.

Regional clubs: There are seventeen regional clubs listed on the parent club's Web site under "Clubs."

Rescue: The "Rescue" page on the parent club's Web site contains links to two national rescue organizations.

Also known as the African Lion Dog, the Rhodesian Ridgeback was developed by Boer farmers in South Africa. Its ancestors include a wide-ranging assortment of working dogs brought by settlers from Germany, Holland, and France. Mastiffs, Great Danes, Bullenbeisser, Greyhounds, and various terrier breeds were bred with indigenous ridged livestock dogs known as Hottentot Dogs. This combination imparted the hardiness and disease resistance that was lacking in transplanted European breeds. The resulting combination produced a dog that was used to protect homes and livestock and hunt Africa's big game. Se-

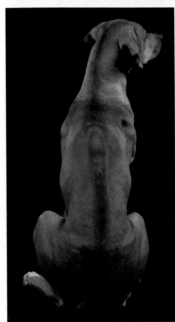

lective breeding eventually stabilized the type of dog we know as the Rhodesian Ridgeback. A standard for the breed was drafted by South African breeders in 1922. The first Rhodesian Ridgebacks were imported to America in 1950. The Rhodesian Ridgeback is the national dog of South Africa.

The Rhodesian Ridgeback is a strong, muscular, well-balanced dog used for hunting, guarding, and companionship. The breed's defining trait is a ridge of hair growing in the opposite direction along the back. The ridge should be clearly defined, symmetrical, and extending from behind the shoulders to the hip bones. The Ridgeback has a strong neck; a deep chest; a firm, powerful back; and a long tail carried with a slight upward curve. It has a moderately long, flat skull; a long, powerful muzzle; round, bright eyes; and high-set, medium-sized ears, tapered to rounded points and carried close to the head.

Working mastiffs have been used to guard, drive, and hold cattle throughout Europe since Roman times. They were defined more by function than breed type, and the Rottweiler was one of many regional breeds that became rare in the nineteenth century as their traditional work disappeared. In 1901, the first club was formed to promote the Rottweiler in Germany, and the breed found a new role as a police dog. The breed has been consistently popular since the 1980s. Today Rottweilers are primarily companions, but they also prove their merit as police dogs, service dogs, therapy dogs, and strong competitors in several dog sports.

This is a power-ful, robust, black and tan dog with a short coat and rectangular pro-portions. The breed has a powerful neck; a firm, level back; a broad chest; a short, docked tail; and  well-arched, round, compact feet. The head is broad and medium in length, with strong, broad jaws; medium-sized, dark, almond-shaped eyes; a broad, black nose; and triangular pendant ears that are held level with the top of skull when the dog is alert. The Rottweiler's expression is noble, alert, and confident.

Year of AKC recognition: 1931

Group: Working

Size: Males—24–27 inches; females—22–25 inches

Coat: The outer coat is coarse, dense, and flat; undercoat is present on the neck and thighs only. The coat should not be wavy and should never be long.

Color: Black with clearly defined mahogany markings

Life expectancy: 9–10 years

Activity level: Moderate. Rottweilers need at least two vigorous twenty-minute exercise sessions daily, preferably with human interaction rather than simply turning the dog out to run in the yard.

Grooming: Weekly brushing is recommended.

Temperament: Personalities range from very affectionate to reserved, but overall, the Rottweiler is calm, confident, courageous, self-assured, and extremely loyal. Rottweilers have strong protective and territorial instincts, which make them excellent watchdogs. Owners must train and guide these protective instincts in a positive manner so as to avoid the dog becoming bossy and domineering. Puppies should have extensive socialization and obedience training. A strong bond with their owners is critical to successful training. Intelligent and adaptable, Rottweilers are quiet, well-behaved housedogs and are good with other pets if socialized to them from puppyhood.

Parent club: American Rottweiler Club (www.amrottclub.org); founded in 1973

Buyers' advice from parent club: Owning a Rottweiler carries greater than average responsibilities. Deal only with a reputable breeder.

Regional clubs: Close to thirty American regional clubs can be found on the ARC's Web site on the "Regional and Local Clubs" page under "About the American Rottweiler Club."

Rescue: RottNet (www.rottnet.net)

RUSSELL TERRIER

Entered into Miscellaneous Class 2010

Size: 10–12 inches

Coat: There are three types of coat: the smooth coat is dense, short, and coarse; the rough coat is harsh and dense; and the broken coat is intermediate in length, somewhere between smooth and rough in texture, and usually includes facial furnishings. All three coat types are weatherproof, with a harsh outer coat and an undercoat.

Color: White with black and/or tan markings

Life expectancy: 12–14 years

Activity level: High. This is a hardy, game working terrier and a good choice for an active family. Russell Terriers do well in an urban environment as long as they get sufficient exercise in the form of daily runs and plenty of interactive play. Their energy and versatility can be channeled successfully into a wide range of dog sports.

Grooming: Brush weekly.

Temperament: This is a breed with prodigious stamina and energy and a strong hunting instinct. Russells are feisty but never quarrelsome. They possess a combination of high intelligence, unsurpassed determination, and problem-solving ability, and this mental and physical energy must be channeled. Highly attuned to their environment, Russells are excellent alarm dogs. Owners must be prepared to provide firm, fair, consistent training.

Parent club: American Russell Terrier Club (www.theartc.org); founded in 1995

Buyers' advice from parent club: "Irish shorties," miniature Russell Terriers, short-legged Russell Terriers, and solid-colored Russell Terriers are not recognized types. Buyers should choose a dog based on health and temperament.

The breed originated in England for foxhunting and was derived from strains of Parson John Russell's terriers. Although the breed shares a background with the Parson Russell Terrier, the Russell has been developed as a separate breed. It was formally separated from the longer-legged Parson Russell type in 2003. Although its ancestry is in Britain, the Russell is considered as having developed in Australia.

This is a hardy, compact terrier characterized by small size, predominantly white color, and a flexible body. It is rectangular in proportion, with an oval-shaped chest that will compress to allow the dog to squeeze into underground tunnels. It has a level back; straight, sturdy legs; and oval-shaped feet. The tail is set high and either docked or undocked. The skull is flat and moderately wide, the muzzle is wide and slightly tapered, and the nose is black. The small, V-shaped ears can be folded forward or carried close to the head. The dark, almond-shaped eyes give the breed a keen, lively, engaging expression.

First described in 1695, the breed was famed for centuries as the heroic, lifesaving dog of the Swiss Alps. Used as a rescue dog, draft dog, and guard by monks, the Saint rescued travelers from avalanches and snowdrifts as they crossed the treacherous Great Saint Bernard Pass over the western Alps. The most famous dog at the monks' hospice, "Barry," was reputed to have saved over forty lives during his career from 1800–1810. A few years later, the entire Saint Bernard gene pool was nearly wiped out due to severe weather, but bringing in similar lines from the lower country restored the quality of the dogs. In 1830, when the breed was in poor condition, the monks decided to crossbreed the Newfoundland to restore the Saint's vigor, thus introducing longhaired Saints. The breed became known by its current name in 1880, and by the late nineteenth century, it was a popular pet and a show dog.

An imposing dog, the Saint Bernard has broad, powerful shoulders; a strong, level back; heavy-boned, sturdy legs; big, broad feet; and a long, bushy tail. The head is massive, with strong, high cheekbones; a short, straight muzzle; loose skin and deep wrinkles over the forehead; and a broad, black nose. Medium-sized, triangular ears are high set, standing slightly away from the head. The eyes are medium sized, dark brown, and deep set, giving the dog a friendly, intelligent expression.

Year of AKC recognition: 1885

Group: Working

Size: Males—28–30 inches, 140–180 pounds; females—26–28 inches, 120–140 pounds. The tallest Saint Bernard had a recorded height of 35 inches; the heaviest one weighed 367 pounds.

Coat: There are two coat types. The Shorthaired is dense, smooth lying, and tough, and the Longhaired is medium length and straight to slightly wavy.

Color: White with red, red with white; brindle patches with white markings

Life expectancy: 8–10 years

Activity level: Moderate. The Saint Bernard must be kept in a fenced yard or walked on a strong lead. These dogs do well in obedience, tracking, agility, draft work, and weight pulling. They have a low tolerance for heat and should not be exercised in hot weather.

Grooming: Weekly brushing is recommended, more often during seasonal shedding in spring and fall.

Temperament: Loyal, gentle, affectionate, and very intelligent, the Saint Bernard responds well to praise and rewards. Puppies must have an early introduction to basic obedience training. They make good watchdogs, but they are not guard dogs. Saint love is accompanied by drool.

Parent club: Saint Bernard Club of America (www.saintbernardclub.org); founded in 1888

Buyers' advice from parent club: Research carefully before buying a puppy. Have a clear idea of what a proper Saint should look like. Puppy buyers should visit the breeder in person and ask many questions. All Saints on the breeder's premises should be friendly and outgoing. Breeders are willing to provide references as well as AKC registration papers and pedigrees.

Regional clubs: Over thirty regional US breed clubs are listed on the parent club's Web site on the "Local Clubs" page under "New to Saints."

Rescue: The Saint Bernard Rescue Foundation (www.saintrescue.org)

SALUKI

Year of AKC recognition: 1929

Group: Hound

Size: Males—23–28 inches; females—considerably smaller

Coat: This breed has two coat varieties. The Feathered variety is smooth, soft, and silky in texture, with feathering on the legs, back of thighs, toes, tail, and ears. The Smooth variety is the same but without the feathering.

Color: White, cream, fawn, golden, red, grizzle and tan, tricolor, and black and tan

Life expectancy: 10–17 years

Activity level: Moderate. The breed is famed for its speed and endurance. Salukis have a strong hunting instinct and will chase; they should never be exercised off lead. Car accidents are the number-one cause of death of young Salukis. Salukis must have daily running in space surrounded by 5–6 foot fencing. They enjoy lure coursing, flyball, oval track racing, scent hurdling, agility, and tracking.

Grooming: Weekly brushing is recommended.

Temperament: This is a spirited, dignified, gentle sighthound with an independent nature. Salukis are affectionate with their owners but reserved with strangers and must have ongoing socialization. Noted for their fastidious habits, they make excellent house dogs. Salukis do best with gentle, patient training from a trusted owner. They respond well to clicker training.

Parent club: Saluki Club of America (www.salukiclub.org); founded in 1927

Buyers' advice from parent club: Educate yourself by meeting experienced Saluki owners and breeders. Consider adopting an adult rescue dog. Find a responsible breeder through the SCOA.

Regional clubs: Regional club information is available under "Other Saluki Organizations" on the parent club's Web site.

Rescue: Information is available on the "Saluki Rescue" page under "About Salukis" on the parent club's Web site.

The Saluki was a highly prized hunting dog throughout the Middle East for thousands of years, used for coursing and hawking. It was known as the Persian Greyhound when it was first imported to Britain in 1840 and was used for hare coursing there. The nineteenth-century breeder Florence Amhurst began importing dogs to Norfolk, England, in 1895. She is credited with promoting the breed at shows and was instrumental in founding the first club and getting it recognized. Salukis were first imported to America from Thebes in 1861.

The breed standard calls for a dog whose appearance gives "an impression of grace and symmetry and of great speed and endurance coupled with strength and activity…". True to its origins, the Saluki is an athletic sighthound with a graceful outline; a broad, muscular back; a slight arch over loin; and a long, low-set tail carried in a curve. It has a long, narrow head; long ears hanging close to the head; and large, oval eyes, giving it a far-seeing expression.

This is a typical Nordic breed, used for centuries by Samoyed tribes for herding, hunting, guarding, and hauling. It first came to public attention when polar explorers began using Samoyed as sled dogs for Arctic and Antarctic expeditions. British dog fanciers became interested in the breed in the late nineteenth century. Most notably, Ernest Kilburn-Scott and his wife were primarily responsible for establishing Samoyed breeding programs in Britain. They imported a number of dogs that ranged in color and type, including a former sled dog that the Kilburns found in an Australian zoo. The Samoyed quickly developed a following after Britain's Queen Alexandra began breeding and showing them in the Edwardian era.

The Samoyed is distinguished by its glistening white coat and appealing expression. It has a broad, wedge-shaped head; a medium-length, tapered muzzle; triangular, erect ears with slightly rounded tips; and sparkling, deep-set,  almond-shaped eyes. Its black lips slightly curve upward at the corners, giving the Samoyed its characteristic smile. It has a deep chest; a level back; large, oval-shaped feet; and a long, heavily coated tail carried up over the back.

Year of AKC recognition: 1906

Group: Working

Size: Males—21–23½ inches, 45–65 pounds; females—19–21 inches, 35–50 pounds

Coat: Heavy and weather-resistant, the Samoyed's full standoff double coat consists of a straight, harsh outer coat and a soft, short, thick undercoat. The males carry more of a ruff around the neck and shoulders, framing the head.

Color: White, white and biscuit, cream, or all biscuit with a silvery sheen to the coat

Life expectancy: 12–14 years

Activity level: Moderate. Samoyed make excellent jogging companions, but puppies should avoid strenuous exercise. Use caution when exercising a Samoyed during the summer. Samoyed do well in obedience, herding, sledding, and weight pulling.

Grooming: Brush weekly, more often during seasonal shedding in spring and fall.

Temperament: Although this is a self-reliant, independent working dog, a Samoyed bonds strongly to its owner. This dignified, graceful dog is extremely loyal and seeks approval and attention from its humans. If ignored, the Sammy can become demanding, as this is a true working dog that is happiest when it has a job to do. This dog is a keenly intelligent problem-solver and will become bored with a limited daily routine.

Parent club: Samoyed Club of America (www.samoyedclubofamerica.org); founded in 1923

Buyers' advice from parent club: Purchase a puppy from a reliable breeder who will provide you with a written contract and health guarantee. Be wary of breeders who represent the Samoyed as easy to keep clean or nonshedding.

Regional clubs: The SCA lists around thirty regional US clubs on its Web site on the "Clubs" page under "About SCA."

Rescue: Rescue information can be found on the "Rescue Groups" page under "About SCA" on the parent club's Web site.

SAMOYED

SCHIPPERKE

Year of AKC recognition: 1904

Group: Non-Sporting

Size: Males—11–13 inches; females—10–12 inches

Coat: The abundant outer coat's texture is straight and slightly harsh, and the undercoat is soft and very dense. The coat's length should be short on the face, ears, front of the forelegs and hocks; of medium length on the body; and longer elsewhere, forming a ruff on the neck, a cape beyond the ruff, a jabot across the chest and down between the forelegs, and culottes on the back of the hind legs.

Color: Black

Life expectancy: 12–14 years

Activity level: Moderate. Schipperkes love to run in a large yard but can adapt to life as an apartment dog.

Grooming: Brush once or twice a week.

Temperament: This is a lively, inquisitive, confident little dog with an independent nature. Faithful and devoted to its owner, the breed can be reserved with strangers. Schipperkes are extremely vigilant and make exceptional watchdogs. They also have a well-developed hunting instinct. Schipperkes can be willful and challenging to train, and owners must have patience and persistence. Obedience training will preempt many potential problems such as excessive barking, begging, or bolting out open doors.

Parent club: Schipperke Club of America (www.schipperkeclub-usa.org); founded in 1929

Buyer's advice from parent club: The parent club's Web site offers a breeder referral service.

Regional clubs: The SCA lists about a dozen breed clubs on its Web site on the "Regional Clubs" page under "Club Info."

Rescue: SCA Rescue and Health Foundation (www.schipperkefoundation.org); the SCA also lists rescue groups on its Web site on the "Rescue Organizations" page under "Rescue Referral."

A miniaturized version of the sheepdogs long used in Belgium, the Schipperke was used to hunt small animals, kill vermin, and guard canal boats that doubled as homes and businesses between Antwerp and Brussels. In Flemish, *schip* is translated as boat. Also known as the Little Captain, the Schipperke was a working-class companion dog until it caught the attention of royal visitors at a Brussels dog show in 1885. At that point, the breed transitioned into a fashionable pet. A few years later, in 1888, the first Schips were imported to America.

The Schipperke is a short-backed, cobby dog with a level or sloping backline; a broad, deep chest; a slightly arched, moderate neck; and a short, docked tail. The breed's unique silhouette is created by its square profile and distinctive coat, complete with ruff, cape, and culottes. It has a slightly rounded, wedge-shaped, foxy head and a questioning, mischievous expression. The eyes are small, dark, and oval shaped, and the ears are high set, small, and triangular.

This ancient breed of Scotland is considered a close relative of the Irish Wolfhound, also developed from ancient Celtic sighthounds to course big game. For centuries, ownership was restricted to nobility. Social, economic, and environmental changes pushed the breed to the brink of extinction by the nineteenth century. It gained new popularity in the Victorian era thanks to the paintings of Sir Edwin Landseer, the writings of Sir Walter Scott, and the patronage of Queen Victoria.

This is a large, rough-coated sighthound with a long neck covered with a mane, a deep chest, and a flexible back. The legs are

long, sturdy, and straight and the toes are well arranged. The long tail is curved but never carried higher than back level. The Deerhound has a long, flat skull and a pointed muzzle with a silky mustache and beard. The ears are set high, covered with black or dark hair, folded back, or held semi-erect when alert. The dark eyes give the Deerhound its characteristic soft expression.

Year of AKC recognition: 1886

Group: Hound

Size: Males—30–32 inches, 85–110 pounds; females—28 inches and up, 75–95 pounds

Coat: This breed's coat is crisp and somewhat wiry, 3–4 inches long, with a slight fringe on the inside of the forelegs and the hind legs.

Color: Dark blue-gray, shades of gray or brindle, yellow, sandy red, or red fawn

Life expectancy: 8–11 years

Activity level: Moderate. This large dog, with its long legs, needs sufficient exercise in a safely fenced, reasonably large area. Puppies are busy and need supervised exercise.

Grooming: Brush weekly using a slicker brush in the direction the hair grows; use a steel comb for longer hair. Only bathe as needed: bathing will remove doggy odor but will soften the coat's naturally harsh texture.

Temperament: The Deerhound was developed as a courageous, hardy coursing dog, but it is famed for its good manners. Loyal, devoted, and willing to please, Deerhounds need plenty of human companionship and they are wonderfully quiet, dignified house dogs at maturity. Puppies are energetic and inquisitive and require the typical amount of supervision. They get along well with other dogs, but true to their natures, they will chase small animals. Training should begin at a young age, focusing on getting the pup's attention and motivating correct responses.

Parent club: Scottish Deerhound Club of America (www.deerhound.org); founded in 1906

Buyers' advice from parent club: All of the research you do before the puppy comes into your home will be well worth your effort. Ask the breeder a lot of questions. Find out whether or not the breeder does health testing; participates in dog sports, such as showing, coursing, or obedience; and belongs to the national club.

Rescue: SDCA Rescue and Placement Committee information can be found on the club's Web site under "Rescue & Placement."

SCOTTISH TERRIER

Year of AKC recognition: 1885

Group: Terrier

Size: 10 inches; males—19–22 pounds; females—18–21 pounds

Coat: Called a broken coat, the Scottish Terrier's coat is made up of a hard, wiry outer coat and a soft, dense undercoat, with characteristic longer coat on the eyebrows, beard, legs, and lower body.

Color: Black, wheaten, or brindle

Life expectancy: 12 years

Activity level: Moderate. Scotties are calm house dogs if they have daily activity in the form of walks, interactive play, or running in a fenced yard. Since Scotties will take off in pursuit of prey, they should always be exercised on lead or in a fenced yard. They are not good swimmers, and pools and hot tubs should be fenced off. Scotties are successful in obedience, agility, and earthdog events.

Grooming: Brush weekly. Scotties must be trimmed or stripped every two months to maintain their distinctive outline. A grooming booklet is available from the parent club.

Temperament: This is a feisty little dog, fearless, determined, and self-confident. Its jaunty demeanor is hard to resist. Scottish Terriers have a strong hunting instinct and can be resolutely territorial. They can be quite vocal and can resort to destructive behavior if bored or neglected. Basic obedience training will go a long way toward preventing behavior problems, but training a Scottie requires patience and determination, as the breed has an independent, self-reliant nature.

Parent club: Scottish Terrier Club of America (http://clubs.akc.org/stca); founded in 1900

Buyer's advice from parent club: Learn as much as possible about the breed. The secret to finding a Scottie is networking through the parent club or a regional club. Consider an adult or rescue dog.

Regional clubs: Regional clubs are listed under "Regional Clubs" on the parent club's Web site.

Rescue: The STCA's Rescue Program is listed under "Rescue" on the club's Web site.

The Scottish Terrier shares its heritage with the other working terriers of Scotland, the Cairn and the West Highland White Terrier. They were gradually separated into distinct breeds in the late nineteenth century. Scotties were first shown in 1860 in classes that included Dandie Dinmont, Yorkshire, and Skye Terriers. The breed's loyal fanciers soon set out on their own, and a club was formed to promote the Scottish Terrier in 1882. The first Scotties imported to America arrived the following year. The most famous Scottie in America was Franklin Delano Roosevelt's Fala. More recently, Americans were regularly treated to the antics of Barney and Miss Beasley, the White House Scotties of the George W. Bush administration.

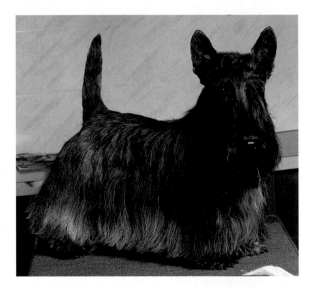

This is a sturdy, compact, short-legged terrier with a wire coat, good bone, and substance. The Scottish Terrier has a long head; a black nose; small, bright, wide-set, almond-shaped eyes; and a piercing, varminty expression. The small, pointed ears are covered in velvety, short hair and carried erect. The breed has a strong, thick, moderately short neck; a moderately short body; a broad, very deep chest; heavy forelegs; and muscular hindquarters. The tail is tapered, 7 inches long, and set and carried high.

The Sealyham Terrier was developed at the Sealyham estate of Captain John Edwardes in Haverfordwest, Wales, between 1850 and 1891. He used a combination of West Highland White Terrier, Wire Fox Terrier, Bull Terrier, and Dandie Dinmont Terrier to create a game, hardy terrier with an easily visible light coat and the speed and tenacity to take on badger, fox, and otter. Sealyhams were imported to America in the early twentieth century and became tremendously popular show dogs almost immediately. The breed has fallen into relative obscurity in recent times but continues to make a mark in show rings in America and Europe.

This is a short-legged and short-coupled wirehaired terrier. It has a flexible, level back; substantial bone and muscle; and a  short, docked tail carried upright. The long, broad head is slightly domed with flat cheeks; powerful, square jaws; and a black nose. The eyes are dark, wide set, and oval shaped, giving the Sealyham a keen terrier expression. The ears are thin with rounded tips, folded with the forward edge held close to cheeks.

Year of AKC recognition: 1911

Group: Terrier

Size: About 10½ inches; males—23–24 pounds; females—slightly less

Coat: Hard, wiry, and weather-resistant outer coat insulated by a soft, dense undercoat

Color: White with lemon, tan, or badger-colored markings on the head and ears

Life expectancy: 12–14 years

Activity level: Moderate. The Sealyham is calmer and quieter than some other terriers. It should have daily walks and interactive play. Fencing must be reinforced at the bottom to prevent digging. Sealyhams are good for urban dog owners.

Grooming: Brush and comb twice a week; have the coat trimmed or stripped monthly. Sealyhams must be familiarized with grooming as puppies. A grooming handbook is available from the SCTA.

Temperament: The Sealyham has all of the hallmark traits of a spirited, strong-willed, independent terrier. Nonetheless, because it was bred to work in packs, it will instinctively cooperate with other dogs. Outgoing, friendly, and adaptable, Sealys are undemanding pets but can be stubborn. Owners must provide firm and fair leadership and consistent positive-reinforcement training. A courageous nature and a deep bark make the Sealyham an excellent watchdog.

Parent club: American Sealyham Terrier Club (http://clubs.akc.org/sealy); founded in 1913

Buyers' advice from parent club: Interested buyers are encouraged to be flexible and patient in their puppy search since the Sealyham is a fairly rare breed. Find a breeder through the ASTC Web site. Most breeders do not place puppies until they are between ten and sixteen weeks of age. Always get a contract and health guarantee. It's worthwhile to consider a rescue or an older dog.

Regional club: Sealyham Terrier Club of Southern California (www.socalsealyham.com)

Rescue: The Sealyhams Forever Foundation can be found on the parent club's Web site on the "Sealyham Rescue" page under "The ASTC."

SEALYHAM TERRIER

SHETLAND SHEEPDOG

Year of AKC recognition: 1911

Group: Herding

Size: 13–16 inches

Coat: The Sheltie's characteristic longhaired, rough coat is a standoff double coat, consisting of a long, straight, harsh outer coat and a short, dense, furry undercoat. The coat on the face, ear tips, and feet is smooth. There's heavier coat on the neck and chest; this mane and frill are more pronounced in males. Coat on the tail is profuse.

Color: Black, blue merle, or sable with varying amounts of white (not to exceed half the body). Sable ranges from golden through mahogany.

Life expectancy: 12–14 years

Activity level: High. This is an energetic dog whose working heritage dictates its need for mental and physical activity. Shelties must have daily attention and exercise in the form of long walks, play, or running time with their owners.

Grooming: Brush twice a week, more often during seasonal shedding.

Temperament: Shelties are devoted, affectionate, intuitive, and adaptable. Because the breed is extremely responsive and trainable, it is one of the most popular breeds for dog sports, excelling in herding, agility, rally, and obedience events. Shelties can be reserved with strangers, and socialization is important. Without proper training and attention, they can develop bad habits such as excessive barking or herding people and pets. Shelties respond well to positive, motivational training. They are very sensitive and intolerant of rough handling.

Parent club: American Shetland Sheepdog Association (www.assa.org); founded in 1929

Buyers' advice from parent club: Research the breed carefully and find a responsible breeder. Consider a rescue Sheltie.

Regional clubs: Over seventy-five regional clubs are listed on the parent club's Web site under "Member Clubs."

Rescue: Sheltie rescue information is available on the parent club's Web site under "Rescue."

The Shetland Sheepdog is a fairly new breed, developed on Scotland's Shetland Islands. Possible ancestors include the Collie, Pomeranian, King Charles Spaniel, and spitz breeds. It was used as an all-purpose farm dog and companion breed. The Sheltie was first described in 1844 and was variously called the Lilliputian Collie, Toonei Dog, Peerie Dog, Fairy Dog, or Shetland Collie. Shelties were first imported to America in 1908 and have been shown in Britain since 1909. The breed's eclectic heritage ensured variety of type, and breeders did not reach a consensus on type until around 1930. Today Shelties are trained as medical-alert dogs, therapy dogs, and assistance dogs.

At first glance, the Shetland Sheepdog resembles a miniature version of the Rough Collie, but there are definite differences. The perfectly symmetrical Sheltie is slightly rectangular in profile with a muscular, arched neck; a deep chest; and compact, oval feet. Its long tail reaches the hock, carried up but not curved over the back. Its long, refined head is shaped like a blunt wedge. The Sheltie's expression is gentle and questioning. It has dark, medium-sized, almond-shaped eyes. The ears are small, high set, and erect at the base with tips folded forward.

This is the smallest and oldest of the native breeds of Japan; it was used for centuries to hunt small game in dense mountain underbrush. Officially recognized in Japan in 1936, the Shiba Inu nearly became extinct during World War II, and only three bloodlines remained to revive the breed. Today it is the most popular Japanese breed in Japan. Shibas were first brought to America in 1954. The first American litter was born in 1979 from two Japanese imports.

Year of AKC recognition: 1992

Group: Non-Sporting

Size: Males—14½–16½ inches, 23 pounds; females—13½–15½ inches, 17 pounds

Coat: The breed's typical Nordic double coat is comprised of a stiff, straight outer coat and a soft, thick undercoat. The tail is well furnished with longer hair that stands open in a brush.

Color: The Shiba comes in three colors: red, black with tan points, and red sesame, which is a red coat with black tipping. All three coat colors should have the desirable cream to white markings (called *Urajiro*) on specific parts of the body.

Life expectancy: 13–16 years

Activity level: Moderate. A Shiba's daily exercise needs will be satisfied by long walks, vigorous interactive play, or running in a safely fenced yard. Shibas will chase small animals and birds—and they are fast. Some are notorious escape artists, so secure fencing is essential. This is a hardy breed, tolerant of weather, thanks to its protective coat.

Grooming: Occasional brushing, including daily brushing during shedding in spring and fall.

Temperament: This is a spirited, self-reliant dog, adaptable and resilient with an independent streak. Shibas bond strongly to their owners and are playful companions. They can be reserved with strangers. Puppies should have consistent socialization and an early introduction to rules. Shibas are easy to house-train, but they have a strong hunting instinct and may not come when called. They may become possessive about food and toys; resource guarding should be discouraged. Shibas may not get along well with other dogs.

Parent club: National Shiba Club of America (www.shibas.org); founded in 1992

Buyer's advice from parent club: Research the breed and find a reputable breeder. Ask informed questions about health and temperament.

Regional clubs: Eight Shiba clubs are listed on the parent club's Web site under "Regional Clubs."

Rescue: Shiba Inu Rescue Resource of America (www.sirra.shibas.org)

This is an alert, agile, compact, sturdy hunting dog with a protective double coat. It has a thick neck of moderate length, a firm back, and a thick, high-set tail that is carried over its back. The legs are straight and parallel, and the feet are round with well-arched toes and thick pads. The Shiba has a broad, flat forehead, with a strong jaw, full cheeks, and a slightly tapered muzzle. It has deep-set, triangular eyes that impart a strong, confident gaze, and its small, pricked ears, proportionate to the head size, are triangular and set well apart and tilt forward.

SHIH TZU

Year of AKC recognition: 1969

Group: Toy

Size: 9–10½ inches, 9–16 pounds

Coat: A long, dense double coat that is luxurious and flowing

Color: All colors

Life expectancy: 10–18 years

Activity level: Moderate. A Shih Tzu can get plenty of exercise running around the house, but do not allow it to jump or climb on furniture, as falling can lead to a concussion or a broken jaw. These dogs should never be exercised outdoors in hot weather.

Grooming: Daily to weekly brushing is recommended, depending on the individual coat texture. Puppies must be supervised carefully and trained to cooperate for grooming at a young age.

Temperament: A true companion breed, the Shih Tzu is a happy, affectionate, lively, and outgoing dog that demands human attention. Its bold and alert nature recommends it as a watchdog. Shih Tzu are right and responsive to training, but they can be stubborn. Owners, enamored of the dog's sweetness and irresistibility, must not be tempted to overlook unwanted behavior.

Parent club: American Shih Tzu Club (www.americanshihtzuclub.org); founded in 1963

Buyers' advice from parent club: Be prepared to take responsibility for a Shih Tzu for up to eighteen years. Become educated about the breed's care, training, and grooming. Find a responsible breeder. "Imperial" and "Teacup" labels, used to describe undersized Shih Tzu, do not denote valuable rarities. Ethical breeders do not intentionally produce dogs that don't conform to the standard.

Regional clubs: Sixteen regional breed clubs are listed on the "Local Shih Tzu Clubs" page under "ASTC" on the parent club's Web site.

Rescue: ASTC Rescue Committee information can be found on the "ASTC Rescue Committee" page under "ASTC."

Ancestors of this ancient Asian breed were sent to China as gifts from Byzantium during the Tang Dynasty. Bred at the Imperial kennels for centuries, the Shih Tzu became the favorite breed of the royal family during the Ming Dynasty (1368–1644). Most Shih Tzu disappeared during the Chinese Revolution in 1911, but a few dogs were taken out of the country and used to establish breeding programs in Britain, Scandinavia, and Australia. The Shih Tzu and Lhasa Apso were originally classified as one breed until the 1930s. The Shih Tzu ranks as one of the most popular breeds today.

This is a compact, solid, short-coupled toy dog, covered with a long, flowing double coat. It has a high head carriage; a level back; a broad chest; straight, sturdy legs; and a profusely coated tail curved over the back. It has a broad, round head; a short square muzzle; large, round, wide-set eyes; and large, dropped, heavily coated ears. The Shih Tzu is prized for its dignified, arrogant demeanor.

The smallest, fastest sled dog on the planet, this ancient breed was used by the Chukchi tribes of Siberia for transportation. They were first introduced to America early in the twentieth century as racing dogs, sparking wide interest in the breed. They are most well known for the 1925 Serum Run, a relay of dog teams that transported serum to Nome, Alaska, during a diphtheria epidemic. A statue of the lead dog, Balto, can be seen in New York City's Central Park. Siberians became popular with amateur sled-dog racers in New England in the 1930s and were used as transport dogs by the Army during World War II.

This is a medium-sized, compact dog with slightly rectangular proportions and moderate bone and substance. It has a slightly

rounded skull; a tapered muzzle; a medium-length, arched neck; a deep chest; a straight, strong back; and a well-furred tail, carried over the back in a graceful sickle curve. The breed's almond-shaped eyes and medium-sized, triangular, erect ears contribute to its friendly, mischievous expression.

Year of AKC recognition: 1930

Group: Working

Size: Males—21–23½ inches, 45–60 pounds; females—20–22 inches, 35–50 pounds

Coat: The Siberian has a medium-length double coat consisting of a smooth, straight outer coat and a dense undercoat. There is no undercoat during shedding season.

Color: All colors from black to white. A variety of markings on the head are common, including many striking patterns not found in other breeds.

Life expectancy: 12–14 years

Activity level: High. This breed has incredible endurance and must have daily running time in a safely fenced yard. Siberians do well in many dog sports, especially outdoor ones such as sledding.

Grooming: Brush three times weekly and daily during shedding seasons.

Temperament: Gregarious, gentle, outgoing, friendly, playful, and good-natured, Siberians get along well with other dogs and are very sociable with people. They are willing workers and respond to positive training. At home, they are fastidiously clean house dogs. If bored or neglected, they can resort to chewing, digging, and howling. Siberians are runners; they have a strong predatory instinct and will chase. They are great problem-solvers and can become adept escape artists if bored. If a Siberian learns to escape from enclosures, it will quickly develop a habit of doing so.

Parent club: Siberian Husky Club of America (www.shca.org); founded in 1938

Buyers' advice from parent club: Buyers should patronize responsible local breeders, who can be found by contacting the SHCA. Prospective owners must be prepared for a breed that sheds and requires secure fencing.

Regional clubs: Over forty regional clubs are listed on the SHCA's Web site on the "Area Clubs" page under "Owning Siberians."

Rescue: Siberian Husky Rescue (www.siberianrescue.com)

SIBERIAN HUSKY

SILKY TERRIER

Year of AKC recognition: 1959

Group: Toy

Size: 9–10 inches, around 10 pounds

Coat: The straight, glossy coat has no undercoat and should drape over the body contours. Hair on the lower legs and feet is shorter. Profuse hair on the top of the head forms a topknot.

Color: Blue and tan. The standard describes the blue as silver blue, pigeon blue, or slate blue.

Life expectancy: 13–15 years

Activity level: Moderate to high. Silky Terriers enjoy being involved in all of the household activities. They have energy to spare and relish retrieving games, walks with their owners, and carefree playtime in a fenced yard. Exercise the Silky on lead, as it's prone to chase any passing vermin or fleet-footed wild life.

Grooming: Bathe and brush regularly.

Temperament: Inquisitive and alert, the Silky is a true toy terrier. It makes an ideal companion for anyone requiring a full-of-life pal. This is a friendly and responsive little dog.

Parent club: Silky Terrier Club of America (www.silkyterriercluboramerica.org); founded in 1955

Buyers' advice from parent club: Always buy a puppy from a concerned, responsible breeder who's working toward the betterment of the Silky. Be sure to get references from other puppy buyers as well as a written sales agreement that includes a health guarantee, the registration numbers of sire and dam, and a description of the puppy. Expect to put your name on a waiting list.

Regional clubs: Information on six regional clubs can be found on the parent club's Web site under "About Silkys."

Rescue: Silky Terrier Rescue (http://silkyrescue.tripod.com)

Compared to many breeds, the Silky Terrier is a fairly new breed. It was developed in Australia early in the twentieth century from a combination of the Australian Terrier and the Yorkshire Terrier. Originally known as the Sydney Silky, its name was officially changed in its home country to the Australian Silky Terrier in 1955. A club to promote the breed in America was formed in 1955.

This is a low-stationed, sturdy, rectangular toy breed with a silky-textured coat. It has a level back; straight, fine-boned legs; round, well-arched, compact feet; and a moderately long, flat, wedge-shaped head. The breed's small, dark, almond-shaped eyes give it a piercing, keen expression. The small V-shaped ears are set high and carried erect. The tail is docked, set high, and carried at twelve to two 'o clock position.

Developed on Scotland's Isle of Skye, this breed was used for centuries to hunt vermin underground. Its short legs were ideal for digging and its protective double coat made it impervious to the harsh climate and terrain. The Skye entered popular culture with the legendary tale of Greyfriar's Bobby. When Edinburgh Constable John Grey died of tuberculosis, his faithful Skye guarded his master's grave for fourteen years. A statue commemorates Greyfriar's Bobby in Edinburgh. The breed became extremely popular in Victorian times, so much so that several varieties were developed. One of the longest established of terrier breeds, the Skye began losing ground when other terriers became recognized. Today it is one of the rarest terrier breeds in England and America.

Twice as long as it is high, the Skye is long, low, and sturdy. Its profuse coat falls straight over its sides and veils its eyes. Its silhouette is instantly recognizable: the high head carriage; the long, graceful neck; the level back; and the long tail covered with feathering. Skyes have short, muscular legs and large, oval-shaped feet perfectly designed for digging. It has a long head; a strong muzzle; strong jaws; a black nose; and dark-brown, medium-sized eyes. The ears may be dropped or erect. Erect ears are medium in size and placed high on the head; dropped ears are larger and set lower and hang flat against the head.

Year of AKC recognition: 1887

Group: Terrier

Size: Males—10 inches; females—9½ inches; 35–45 pounds

Coat: The Skye Terrier has a hard, straight, flat outer coat that is 5½ inches long and a short, soft, woolly undercoat. The long feathering on the ears and tail contributes to the Skye's unique appearance.

Color: Black, blue, shades of gray, silver platinum, fawn, or cream

Life expectancy: 12–14 years

Activity level: Moderate. The Skye Terrier must have daily walks or play with its owners. It will chase after squirrels, stray cats, and passing vermin, so it must always be exercised on lead or kept in a fenced yard. Puppies should not have strenuous exercise. The breed is relatively calm and quiet indoors. Skyes do well in obedience, tracking, and agility events.

Grooming: Weekly brushing is recommended.

Temperament: This is a dedicated, fearless worker that is clever, resourceful, and absolutely devoted to its owner. A Skye enjoys daily interaction with its family, which should be strongly encouraged. Skyes are naturally reserved and suspicious of strangers and are typically slow to warm up to new people. They can be dominant and require firm, fair, and consistent leadership, but they are very sensitive and will strongly resist heavy-handed training. Owners must have character equal to this breed.

Parent club: Skye Terrier Club of America (http://clubs.akc.org/skye); founded in 1938

Buyers' advice from parent club: Buy from a reliable, established breeder. Choose a happy, outgoing puppy that is not thin or poorly coated.

Rescue: Information on the Skye Terrier Club of America's Rescue Program can be found on the club's Web site under "Rescue News."

SKYE TERRIER

SOFT COATED WHEATEN TERRIER

Year of AKC recognition: 1973

Group: Terrier

Size: Males—18–19 inches, 35–40 pounds; females—17–18 inches, 30–35 pounds

Coat: The breed's namesake coat is an abundant, slightly wavy single coat with a soft, silky texture.

Color: Shades of wheaten, clear with no other colors in the adult coat (by two years of age). Puppies under a year of age may carry deeper coloring and occasional black tipping; adolescents under two years of age are often quite light in color.

Life expectancy: 10–12 years

Activity level: Moderate. The Soft Coated Wheaten Terrier is adaptable to an urban or rural lifestyle as long as it receives adequate daily exercise. This breed will chase small animals and must be exercised on lead or in a fenced yard.

Grooming: Daily brushing is required, as is trimming or clipping every six to eight weeks. Detailed information on grooming is available from the parent club.

Temperament: This is a steady, self-confident, sociable breed that is less scrappy than some other terriers. Wheatens are happy, bouncy, and exuberant, and if they get into the habit of jumping, it can be hard to discourage. Like most terriers, they can be stubborn and headstrong as well as possessive with food and toys. They make reliable watchdogs and will bark when strangers approach the home or property. Early socialization and firm, gentle, consistent training are musts.

Parent club: Soft Coated Wheaten Terrier Club of America (www.scwtca.org); founded in 1962

Buyers' advice from parent club: Shop carefully and discuss the breed with many owners and breeders before making a decision to add a Wheaten to your family. Contact the club for a list of reputable breeders.

Regional clubs: Eight breed clubs are listed on the parent club's Web site on the "US Local Clubs" page under "Other Wheaten Clubs."

Rescue: Breed rescue information can be found under "Rescue" on the parent club's Web site.

Known in Ireland for more than 200 years, the Soft Coated Wheaten was an all-purpose farm dog. It hunted small game, patrolled the homestead, and provided entertaining companionship. Closely related to the Irish Terrier and Kerry Blue Terrier, the breed was selected for working ability rather than for consistent appearance. The first Soft Coat to be exhibited at an Irish Kennel Club show did so on March 17, 1937, St. Patrick's Day. The Soft Coated Wheaten was first imported to the United States in 1946.

This is a medium-sized, well-balanced, moderate dog with a square outline. It has a strong, level back; a deep chest; round, compact feet; and a docked tail carried up but not over the back. The head is moderately long and rectangular with a powerful muzzle; a black nose; and wide-set, slightly almond-shaped eyes. The ears are erect at the base and folded over, with the tips dropping forward and lying next to the cheek.

The Spinone Italiano, or Italian Pointer, is an all-purpose gundog developed in northwestern Italy's Piedmonte region and renowned for its ability to pursue game in thick brush. Depictions of Spinone-type dogs date back to around 500 B.C. The breed's name evolved from *bracco spinosa*, or "prickly pointer," which refers to the dog's harsh coat texture or the thorny brush in which the dog is hunted. The Società Braccofila wrote the first breed standard in 1897. The breed was imported to America by Dr. Nicola Gigante in 1931 and entered the AKC Miscellaneous Class, where it remained for forty-five years, in 1955.

This is a large, rugged, houndy-looking dog with a strong, straight back and a slight arch over the loin. The chest is deep; the legs are straight, strong, and long; and the feet are round and well arched. The docked tail is carried level with the back or slightly higher. The Spinone has  a large, long head with a square muzzle and strong jaws. The large, high-set, dropped hound ears hang close to the cheeks. The eyes are framed by bushy eyebrows, giving the Spinone a soft, sweet, intelligent expression.

Year of AKC recognition: 2000

Group: Sporting

Size: Males 23–27; females 22–25 inches

Coat: This breed has a dense, stiff single coat, ideally 1½–2½ inches long on the body, with shorter coat on the head, ears, muzzle, front of legs, and feet.

Color: Solid white; white and orange; orange roan, with or without orange markings; white with brown markings; brown roan with or without brown markings

Life expectancy: 10–12 years

Activity level: High. This is a versatile dog with the stamina to hunt all day. Spinoni must have sufficient daily exercise. They should not be exercised off lead, and some will jump fences.

Grooming: Brush weekly and trim minimally to neaten the coat around the tail, legs, and feet. Use a steel comb on the facial furnishings. Do not over-bathe a Spinone, or its skin will become too dry.

Temperament: Friendly and good-natured, the Spinone is a loyal friend and a playful, entertaining companion. Spinoni have a strong hunting instinct and can be somewhat independent. They learn quickly and respond well to positive training and will not tolerate harsh treatment or excessive reprimands. Spinoni typically get along well with other dogs. They may be standoffish with strangers. Socialization should start in puppyhood and be ongoing.

Parent club: Spinone Club of America (www.spinoneclubofamerica.com)

Buyers' advice from parent club: The club's Web site includes listings of breeders and litters; the club states that the breeders are reliable and are members in good standing.

Rescue: The Spinone Rescue Club of America, Inc. is located on the parent club's Web site under "Rescue."

STAFFORDSHIRE BULL TERRIER

Year of AKC recognition: First registered in 1936, the American Staffordshire Terrier and Staffordshire Bull Terrier were divided into separate breeds in 1975.

Group: Terrier

Size: Males—14–16 inches; males—28–38 pounds; females—24–34 inches

Coat: Short, smooth, hard, and glossy

Color: Any color, which can mean solid, parti-colored, or patched

Life expectancy: 12–14 years

Activity level: High. This is a playful, robust dog that must have vigorous daily exercise, preferably with its owner. Staffords enjoy dog sports such as flyball, agility, and obedience.

Grooming: Weekly brushing is recommended.

Temperament: This is a tough, versatile, all-purpose dog that requires plenty of exercise and firm and consistent positive training. Exuberant, impulsive, and exceptionally strong for their size, Staffords need basic obedience training. They have powerful jaws, and a lack of training and supervision will lead to destructive chewing. Owners must be prepared to enforce boundaries and to take a patient approach to training. This is a sensitive, people-oriented breed that best responds to praise and rewards. Harsh training methods are unlikely to succeed and can ruin the breed's character. Staffords have a strong protective instinct and make excellent watchdogs, especially females. Some will live peaceably with other animals, but this varies within the breed, and owners should be prepared to supervise. Staffords are known to be sensitive to weather extremes.

Parent club: Staffordshire Bull Terrier Club of America (www.sbtca.com); founded in 1974

Buyers' advice from parent club: Look for a friendly, healthy puppy or adult. Staffords of any age should be bursting with energy and enthusiam.

Rescue: Rescue information is located under "SBT Rescue" on the parent club's Web site.

The breed originated in the nineteenth century in Staffordshire, England. It was developed from a combination of old-style Bulldog used for bull-baiting and agile, game, smooth-coated terriers to produce a breed with bull-dog tenacity and terrier nimbleness. Known as the Bull and Terrier, Half and Half, or Bulldog Terrier, the breed was used for pit sports and dog fighting until these activities were banned in 1836. Today the Stafford is among England's most popular breeds, though it is less common in the United States.

This is a very strong, muscular, stocky dog, powerful but equally agile and graceful. It has a short, slightly slop-ing back; a deep, a broad chest; strong legs with round bone; and a short, low-set, tapered tail. The head is broad with very pronounced cheek muscles, well-defined jaws, and a black nose. The ears are cropped or uncropped but cannot be drop. The eyes are dark, round, and wide set.

The oldest of the three schnauzer breeds, the Standard Schnauzer was developed in Germany from a combination of German Poodles, spitzen, and wirehaired Pinschers. The breed was traditionally a ratter, watchdog, and all-purpose farm dog. During World War I, Standard Schnauzers were recruited as messenger dogs and were later used for police work. The breed was first imported to America around 1900, but it did not become well known in America until after World War I. Today Standard Schnauzers are trained as search and rescue dogs, detection dogs, therapy dogs, and service dogs.

This is a sturdy, compact, squarely built dog with plenty of muscle and bone and a dense, harsh coat. The tail is docked between 1-2 inches in length. The Schnauzer has a flat, rectangular head with a muzzle shaped  like a blunt wedge; a large, black nose; and a characteristic beard and mustache. The ears are set high and carried erect if cropped or folded forward if uncropped. Medium-sized, dark brown, oval-shaped eyes are accentuated by the breed's bushy eyebrows.

Year of AKC recognition: 1904

Group: Working

Size: Males—18½–19½ inches, 35–50 pounds; females—17½–18½ inches, 30–45 pounds

Coat: This breed has a hard, wiry, thick outer coat and a soft undercoat, along with characteristic mustache, beard, and eyebrows.

Color: Black or pepper and salt (a combination of white and black hairs and white hairs banded with black)

Life expectancy: 13–16 years

Activity level: High. The Standard Schnauzer has stamina and can thrive in most any environment due to its protective, weather-resistant coat and its working heritage. Schnauzers need plenty of activity, interaction, and mental challenges. They do well in obedience, rally, tracking, and herding.

Grooming: Weekly brushing is recommended; the facial hair should be washed frequently. The coat should be stripped twice a year. The pet Standard Schnauzer can be clipped instead, but clipping will alter the coat's natural color and harsh texture. A grooming guide is available from the parent club.

Temperament: Standard Schnauzers are spirited, sociable, alert, and playful, noted for their sense of humor. Intelligent, reliable, and versatile, they can be trained for a wide range of jobs and sports. They are quick learners with excellent problem-solving ability and fierce determination. This is a strong-willed, independent breed, and owners must provide firm, fair, and consistent leadership. Due to their instincts and keen senses, Standard Schnauzers make excellent watchdogs.

Parent club: Standard Schnauzer Club of America (www.standardschnauzer.org); founded in 1925

Buyers' advice from parent club: Buy a puppy from a reputable breeder. The SSCA maintains a breeder referral list.

Regional clubs: Information on eight regional clubs can be accessed under "Regional Clubs" on the parent club's Web site.

Rescue: SSCA Rescue information can be found under "Rescue" on the parent club's Web site.

STANDARD SCHNAUZER

SUSSEX SPANIEL

Year of AKC recognition: 1884

Group: Sporting

Size: 13–15 inches, 35–45 pounds

Coat: Abundant, flat or slightly wavy body coat with longer coat on the legs, ears, tail, and neck

Color: Golden liver

Life expectancy: 13–15 years

Activity level: Moderate. Sussex love daily outdoor running, but they are calm and well-mannered house dogs. They compete in obedience, rally, agility, hunting tests, tracking, and fieldwork. Many Sussex like to propel themselves forward with their front legs while dragging their hind legs outstretched behind them—this is known as kippering and it is a normal breed trait.

Grooming: Weekly brushing is recommended.

Temperament: Typical of spaniels, this is a cheerful, friendly, tractable breed. Sussex are polite and dignified, but they can get bossy. They can be stubborn and are far stronger than they look. Sussex Spaniels are moderately difficult to train; females are harder to house-train than males. Training is essential, and short, positive training sessions are recommended. This breed's soft temperament does not lend itself to heavy correction.

Parent club: Sussex Spaniel Club of America (www.sussexspaniels.org); founded in 1981

Buyers' advice from parent club: Sussex need companionship and will bark and howl if neglected. They mature slowly into an impressive, powerful dog. Be prepared to wait for a puppy, as only seventy-five puppies are born in the United States each year. The breeder will have a lot of questions for the potential owner, so it's important to do your research and know that you are the right owner for a Sussex.

Regional clubs: Links to three American regional clubs can be found on the "Sussex in America & Favorite Links" page on the parent club's Web site.

Rescue: Rescue and placement contact information can be found on the parent club's home page.

The breed was primarily developed by one breeder in Sussex, England, in the eighteenth century. Noted for its rich golden-liver color and distinctive full voice, the Sussex was used to hunt in thick hedgerows and underbrush. It became celebrated for its steadiness, determination, and keen scenting ability. The Sussex could be easily followed on foot and would instinctively bark to signal the hunter when it found the scent of the quarry. It was one of the first breeds recognized by the AKC. But its popularity was overshadowed by faster gundogs in the nineteenth century. Only a handful of breeders maintained the breed in America throughout the 1930s and 1940s. The breed's revival in America took place in the early 1970s, when foundation stock from England was imported. It remains a rare breed and is classified as a vulnerable native breed in Britain.

This is a long, low, massively built dog with a short, strong neck; a level back; a round chest; short legs; large, round feet; and a low-set tail docked 5–7 inches. The breed's trademark somber, frowning expression is produced by a combination of head traits: a long, wide skull with heavy brow; a broad, square muzzle, 3 inches long; large, hazel-colored eyes; and large, thick, low-set ears.

This is an ancient farm breed, used for almost a thousand years to herd cattle and sheep in its native land. The Swedish Vallhund is one of the original breeds of Sweden, dating back to the era of the Vikings. Historians believe that the breed is connected to the more popular Corgi breeds of Wales, crediting the Vallhund as the older breed. For years, the breed was hardly known in Sweden or elsewhere, and in the early 1940s, the efforts of Bjorn von Rosen and K.G. Zettersten revived the breed from the few existing Vallhunds in Sweden. By 1943, the Swedish Kennel Club recognized the Svensk Vallhund; twenty years later, the breed's name was changed to Västgötaspets to recognize the province where the breed's revival occurred. Marilyn Thell of Rhode Island imported the first two Vallhunds into the United States in 1984.

This small, powerful spitz breed has rectangular, balanced proportions and a close-fitting, medium-length, hard coat. It has a long, muscular neck; a level back; an oval-shaped chest; and short, powerful legs. The tail may be naturally bob,  stub, or long, or it may be docked. The natural long tail may curl over the back. The head is rather long and wedge shaped with medium-sized prick ears, a black nose and lips, and medium-sized oval-shaped eyes.

Year of AKC recognition: 2007

Group: Herding

Size: Males—12½–13¾ inches; females—11½–12¾ inches

Coat: The Vallhund's typical Nordic double coat consists of a medium-length, harsh top coat and a soft, dense undercoat. The coat is slightly longer on the neck, chest, and back of the hind legs.

Color: Any color from gray to red, marked in a sable pattern

Life expectancy: 12–15 years

Activity level: Moderate. The Vallhund should have long daily walks. The breed does well in competitive dog sports including tracking, obedience, herding, and flyball.

Grooming: Weekly brushing is recommended, more often during seasonal shedding.

Temperament: This versatile breed is attentive and receptive to training. With its owner, the Vallhund is devoted and affectionate, but it can be wary of strangers. Curious, playful, and bright, the breed is noted for its delightful sense of humor.

Parent club: Swedish Vallhund Club of America (www.swedishvallhund.org); founded in 1987

Buyers' advice from parent club: The parent club Web site includes links to participating breeders as well as available puppies and upcoming litters. New owners are strongly encouraged to investigate their chosen breeder carefully and to ask many questions.

Rescue: SVCA Rescue information can be found under "Rescue" on the club's Web site.

SWEDISH VALLHUND

Year of AKC recognition: 2006

Group: Working

Size: Males—minimum 26 inches; females—minimum 24 inches

Coat: The immense, harsh-textured double coat is weather resistant, consisting of an outer coat of long, coarse guard hairs and a heavy, soft, woolly undercoat. The TM has a heavy mane on the neck and shoulders, and heavy feathering and dense coat on the tail and britches.

Color: Black, brown, or blue/gray with or without tan markings

Life expectancy: 10–12 years

Activity level: Moderate. Tibetan Mastiffs are very active outdoors. Because they have a low tolerance for heat, Tibetan Mastiffs should not be exercised in hot weather. They are escape artists who must have *secure* fencing and can never be walked off lead. They may not come when called and will wander if they can. The breed is independent by nature.

Grooming: Weekly brushing; more often during the heavy annual shedding period.

Temperament: This is an ancient guardian breed. TMs are very independent, strong willed, reserved toward strangers, territorial, and extremely protective of their pack and may not allow visitors into your home. They are generally calm house dogs, though they may bark at night. This is a large, strong breed, and obedience training is essential. These dogs have minds of their own and are quite sensitive. Puppies need extensive socialization, attention, and a structured daily routine. If bored or unsupervised, they can be quite destructive. TMs generally do well with cats and small dogs, especially other Tibetan breeds.

Parent club: American Tibetan Mastiff Association (www.tibetanmastiff.org); founded in 1974

Buyers' advice from parent club: This is a complicated large breed that is not a good choice for first-time dog owners. A breeder referral page can be found on the parent club's Web site.

Rescue: Tibetan Mastiff Rescue, Inc., is located under "TM Rescue" on the ATMA's Web site.

An ancient breed developed in the Himalayan mountains as a protector and flock guardian, the Tibetan Mastiff may well be the source from which most modern working breeds descend. Skeletal remains discovered in China place the dog's ancestors in the Stone and Bronze Ages. There are many accounts of Tibetan Mastiffs accompanying the armies of the Greeks, Romans, Assyrians, and Persians. The first dogs to be sent to England arrived in 1847 as gifts to Queen Victoria, and it was there that the breed's current name came to be used. The first known TMs to enter the United States did so in the late 1950s as gifts to President Dwight D. Eisenhower, though it is to imports from the 1970s that current-day breeders trace their lines.

The breed standard begins "Noble and impressive," which well captures this powerful, large dog. Slightly longer than tall, the TM is well muscled and substantial, with a sturdy, level back, a rather deep chest, straight legs with substantial bone, round feet, and a well-feathered, medium-length tail, carried over the back. The head is broad and massive with a square muzzle and deep-set, almond-shaped eyes, giving it a solemn, watchful expression. The ears are medium sized, thick, high set, V shaped and hanging close to the head.

This ancient breed, related to the Pekingese and the Japanese Chin, can be traced as far back as the Shang Dynasty (1766–1122 BC). Tibetan Spaniels were bred in Tibetan villages and prized as companions, noted for their resemblance to miniature lions. They were also used as watchdogs at the monasteries and were sent as gifts to neighboring rulers. In 1898, Mrs. McLaren Morris became the first person to bring Tibetan Spaniels to England, though it took until the 1940s to establish the breed there. The first breed members arrived in America in 1966.

This is a small, well-balanced dog, with a moderately long, silky double coat. It is slightly longer than tall, with a short, strong neck; a level back; and a long, well-plumed,  high-set tail, carried over the back. Its forelegs are slightly bowed and the feet are small and oval shaped. It has a small, slightly domed head and a medium-length, blunt muzzle. Its dark brown eyes are wide set and oval shaped. The ears are medium size, well feathered, and set fairly high.

Year of AKC recognition: 1984

Group: Non-Sporting

Size: 10 inches, 9–15 pounds

Coat: The Tibetan Spaniel has a silky double coat with smooth coat on the face and front of the legs, a body coat that is flat and of moderate length, a longer mane on the neck, and a long, profuse plume on the tail. There is long feathering on the ears, back of the legs, and feet.

Color: All colors and combinations of colors are allowed in competition.

Life expectancy: 12–15 years

Activity level: Moderate. Tibetan Spaniels should have daily walks or playtime in a fenced yard.

Grooming: Weekly brushing is sufficient. During their twice-annual shed, daily brushing and combing, plus a good bath, will prevent matting.

Temperament: The parent club describes the Tibbie as "50% terrier, 50% monkey, and 50% cat." This is a self-possessed, dignified little dog, loyal and devoted to its family but aloof with strangers. The Tibetan Spaniel thrives on human companionship. Tibbies are vigilant dogs, seriously committed to protecting their home and family. They are quiet but won't hesitate to bark a warning if they detect an intruder. They have keen senses and love to sit on high places to survey their domain. Typically quiet and well-mannered house dogs, they are good for urban dog owners.

Parent club: Tibetan Spaniel Club of America (http://tsca.ws); founded in 1971

Buyers' advice from parent club: Email the parent club for a breeder's directory. Consider the disadvantages of this breed, including the fact that Tibbies are very smart but *not* obedient; they must be kept indoors, where they prefer to sleep on your furniture; they are dog-aggressive; and they can never be walked off-lead because they cannot be trusted to come back.

Regional clubs: Links to two regional clubs can be found under "Links" on the TSCA's Web site.

Rescue: TSCA rescue information can be found under "Rescue-Rehoming" on the club's Web site.

TIBETAN SPANIEL

TIBETAN TERRIER

Year of AKC recognition: 1973

Group: Non-Sporting

Size: Males—14–17 inches; 18–30 pounds; females slightly smaller

Coat: The Tibetan Terrier's protective double coat consists of a soft, woolly undercoat and a profuse and fine-textured outer coat, which can be wavy or straight.

Color: Any color—from white to black—or any combination of colors

Life expectancy: 15–16 years

Activity level: Moderate. Capable of speed and endurance, the TT thrives on daily walks, interactive play, and running in a fenced yard, preferably with its family.

Grooming: Daily brushing to keep the coat shiny and untangled is recommended. The coat can be trimmed to minimize grooming but still requires frequent brushing and bathing.

Temperament: Intelligent, loyal, devoted, and affectionate, TTs make wonderful companion dogs and are terriers in name only. They are sensitive and responsive to their owner's moods and are likely to take offense if treated unfairly. TTs respond well to positive training and do well in agility and obedience trials. They insist on being part of the family and will complain if neglected. Generally playful, they get along well with other dogs, but they can be standoffish with strangers. Puppies should have plenty of socialization to offset any tendencies to wariness.

Parent club: Tibetan Terrier Club of America (www.ttca-online.org); founded in 1957

Buyers' advice from parent club: Buyers must be prepared for the time and expense of raising and caring for a dog. Buyers may face a wait for a TT puppy. Talk to more than one breeder before making a decision.

Regional clubs: Information on four regional clubs can be found on the TTCA's Web site under "Regional Groups."

Rescue: TTCA Rescue Program information is available under "Rescue" on the club's Web site.

This is an ancient breed that was raised by Tibetan monks for centuries. TTs found their way to neighboring countries as gifts, but the breed was unknown to the Western world until the 1920s when Dr. A.R.H. Greig received one as a gift while working in India. She subsequently began breeding them in India and later brought the first breed members to Britain to establish the famous Lamleh Kennel. The first Tibetan Terriers were imported to America from this kennel in 1956.

This is a medium-sized, well-balanced, compact dog with square proportions, completely covered with a profuse double coat. The Tibetan Terrier has a level back; a well-feathered tail, curled and carried forward over the back; and unique, large, flat, round feet (sometimes described as snowshoe feet because they provide plenty of traction). It has a medium-length muzzle; a black nose; and large, wide-set, dark eyes. Long coat covers the eyes and face, and the dropped ears are heavily feathered.

The Toy Fox Terrier is an all-American breed developed by crossing Smooth Fox Terriers with a combination of toy breeds, including the Miniature Pinscher, Italian Greyhound, Chihuahua, and Manchester Terrier. The resulting little dog sparkles with the gameness of its Fox Terrier forebears and the milder, easy-to-live-with charm of its toy parent breeds. This big dog in a tiny package has been popular for decades in the United States as a companion, a show dog, and a part-time mouser.

This is a small, compact, agile, smooth-coated dog with square proportions; it is well balanced and sturdy. The TFT has a slightly arched, gracefully curved neck; a deep, muscular chest; a level back; and a high-set, short, docked tail. Its elegant head is wedge shaped and slightly rounded, with flat cheeks and a skull and muzzle equal in length. The eyes are bright, dark, round, and wide set, giving the TFT an intelligent, mischievous expression. The ears are erect, pointed, and high set.

Year of AKC recognition: 2003

Group: Toy

Size: 8½ –11½ inches

Coat: Fine textured, short, and smooth.

Color: Tricolor (white body with black head and tan markings); white, chocolate, and tan (white body with chocolate head and tan markings); white and tan (white body and tan head); white and black (white body and black head)

Life expectancy: 13–15 years

Activity level: Moderate. Toy Fox Terriers should have two or three daily walks or running time in a fenced yard. They will chase passing small animals or birds and should not be exercised off lead. TFTs are sensitive to cold and should wear a coat or sweater when exercised in inclement weather. They do well in obedience, agility, and flyball.

Grooming: A quick brushing once a week will help to prevent shedding. Bathe occasionally, keeping in mind that TFTs do not like to be wet.

Temperament: A blend of toy and terrier temperament, TFTs are affectionate, devoted companions. They are animated and entertaining, typically playful for their entire lives. Even though they possess the spirited nature, courage, and self-confidence of a terrier, they get along well with other pets and in general are outgoing and friendly. They have a strong hunting instinct and react quickly if they sense anything is amiss in their territory. TFTs are bright and receptive to training, but will not tolerate harsh treatment or bullying. They house-train easily.

Parent club: American Toy Fox Terrier Club (www.atftc.com); founded in 1994

Buyers' advice from parent club: Research the breed thoroughly before deciding on a Toy Fox Terrier. Research your selected breeder, as well, and insist on credible references and peer referrals. A good breeder will provide you with AKC registration and litter papers when purchasing a dog. The parent club's Web site includes a state-by-state directory of breeders.

Rescue: The TFT Rescue Program is located under "TFT Rescue" on the parent club's Web site.

TREEING WALKER COONHOUND

Entered Miscellaneous Class in 2009

Size: Males—22–27 inches; females—20–25 inches pounds; 50–90 pounds

Coat: Smooth, glossy, short, hard, close fitting, and protective

Color: Treeing Walkers are usually tricolor, either white with black and tan markings or black with white and tan markings. White with tan or black spots is also seen.

Life expectancy: 12–13 years

Activity level: High. Treeing Walker Coonhounds are fast, agile, tireless workers, and they must have plenty of daily running in a securely enclosed area. When trailing a scent, they will ignore commands to return; they can also scale fencing, so fencing must be at least 6 feet high.

Grooming: Brush weekly.

Temperament: This is a courageous, determined hunter that also makes a great family pet for owners who are prepared to provide enough exercise. Treeing Walkers can become very destructive without sufficient activity. If their exercise needs are met, they are calm, quiet house dogs that love nothing more than curling up for a snooze on the sofa. Affectionate, even-tempered, and tolerant, they get along well with children and other dogs. They are smart and eager to please, responding well to training, but they can also be opportunistic and manipulative if owners fail to provide consistent leadership. The Treeing Walker is a very vocal breed that will instinctively bark when it detects an interesting track.

The Treeing Walker Coonhound is a descendant of the English Foxhounds imported into America before the Revolutionary War. From these English hounds came the Virginia Hounds and then the Walker Hounds from which the Treeing Walkers were developed. An outcross to a dog of unknown ancestry known as "Tennessee Lead" was made to add gameness to the breed. Treeing Walkers were grouped with English Coonhounds until 1945, when Walker breeders established their own distinct breeding programs.

This is a determined treeing and trailing dog that is extremely popular for competitive coonhound events. It has straight, lean legs; a deep chest; a strong, muscular, level back; and a moderately long, high-set tail carried up in a curve, like a saber. The head is broad with a medium-length, square muzzle and a black nose. The ears are moderately low set, reaching nearly to the tip of the nose when pulled forward and hanging gracefully toward the muzzle. The large, wide-set eyes in brown or black give it a gentle, soft expression.

Also known as the Hungarian Pointer, the Vizsla was developed in medieval Hungary as a hawking dog and later came into use as a gun-dog. It was celebrated for its excellent pointing and retrieving ability. The breed became rare after World War I and only survived World War II thanks to dedicated breeders who took dogs out of the country during the Hungarian occupation. Vizslas were first imported to America in the 1950s and have been used for hunting upland game, rabbits, and waterfowl. They are also trained for search and rescue work today.

Year of AKC recognition: 1960

Group: Sporting

Size: Males—22–24 inches; females—21–23 inches

Coat: Short, dense, and smooth. This breed has no undercoat.

Color: Shades of golden rust

Life expectancy: 12–14 years

Activity level: High. The Vizsla needs plenty of daily exercise, not just a long walk on a leash. If you want to read the *New York Sunday Times* without being bothered, take your Vizsla for a run before you sit down on the couch. If this exercise requirement is fulfilled, the breed makes an excellent house dog, noted to be clean and well mannered. The breed is sensitive to cold. In addition to hunting, Vizslas excel in field trials, obedience, rally, agility, flyball, and tracking events.

Grooming: Weekly brushing is recommended.

Temperament: Lively, gentle, and affectionate, the Vizsla is a devoted companion. The breed is noted to be tractable and willing to please. Vizslas respond well to positive training but are very sensitive and cannot tolerate harsh handling. The breed is famed for its aptitude as both a pointer and a retriever, on land or in water. Vizslas have a strong protective instinct and make great watchdogs.

Parent club: Vizsla Club of America (www.vcaweb.org); founded in 1953

Buyers' advice from parent club: Always buy from a reputable breeder; contact a regional Vizsla club for breeder referrals. If looking for a field prospect, look at the puppy's pedigree to determine whether there are proven field dogs in the background. An ethical breeder will be more than willing to discuss the background of puppies he or she is producing.

Regional clubs: Close to forty regional breed clubs are listed on the VCA's Web site under "Regional Clubs."

Rescue: Vizsla National Rescue Committee information can be found under "Vizsla Rescue" on the VCA's Web site.

A lithe, lean, graceful, athletic hunting dog, the Vizsla is medium sized and muscular, with a short, close-fitting single coat. Light-footed and graceful on the move, it has a smooth, well-muscled neck; a short back rounded at the loin; and compact, round feet. The tail is docked one-third off and carried horizontally. The eyes, nose, and nails blend with the coat in color. The head is lean, with a square muzzle; the skull and muzzle are approximately equal in length. The eyes are medium sized, and the ears are long, thin, and silky with rounded tips; set low; and hanging close to the head.

WEIMARANER

Year of AKC recognition: 1943

Group: Sporting

Size: Males—25–27 inches; females—23–25 inches

Coat: Short, smooth, and sleek

Color: The "Gray Ghost" is solid in color in shades ranging from mouse gray to silver gray.

Life expectancy: 10–13 years

Activity level: High. According to the standard, the Weimaraner must be built for speed and endurance. This is an energetic breed that needs to run. Weimaraners will range in search of game and must be exercised in a fenced area. They do well in rally, agility, tracking, and obedience as well as in hunt tests and field trials. They also make great jogging and hiking companions. Without sufficient exercise, a Weimaraner will resort to habits such as excessive barking or chewing.

Grooming: Weekly brushing is recommended.

Temperament: This is a sensitive, devoted dog that is extremely affectionate with its family. Highly alert, the Weimaraner has a stronger protective instinct than some other gundogs and makes an excellent watchdog. This is an extremely intelligent dog, bred for versatility, but obedience training is essential. Weimaraners have a lot of character and can be assertive and headstrong without consistent training. They may tolerate small pets, but caution is always advisable.

Parent club: Weimaraner Club of America (www. weimclubamerica.org); founded in 1942

Buyers' advice from parent club: Ask to see the mother and verify that the parents have been screened for health. Look at pedigrees to determine whether the breeder participates in dog shows, obedience, or field trials. Participation in any or all of these is a plus. Always get a contract and health guarantee for any puppy purchased.

Regional clubs: There are around forty regional breed clubs, information about which can be found under "Local Clubs" on the WCA's Web site.

Rescue: Weimaraner Rescue (www.weimrescue.org)

Originally known as the Weimar Pointer, the breed was developed in the early nineteenth century by nobility associated with the court of Weimar determined to create one breed with scenting ability, speed, courage, and intelligence. Its ancestry includes a combination of Bloodhound and German hunting dogs such as the German Shorthaired Pointer. Used not only for upland shooting and water retrieving, the Weimaraner was a proficient hunter of big game. For decades, breeding programs were strictly controlled and exportation of Weimaraners from Germany was banned. Not until 1929 was an American admitted to the elite club of Weimaraner owners and permitted to bring two dogs to the United States. The breed swiftly developed a reputation as a top-class obedience contender, and it remains prized as a hunting dog and field-trial competitor.

The Weimaraner has a moderately long head with the skull and muzzle approximately equal in length. It has long, high-set ears; amber, gray, or blue-gray eyes; and a kind, keen, intelligent expression. The Weimaraner has a moderately long, level back; a deep chest; straight, sturdy legs; firm, compact feet with webbed toes; and a confidently carried tail, docked to approximately 6 inches.

The Welsh Springer Spaniel is one of the oldest types of land spaniels developed during the Renaissance for netting and falconry. It was widely used as a hunting dog in England in the 1700s, but its popularity declined in the following century and the breed was perpetuated by a few devoted fanciers. It was shown in combined classes with the English Springer Spaniel at early dog shows and was revived in America after World War II.

Compact, with slightly rectangular proportions and hard muscle, the Welsh Springer has a long, slightly arched neck and a level back. The tail is gener-

ally docked and carried nearly horizontal. The Welsh Springer has a medium-length, slightly domed head; oval-shaped, medium-sized eyes; and a soft expression. The ears are set at eye level and hang close to the cheeks.

Year of AKC recognition: 1914

Group: Sporting

Size: Males—18–19 inches, 40–55 pounds; females—17–18 inches, 35–50 pounds

Coat: The dense, protective coat is straight, flat, and soft, with feathering on the back of the legs, chest, underside, ears, and tail.

Color: Rich red and white; any pattern is acceptable in competition

Life expectancy: 12–15 years

Activity level: High. The Welsh Springer is generally calmer than other spaniel breeds, but it is built for hard work and endurance and must have plenty of daily exercise. This is an excellent personal hunting dog. Welsh Springers also make great hiking and jogging companions, but owners should not allow puppies to partake in strenuous exercise until one year of age.

Grooming: Brush and comb twice a week to prevent the silky coat from tangling or matting. Good grooming habits can minimize the cottony texture that sometimes develops on spayed or neutered dogs.

Temperament: A loyal, affectionate dog, and a willing worker, the Welsh Springer has a strong hunting instinct but is noted for its even, balanced disposition. As a companion, the Welsh is a sensitive, sensible dog, utterly faithful and devoted to its family but typically reserved with strangers. It is a versatile hunting dog, but it must have consistent training from a young age to cultivate focus and attention.

Parent club: Welsh Springer Spaniel Club of America (www.wssca.com); founded in 1961

Buyers' advice from parent club: Be prepared for a "Velcro" dog that prefers to be with its family. The choice between male and female is personal—male puppies tend to be more easygoing while female puppies can be busier and more inquisitive.

Rescue: WSSCA Breed Rescue information can be found on the club's Web site under "Breed Rescue."

WELSH SPRINGER SPANIEL

WELSH TERRIER

Year of AKC recognition: 1888

Group: Terrier

Size: Males—15 inches, 20 pounds; females—proportionally smaller

Coat: Hard, wiry, and dense with a short, soft undercoat and dense, wiry furnishings on the muzzle, legs, and quarters.

Color: Black or grizzle on the body, with clear tan on the legs, quarters, and head

Life expectancy: 12–15 years

Activity level: High. The Welsh Terrier has a long heritage as a diligent worker. This is a zippy little dog, always looking for action. It must have daily exercise and cannot be exercised off lead. Fencing must be reinforced 6 inches below ground to prevent tunneling underneath. A Welsh Terrier will ignore invisible fencing. Most Welsh love dog sports as an outlet for their working drive.

Grooming: Comb twice a week. The coat should be plucked several times a year.

Temperament: This is an intelligent, alert, spirited, and courageous terrier. Friendly, outgoing, and willing to please, the Welsh has a pronounced working drive, but it is a well-balanced companion. Although noted for its gameness, the Welsh also willingly works with other dogs. The breed is known to be easily distracted, so patient, positive obedience training will ensure a well-mannered dog in the home. The Welsh will respond aggressively to rough handling.

Parent club: Welsh Terrier Club of America (clubs.akc.org/wtca); founded in 1900

Buyers' advice from parent club: Buy a puppy from a responsible WTCA member breeder. To evaluate the quality of a puppy, evaluate the quality of the breeder. Deal directly with the breeder, who will ensure that you are aware of the responsibilities of owning a Welsh. Take your time.

Regional clubs: Information on seven regional breed clubs is listed on the parent club's Web site under "Regional Club Contacts."

Rescue: WTCares—Welsh Terrier Rescue Service (http://wtcares.blogspot.com)

The Welsh Terrier is an old breed, traditionally known as the Old English Terrier or the Black and Tan Wirehaired Terrier. For quite a while, these names were used interchangeably to denote the long-legged sporting terriers of Wales that were used to hunt otter, fox, and badger. Welsh Terriers were first imported to America in 1888 by Prescott Lawrence and shown in the Miscellaneous Class. More regular imports began to appear about ten years later.

This is a sturdy, compact, long-legged terrier with square proportions. It has a slightly arched, graceful neck; a level back; small, round feet; and a high-set, docked tail carried upright. The head is rectangular with a strong, squared-off muzzle with wiry furnishings and a black nose. The eyes are small, dark, wide set, and almond shaped, giving the Welsh its characteristic steady, confident, alert expression. Its small, V-shaped ears are carried folded forward with the tips falling near the outside corners of the eyes.

The West Highland White, Cairn, Dandie Dinmont, and Scottish Terriers trace their ancestry back to the hardy working terriers of Scotland. In the nineteenth century, these regional types were separated into individual breeds, but this was a lengthy, contentious process. The Westie was selected for light color so that it could be easily spotted in the field and not mistaken for the quarry. Originally known as the Poltalloch or Roseneath Terrier, which was the breed's name when it was first recognized by the AKC, the West Highland White Terrier officially acquired its current name 1909.

This is a small, compact, well-balanced, short-legged terrier. Game, sporty, and short coupled, the Westie has a muscular neck; a flat, level back; short, sturdy legs; and strong, round feet. The short tail is shaped like a carrot, set high and carried up but  not curled over the back. The head is broad and slightly domed, and the coat on the head is shaped round. The blunt muzzle is slightly shorter than the skull and subtly tapers to a large, black nose. The breed's hallmark piercing, inquisitive expression is produced by dark, wide-set, medium-sized, almond-shaped eyes, accentuated by heavy eyebrows and small, wide-set, erect ears.

Year of AKC recognition: 1908

Group: Terrier

Size: Males—11 inches; females—10 inches; 15–20 pounds

Coat: A hard, straight outer coat that is 2 inches long and shorter on the neck and shoulders. The undercoat is plentiful and soft. The furnishings are somewhat longer and softer.

Color: White

Life expectancy: 13–15 years

Activity level: Moderate to high. This hardy working terrier is tolerant of cold, thanks to its protective coat. Westies must have daily activity or may resort to excessive barking or digging. Westies have strong prey drive and must be exercised on lead or in a fenced yard. They do well in sports such as agility, earthdog, obedience, rally, and flyball.

Grooming: Daily brushing, along with professional grooming every four to six weeks. Westies should not be bathed more than once a month.

Temperament: A typical terrier: self-confident, spunky, and determined. The Westie's lighthearted, happy nature makes for enjoyable company. Devoted to their owners, Westies are generally sociable with others and usually get along well with dogs and cats. They can become bossy if their owners are too indulgent. They respond best to reward-based training but can be stubborn.

Parent club: West Highland White Terrier Club of America (www.westieclubamerica.com); founded in 1909

Buyers' advice from parent club: Contact Team Westie, the parent club's educational resource network, for advice, information, and references. Research the breed and confirm that it will fit well into your lifestyle; never buy on impulse. Contact local dog clubs and regional Westie clubs, and attend dog shows to learn more about the breed.

Regional clubs: Almost two dozen US clubs can be found on the parent club's Web site on the "Regional Clubs" page under "The WHWTCA."

Rescue: The National Rescue Committee can be found on the WHWTCA's Web site under "Rescue."

WHIPPET

Year of AKC recognition: 1888

Group: Hound

Size: Males—19–22 inches; females—18–21 inches

Coat: Short and smooth

Color: Any color

Life expectancy: 12–15 years

Activity level: Moderate. This is an athletic breed, capable of high speed. A Whippet does not need long periods of exercise, but it must have daily exercise and regular opportunities for free running in a safely enclosed area. Whippets cannot be trusted off leash, as they will take off in pursuit of any perceived "prey." Whippets do well in dog sports such as lure coursing, racing, flyball, disc dog, and agility. However, they are also wonderfully clean, quiet house dogs, and they love nothing better than curling up beside their owners for a nap. For outdoor exercise, owners must consider that the Whippet does not have a protective coat and cannot tolerate prolonged exposure to cold.

Grooming: Brush weekly. Trim nails as needed.

Temperament: Friendly, gentle, and affectionate, Whippets are comfort-loving dogs and excellent companions. They are versatile and can adapt to a range of lifestyles. They get along well with other dogs, and many Whippets live amicably with cats, but they should be introduced to other pets under supervision. They are quite sensitive and must be trained with gentle, positive methods.

Parent club: American Whippet Club (www.americanwhippetclub.com); founded in 1930

Buyers' advice from parent club: The American Whippet Club provides breeder referrals through its Web site. The club encourages potential owners to make an informed decision about this breed. The club also recommends that new owners consider adopting a Whippet through breed rescue.

Regional clubs: About twenty US regional Whippet clubs can be found on the parent club's Web site under "Independent Clubs."

Rescue: Whippet Rescue and Placement (www.whippet-rescue.com)

Although dogs of Whippet type date back to ancient times, the Whippet as a distinct breed emerged over two centuries ago, developing for about 100 years before official British recognition in 1891. Established in northern Britain, the Whippet was also known in its early days as the "snap dog" or "rag dog." Once called a "Greyhound in miniature" or the "poor man's Greyhound," early Whippets were occasionally crossed with terriers to add more tenacity. The breed was traditionally used for poaching, rabbit coursing, and most of all, racing. Whippet racing was a fantastically popular amateur sport in the nineteenth century, both in Britain and America. Whippets were first imported to America in the nineteenth century, where mill towns such as Lowell, Massachusetts, became centers of Whippet racing.

This is a medium-sized, elegant, athletic sighthound with a distinctive, graceful outline. It has moderate bone and substance; a long, well-arched neck; a firm, flexible back with a smooth natural arch from loin to croup; and a deep chest that curves up to a definite waistline. The long, tapered tail is carried low in a gentle curve. The Whippet's head is long and lean, with a powerful muzzle and large, dark eyes. Its small, fine-textured ears are carried folded back along the neck.

The Wirehaired Pointing Griffon was developed in the late nineteenth century by one of the world's most innovative dog breeders, E.K. Korthals (1851–1896), a Dutch banking heir. Inspired by his work managing a large kennel of hunting dogs in Germany, Korthals devoted his life to creating a tough, versatile sporting dog. In 1874, his eight foundation dogs, which included setters, spaniels, pointers, and an Otterhound, were hand-picked based on their working aptitude. He maintained meticulous records on each generation as he developed the Korthals Griffon. He designed working trials to test their hunting skills, and his dogs were already widely admired by hunters when he began exhibiting them at dog shows. He wrote the breed standard in 1886 and formed an international breed club two years later. The first Griffon arrived in America in 1887.

This is a rugged, athletic, medium-sized, shaggy-looking dog with rectangular proportions. It has a long, slightly arched neck; a firm, gently sloping back; and a tail that is docked by one-third to  half its length and carried out or slightly raised. The head is square-shaped, with a profuse mustache and eyebrows that impart a roguish, friendly expression. The eye color ranges from yellow to brown, and the medium-sized ears are set high and lie flat against the head.

Year of AKC recognition: 1887

Group: Sporting

Size: Males—22–24 inches, 50–70 pounds; females—20–22 inches, 35–50 pounds

Coat: This breed has a medium-length, straight, harsh, protective outer coat and a fine, thick, downy, insulating, water-resistant undercoat. Longer undercoat on the face provides the characteristic eyebrows and mustache.

Color: Steel gray with brown, white and brown, or white and orange markings

Life expectancy: 12–15 years

Activity level: High. This is an athletic, rugged, versatile hunting dog that needs daily exercise. Griffons enjoy running, jogging, swimming, and interactive play and are quiet, well-behaved house dogs as long as their exercise needs are met. They do well in tracking, agility, obedience, hunting tests, and field trials.

Grooming: Brush and "roll" the coat (strip out dead hairs by hand) regularly. Bathe about once a month. Trim any excess hair from between the foot pads as needed. Detailed grooming information is available on the parent club's Web site.

Temperament: Griffons are highly intelligent, receptive to training, and eager to please. They make great family pets, thriving on attention from and interaction with their owners; they do best if treated as members of the household. They are sociable and friendly. Griffons are versatile gundogs and excellent water retrievers that can be trained to work any type of game.

Parent club: American Wirehaired Pointing Griffon Association (www.awpga.com); founded in 1991

Buyers' advice from parent club: This is a rare breed, and only a few litters are born each year. Learn as much as you can about the breed before making a decision. Find a reputable breeder through the parent club or consider a rescue Griffon.

Rescue: The American Wirehaired Pointing Griffon Association's USA Rescue Program can be found on the parent club's Web site under "Get a Griff!"

WIREHAIRED POINTING GRIFFON

XOLOITZCUINTLI

Entered Miscellaneous Class in 2009

Size: Toy—10–14 inches, 10–15 pounds; Miniature—14–18 inches, 15–30 pounds; Standard—18–23 inches, 30–55 pounds

Coat: The Hairless variety has smooth, tough, protective, close-fitting skin. There may be a small amount of very short, coarse hair on the top of the head, the tail tip, and the toes. The Coated variety is completely covered with a short, flat coat.

Color: Black, gray, slate, red, liver, or bronze, with or without white spots and markings.

Life expectancy: 13–18 years

Activity level: High. Xolos must have daily exercise, long walks, interactive play, or running time in a fenced area. Fencing must be at least 6 feet high, as Xolos of all sizes are expert climbers and jumpers. They have a very high tolerance for heat but should wear a coat or sweater when going out in inclement weather. Xolos excel in agility.

Grooming: Hairless Xolos should be bathed biweekly. Coated Xolos need weekly brushing.

Temperament: The Xolo has the typical temperament traits of a primitive breed—strong natural instincts, natural wariness, and extreme devotion to its owner. Xolos are reserved with strangers but should never be timid or aggressive. They should be introduced to other pets under supervision. Xolos have a strong prey drive, and some are dog-aggressive. Adults are calm and dignified; puppies are extremely energetic and can be very destructive without careful supervision and a structured routine. The Xolo is noted for its clean, fastidious habits and is easy to house-train.

Parent club: Xoloitzcuintli Club of America (http://xoloitzcuintliclubofamerica.com); founded in 1986

Buyers' advice from parent club: Check registration and pedigree before purchase. Xolos from unregistered lines may not be purebred or eligible for registration. Choose a puppy that has been well socialized in a home environment.

Regional clubs: There are regional clubs in Northern California and one in Southern California.

Rescue: Xoloitzcuintli Club of America National Rescue (http://xoloitzcuintliclubofamerica.com)

The Xoloitzcuintli (*show-low-eets-queen-tlee*) evolved in western Mexico about 3,000 years ago. Its name is derived from the name of the Aztec Indian god *Xolotl* and the Aztec word for dog, *Itzcuilti*. The breed is well documented in the art and customs of many Mexican cultures and has remained virtually unchanged for centuries. It was among the first breeds accepted into the AKC stud book in 1887; at that time it was known as the Mexican Hairless. The Xolo lost its AKC status in 1959. Three years earlier, in 1956, it was officially recognized in its native land and is now designated as Mexico's national breed.

This is a moderately built, athletic dog, distinguished by hairlessness. The recessive form of the trait produces a short, smooth coat. Both varieties are rectangular in proportion, sturdy, and well muscled. The back is level with a slight arch at the loin, and the long,  whiplike tail is set low and carried out or up but never over the back. The head is wedge shaped with strong jaws; oval-shaped eyes; and very large, erect, high-set ears.

The Yorkshire Terrier was developed from now-extinct terrier breeds—the Clydesdale Terrier, the Paisley Terrier, the Old English Terrier, and the Waterside Terrier—in northern England in the nineteenth century. Breeders in Yorkshire were responsible for stabilizing and refining the small size and the distinctive silky blue and tan coat now associated with the breed. The Yorkie quickly became popular in Britain, America, and as far away as Australia. The breed arrived in the United States in the late 1800s and was shown at the first Westminster show in 1877. It remains one of the most popular breeds in America.

This is a sturdy, compact, toy terrier, covered with a long, straight, blue and tan coat. It has a small, slightly rounded head; a moderate-length, tapered muzzle; a black nose; dark, sparkling, medium-sized eyes; and small, erect, V-shaped ears. The back is short and level. The

legs are sturdy and straight, with round feet and black nails. The docked tail is carried slightly higher than the back.

Year of AKC recognition: 1885

Group: Toy

Size: Not to exceed 7 pounds

Coat: Fine, silky, glossy, long, and straight

Color: Dark steel blue on the body; rich golden tan on the head, face, chest, and legs. Yorkie puppies are born dark and gradually develop their adult coloring as they mature.

Life expectancy: 11–15 years

Activity level: Moderate. Daily walks and play will satisfy a Yorkie's exercise needs. The Yorkie's coat is not weather protective and it should not be exercised outdoors in weather extremes. The breed does well in agility, rally, and obedience.

Grooming: This is a fine-textured coat that mats easily and should be brushed daily and bathed weekly. Coats can be maintained in a pet trim for easier grooming. Detailed grooming information and trimming patterns are available on the parent club's Web site.

Temperament: This is a bold, lively, self-confident toy terrier. While Yorkies are responsive and trainable, owners should resist the urge to overlook unwanted behavior. Consistent socialization will ensure a well-balanced, outgoing temperament.

Parent club: Yorkshire Terrier Club of America (www.ytca.org); founded in 1951

Buyers' advice from parent club: Teacup, red, chocolate, parti-color, and rare gold Yorkies are not recognized types, acceptable variations, or valuable rarities. Responsible breeders do not intentionally perpetuate these traits, which can be associated with health issues. Buy from a responsible breeder; such a breeder will not release a puppy less than twelve weeks of age to a new home.

Regional clubs: There are about twenty regional Yorkie clubs; links to each one can be found on the parent club's Web site under "Regional Clubs and Their Show Results."

Rescue: Yorkshire Terrier Club of America Rescue information can be found on the club's Web site under "Rescue."

YORKSHIRE TERRIER

Photo Credits

*for breed profiles, pages 16–193

Affenpinscher (adult: courtesy Affenpinscher Club of America; puppy: Carol Ann Johnson) • Afghan Hound (adult: © Roger Rechler/photo by Susan Sprung; puppy: Anna Stromberg/courtesy Afghan Hound Club of America) • Airedale Terrier (courtesy Airedale Terrier Club of America, Inc.) • Akita (courtesy Akita Club of America) • Alaskan Malamute (adult: courtesy Alaskan Malamute Club of America; puppy: Isabelle Francais for AKC) • American English Coonhound (adult: Curt Willis; puppy: Isabelle Francais) • American Eskimo Dog (adult: Isabelle Francais; puppy: Chet Jezierski © AKC) • American Foxhound (adult: Tara Darling; puppy: Isabelle Francais) • American Staffordshire Terrier (Isabelle Francais) • American Water Spaniel (adult: Mary Bloom © AKC; puppy: Tara Darling) • Anatolian Shepherd (courtesy Anatolian Shepherd Dog Club of America) • Australian Cattle Dog (Cheryl Kurpas/courtesy Australian Cattle Dog Club of America) • Australian Shepherd (adult: Mary Bloom © AKC; puppy: Diane Lewis for AKC) • Australian Terrier (courtesy Australian Terrier Club of America)

Basenji (courtesy Basenji Club of America) • Basset Hound (courtesy Basset Hound Club of America) • Beagle (courtesy National Beagle Club of America) • Bearded Collie (adult: © 2005 Chet Jezierski; puppy: © 2010 Chet Jezierski) • Beauceron (adult: Isabelle Francais for AKC; puppy: Tara Darling) • Bedlington Terrier (adult: Tara Darling; puppy: Mary Bloom © AKC) • Belgian Malinois (adult: Mary Bloom © AKC; puppy: Isabelle Francais) • Belgian Sheepdog (courtesy Belgian Sheepdog Club of America) • Belgian Tervuren (© Karen P. Johnson for the American Kennel Club/courtesy American Belgian Tervuren Club) • Bernese Mountain Dog (adult: © R. Nielsen 2010; puppy: © M. Eschweiler 2010/courtesy Bernese Mountain Dog Club of America) • Bichon Frise (adult: R.J. Hamilton; puppy: courtesy Bichon Frise Club of America) • Black and Tan Coonhound (courtesy Black and Tan Coonhound Club of America) • Black Russian Terrier (adult: Mary Bloom © AKC; puppy: Isabelle Francais) • Bloodhound (adult: Isabelle Francais; puppy: Isabelle Francais for AKC) • Bluetick Coonhound (adult: courtesy Amanda Alexander; puppy: courtesy Cynthia Grooms)

• Border Collie (Isabelle Francais) • Border Terrier (adult: © Jean Clark; puppy: courtesy Border Terrier Club of America) • Borzoi (courtesy Borzoi Club of America) • Boston Terrier (adult: © AKC; puppy: Isabelle Francais) • Bouvier des Flandres (adult: Mary Bloom © AKC; puppy: Isabelle Francais) • Boxer (adult: © 2003 Nancy Spelke, Custom Dog Designs; puppy: courtesy American Boxer Club) • Boykin Spaniel (Bill Simmons/courtesy Boykin Spaniel Club and Breeders Association of America) • Briard (courtesy Briard Club of America) • Brittany (courtesy American Brittany Club) • Brussels Griffon (courtesy American Brussels Griffon Association) • Bull Terrier (adult: Mary Bloom © AKC; puppy: Isabelle Francais) • Bulldog (© AKC) • Bullmastiff (adult: courtesy American Bullmastiff Association; puppy: Mary Bloom © AKC)

Cairn Terrier (Mary Bloom © AKC) • Canaan Dog (courtesy Canaan Dog Club of America) • Cane Corso (courtesy Cane Corso Club of America) • Cardigan Welsh Corgi (courtesy Cardigan Welsh Corgi Club of America) • Cavalier King Charles Spaniel (adult: © Calvin J. Sampson III, Still Motion Photography/courtesy American Cavalier King Charles Spaniel Club; puppy: courtesy American Cavalier King Charles Spaniel Club) • Cesky Terrier (Tara Darling) • Chesapeake Bay Retriever (© DennisGlennon.com) • Chihuahua (© Patricia W. Witter/courtesy Chihuahua Club of America) • Chinese Crested (Mary Bloom © AKC) • Chinese Shar-Pei (courtesy Chinese Shar-Pei Club of America) • Chinook (courtesy Chinook Club of America) • Chow Chow (adult: Mary Bloom © AKC; puppy: AKC file photo) • Clumber Spaniel (adult: © Eileen Sutherland/courtesy Clumber Spaniel Club of America; puppy: © Tonya Pet Photography) • Cocker Spaniel (adult: Mary Bloom © AKC; puppy: Isabelle Francais for AKC) • Collie (courtesy Collie Club of America) • Curly-Coated Retriever (adult: Mary Bloom © AKC; puppy: Gary and Mary Meek)

Dachshund (courtesy Dachshund Club of America) • Dalmatian (adult: Mary Bloom © AKC; puppy: Meghan Lyons © AKC) • Dandie Dinmont Terrier (courtesy Dandie Dinmont Terrier Club of America) • Doberman Pinscher (adult: © Rita Kay Adams/courtesy Doberman Pinscher Club of America;

puppy: Isabelle Francais for AKC); Dogue de Bordeaux (courtesy Dogue de Bordeaux Society of America)

English Cocker Spaniel (© Kerrin Winter-Churchill) • English Foxhound (Isabelle Francais for AKC) • English Setter (adult: courtesy Melissa D. Newman, puppy: Isabelle Francais for AKC) • English Springer Spaniel (adult: © Ruth Dehmel; puppy: Tara Darling) • English Toy Spaniel (adult: Mary Bloom © AKC; puppy: Carol Ann Johnson) • Entlebucher Mountain Dog (courtesy National Entlebucher Mountain Dog Association)

Field Spaniel (© Mary Bloom/courtesy Field Spaniel Society of America, Inc.) • Finnish Lapphund (© Lynn Drumm Photography/courtesy Finnish Lapphund Club of America) • Finnish Spitz (courtesy Finnish Spitz Club of America) • Flat-Coated Retriever (adult: Tara Darling; puppy: Carol Ann Johnson) • Fox Terrier (courtesy American Fox Terrier Club) • French Bulldog (© Allen Weinberg/courtesy French Bull Dog Club of America)

German Pinscher (Janet Oatney © GPCA 2010/courtesy German Pinscher Club of America) • German Shepherd Dog (courtesy German Shepherd Dog Club of America/Valerie Harrington) • German Shorthaired Pointer (property of CheckSix Shorthairs/courtesy German Shorthaired Pointer Club of America, Inc.) • German Wirehaired Pointer (© Liz Dixon) • Giant Schnauzer (© Gay Glazbrook) • Glen of Imaal Terrier (adult: Mary Bloom © AKC; adult and puppies: Isabelle Francais for AKC) • Golden Retriever (adult: © James Soderberg; adult and puppy: © Gloria Kerr) • Gordon Setter (adult: courtesy Gordon Setter Club of America; puppy: Sara Carlson/courtesy Gordon Setter Club of America) • Great Dane (adult: Isabelle Francais; puppy: Isabelle Francais for AKC) • Great Pyrenees (courtesy Great Pyrenees Club of America) • Greater Swiss Mountain Dog (courtesy Greater Swiss Mountain Dog Club of America) • Greyhound (adult: Helios Photo 2008/courtesy Greyhound Club of America; puppy: Helios Photo 2009/courtesy Greyhound Club of America)

Harrier (courtesy Harrier Club of America) • Havanese (adult: Marie A. Fiore/courtesy Havanese Club of

America; puppy: Isabelle Francais) Ibizan Hound (courtesy Ibizan Hound Club of the United States) • Icelandic Sheepdog (adult: Agust Agustsson; puppy: Jorgen Metzdorff/courtesy Icelandic Sheepdog Association of America) • Irish Red and White Setter (courtesy Irish Red and White Setter Association) • Irish Setter (adult: Mary Bloom © AKC; puppies: Isabelle Francais for AKC) • Irish Terrier (courtesy Irish Terrier Club of America) • Irish Water Spaniel (© 2010 Jeremy Kezer/courtesy Irish Water Spaniel Club of America)• Irish Wolfhound (© Irish Wolfhound Club of America) • Italian Greyhound (© Anne Marie Shute/courtesy Italian Greyhound Club of America)

Japanese Chin (adult: Tara Darling; puppy: © Scott Toney, Midweed Japanese Chin/courtesy Japanese Chin Club of America)

Keeshond (Isabelle Francais for AKC) • Kerry Blue Terrier (adult: Mary Bloom © AKC; puppy: Michael Trafford) • Komondor (Isabelle Francais for AKC) • Kuvasz (Isabelle Francais)

Labrador Retriever (adult: Mary Bloom © AKC; puppy: © AKC)• Lakeland Terrier (TopDogPhotos/courtesy United States Lakeland Terrier Club) • Leonberger (courtesy Leonberger Club of America) • Lhasa Apso (adult: courtesy American Lhasa Apso Club; puppy. © Darling Photos/courtesy American Lhasa Apso Club) • Löwchen (Isabelle Francais)

Maltese (adult: © AKC; puppy: Isabelle Francais) • Manchester Terrier (adult: Mary Bloom © AKC; puppy: Isabelle Francais for AKC) • Mastiff (Isabelle Francais) • Miniature Bull Terrier (Isabelle Francais) • Miniature Pinscher (adult: Mary Bloom © AKC; puppy: Isabelle Francais) • Miniature Schnauzer (Isabelle Francais)

Neapolitan Mastiff (adult: Mary Bloom © AKC; puppy: Isabelle Francais for AKC) • Newfoundland (Mary Bloom © AKC; puppy: Isabelle Francais) • Norfolk Terrier (© Derek Glas/courtesy Norfolk Terrier Club) • Norwegian Buhund (adult: Carol Ann Johnson; puppy: Tara Darling) • Norwegian Elkhound (courtesy Norwegian Elkhound Association of America) • Norwegian Lundehund (adult: Alice van Kempen; puppy:

courtesy Boromir Kennel)• Norwich Terrier (adult: Mary Bloom © AKC; puppy: Isabelle Francais) • Nova Scotia Duck Tolling Retriever (AKC file photos)

Old English Sheepdog (Isabelle Francais) • Otterhound (adult: courtesy Otterhound Club of America; puppy: Diane Hoy/Otterhound Club of America)

Papillon (adult: © AKC; puppy: Isabelle Francais) • Parson Russell Terrier (adult: Mary Bloom © AKC; puppy: Isabelle Francais) • Pekingese (adult: courtesy Pekingese Club of America; puppy: © Tony Rosato/courtesy Pekingese Club of America) • Pembroke Welsh Corgi (courtesy Pembroke Welsh Corgi Club of America) • Petit Basset Griffon Vendéen (adult: © 2007 Bob Cohen/courtesy PBGV Club of America; puppy: © 2006 Bob Cohen/courtesy PBGV Club of America • Pharaoh Hound (adult: © Pet Action Shots/courtesy Pharaoh Hound Club of America/ puppy: courtesy Pharaoh Hound Club of America) • Plott (adult: Mary Bloom © AKC; puppy: Isabelle Francais) • Pointer (adult: © Jackie Paul/courtesy American Pointer Club) • Polish Lowland Sheepdog (adult: Mary Bloom © AKC; puppy: Isabelle Francais) • Pomeranian (adult: Mary Bloom © AKC; puppy: © AKC) • Poodle (© Leslie Newing Photography/ courtesy Poodle Club of America) • Portuguese Water Dog (adult: Creative Indulgence; puppy: Glen Boedecker; Courier Magazine, Sept./Oct. 2009) • Pug (courtesy Pug Dog Club of America) • Puli (Isabelle Francais) • Pyrenean Shepherd (Isabelle Francais)

Rat Terrier (courtesy Rat Terrier Club of America) • Redbone Coonhound (Christine Smith/courtesy Redbone Coonhound Association) • Rhodesian Ridgeback (courtesy Rhodesian Ridgeback Club of the United States) • Rottweiler (Isabelle Francais) • Russell Terrier (JoAnn Stoll/courtesy American Russell Terrier Club)

Saint Bernard (© Nancy Nosiglia/ courtesy Saint Bernard Club of America) • Saluki (adult: Mary Bloom © AKC; puppy: Isabelle Francais) • Samoyed (courtesy Samoyed Club of America) • Schipperke (adult: Mary Bloom © AKC; puppy: Isabelle Francais for AKC) • Scottish Deerhound (adult: Mary Bloom © AKC; puppy: Carol Ann Johnson) •

Scottish Terrier (adult: Tara Darling; puppy: Mary Bloom © AKC) • Sealyham Terrier (adult: Isabelle Francais; puppy: courtesy American Sealyham Terrier Club) • Shetland Sheepdog (© 2010, Pete Culumovic Photos/courtesy American Shetland Sheepdog Association) • Shiba Inu (adult: courtesy Leslie Ann Engen; puppy: Mary Bloom © AKC) • Shih Tzu (courtesy American Shih Tzu Club) • Siberian Husky (adult: Mary Bloom © AKC; puppy: courtesy Siberian Husky Club of America) • Silky Terrier (courtesy Silky Terrier Club of America) • Skye Terrier (adult: Tara Darling; puppy: Alice van Kempen) • Soft Coated Wheaten Terrier (courtesy Soft Coated Wheaten Terrier Club of America, Inc.) • Spinone Italiano (adult: courtesy Spinone Club of America; puppy: © Phil Perham/courtesy Spinone Club of America) • Staffordshire Bull Terrier (adult: Mary Bloom © AKC; puppy: Isabelle Francais) • Standard Schnauzer (courtesy Standard Schnauzer Club of America) • Sussex Spaniel (courtesy Sussex Spaniel Club of America) • Swedish Vallhund (adult: Mary Bloom © AKC; puppy: Isabelle Francais)

Tibetan Mastiff (© American Tibetan Mastiff Association) • Tibetan Spaniel (courtesy Tibetan Spaniel Club of America, Inc.) • Tibetan Terrier (adult: Backstage Photo; puppy: David Murray) • Toy Fox Terrier (adult: Isabelle Francais for AKC; puppy: Isabelle Francais) • Treeing Walker Coonhound (adult: Curt Willis; puppy: Isabelle Francais)

Vizsla (Mary Bloom © AKC; puppy: Isabelle Francais for AKC)

Weimaraner (Isabelle Francais) • Welsh Springer Spaniel (courtesy Welsh Springer Spaniel Club of America) • Welsh Terrier (adult: Carol Ann Johnson; puppy: Isabelle Francais for AKC) • West Highland White Terrier (adult: © AKC; puppy: Chet Jezierski © AKC) • Whippet (adult: courtesy American Whippet Club; puppy: © A. Diehl/courtesy American Whippet Club) • Wirehaired Pointing Griffon (adult: Mary Bloom © AKC; puppy: Isabelle Francais)

Xoloitzcuintli (adult: courtesy Amy Fernandez; puppy: Shannon Larson)

Yorkshire Terrier (adult: © AKC; puppy: Isabelle Francais)

Resources

Books

The Complete Dog Book, 20th edition (New York: Ballantine Books, 2006)
This official publication of the AKC, first published in 1929, includes the complete histories and breed standards of 153 recognized breeds as well as information on general care and the dog sport.

The Complete Dog Book for Kids (New York: Howell Book House, 1996)
Specifically geared toward young people, this official publication of the AKC presents 149 breeds and varieties as well as introductory owners' information.

Citizen Canine: Ten Essential Skills Every Well-Mannered Dog Should Know by Mary R. Burch, PhD (Freehold, New Jersey: Kennel Club Books, 2010)
This official AKC publication is the definitive guide to the AKC's Canine Good Citizen program, recognized as the gold standard of behavior for dogs, with more than half a million dogs trained.

Dog Care & Training (New York: Howell Book House, 2002)
This official publication of the AKC is an excellent resource for new owners when they research and bring home a new puppy. Covering everything from puppy-care basics to training and health, and everything in between, this is a must-have guide to responsible pet ownership.

DOGS: The First 125 Years of the American Kennel Club (Freehold, New Jersey: Kennel Club Books, 2009)
This official AKC publication presents an authoritative complete history of the AKC, including detailed information not found in any other volume.

Dogs for Kids! Everything You Need to Know About Dogs by Kristin Mehus-Roe (Irvine, California: BowTie Press, 2007)
An entertaining and educational reference tool for children and their parents, including hundreds of color photographs on nearly 400 pages.

The Original Dog Bible: The Definitive Source for All Things Dog, 2nd edition, by Kristin Mehus-Roe (Irvine, California: BowTie Press, 2009)
This 831-page magnum opus includes over 250 breed profiles, hundreds of color photographs, and a wealth of information on every dog topic imaginable—thousands of practical tips on grooming, training, care, and much more.

Periodicals

American Kennel Club Gazette
Every month since 1889, serious dog fanciers have looked to the *Gazette* for authoritative advice on training, showing, breeding, and canine health. Each issue includes the breed columns section, written by experts from the respective breed clubs.

AKC Family Dog
This is a bi-monthly magazine for dog lovers whose special dog is "just a pet." Helpful tips, how-tos, and features are written in an entertaining and reader-friendly format. It's a lifestyle magazine for today's busy families who want to enjoy the most rewarding, mutually happy relationship with their canine companions.

Dog Fancy
The world's most widely read dog magazine, *Dog Fancy* celebrates dogs and the people who love them. Each monthly issue includes cutting-edge medical developments, health and fitness (with a focus on prevention, treatment, and natural therapy), behavior and training, travel and activities, breed profiles and dog news, issues and trends for purebred and mixed-breed dog owners. The magazine informs, inspires, and entertains readers while promoting responsible dog ownership. Throughout its more than forty-year history, *Dog Fancy* has garnered numerous honors, including being named the Best All-Breed Magazine by the Dog Writers Association of America.

Dog World
With more than ninety-five years of tradition as the top magazine for active people with active dogs, *Dog World* provides authoritative, valuable, and entertaining content to the community of serious dog enthusiasts and participants, including breeders; conformation exhibitors; obedience, agility, herding, and field trial competitors; veterinarians; groomers; and trainers. This monthly magazine is the resource to turn to for up-to-date information about canine health, advanced training, holistic and homeopathic methods, breeding, and conformation and performance sports.

Dogs in Review
For more than ten years, *Dogs in Review* has showcased the finest dogs in the U.S. and from around the world. The emphasis has always been on strong editorial content, with input from distinguished breeders, judges, and handlers worldwide. This global perspective distinguishes this monthly publication from its competitors—no other North American dog-show magazine gathers together so many international experts to enlighten and entertain its readership.

Dogs USA
Dogs USA is an annual lifestyle magazine published by the editors of *Dog Fancy* that covers all aspects of the dog world: culture, art, history, travel, sports, and science. It also profiles breeds to help prospective owners choose the best dogs for their future needs, such as a potential show champion, super service dog, great pet, or competitive star.

Natural Dog
Natural Dog is the magazine dedicated to giving a dog a natural life. From nutritional choices to grooming to dog-supply options, this publication helps readers make the transition from traditional to natural methods. The magazine also explores the array of complementary treatments

available for today's dogs: acupuncture, massage, homeopathy, aromatherapy, and much more. *Natural Dog* appears as an annual and also as the flip side of *Dog Fancy* magazine four times a year (in February, May, August, and November).

Puppies USA
Also from the editors of *Dog Fancy*, this annual magazine offers essential information for all new puppy owners. *Puppies USA* is lively and informative, including advice on general care, nutrition, grooming and training techniques for all puppies, whether purebred or mixed breed, adopted, rescued, or purchased. In addition, it offers family fun through quizzes, contests, and much more. An extensive breeder directory is included.

Web Sites

www.akc.org
The American Kennel Club's (AKC's) Web site is an excellent starting point for researching dog breeds and learning about puppy care. The site lists hundreds of breeders, along with basic information about breed selection and basic care. The site also has links to the national breed club of every AKC-recognized breed; breed-club sites offer plenty of detailed breed information as well as lists of member breeders. In addition, you can find the AKC National Breed Club Rescue Network at this link: www.akc.org/breeds/rescue.cfm.

www.dogchannel.com
Dog Channel is "the website for dog lovers," where hundreds of thousands of visitors each month find extensive information on breeds, training, health and nutrition, puppies, care, activities, and more. Interactive features include forums, Dog College, games, puzzles, and Club Dog, an exclusive free club where dog lovers can create blogs for their pets and earn points to buy products. DogChannel is the definitive one-stop site for all things dog.

www.meetthebreeds.com
The official Web site of the Meet the Breeds event, hosted by the American Kennel Club (AKC) and the Cat Fanciers' Association (CFA) in the Jacob Javits Center in New York City in October. The first event took place in 2009. The Web site includes information on every recognized breed of dog and cat, alphabetically listed, as well as the breeders, demonstration facilitators, sponsors, and vendors participating in the annual event.

AKC-Affiliated Organizations

The AKC Humane Fund unites a broad spectrum of animal lovers in promoting the joy and value of responsible and productive pet ownership through education, outreach, and grant-making. Monies raised may fund grants to organizations that teach adults and children about responsible pet ownership; provide for the health and well-being of all dogs; and preserve and celebrate the human-animal bond and the evolutionary relationship between dogs and humankind.

The American Kennel Club Companion Animal Recovery (CAR) Corporation is an affiliate organization of AKC, dedicated to reuniting lost microchipped and tattooed pets with their owners. AKC CAR maintains a permanent-identification database and provides lifetime recovery services 24 hours a day, 365 days a year, for all animal species, regardless of age or size. Millions of microchipped and tattooed pets are enrolled in the program. Coordinators have recovered hundreds of thousands of pets since the program's inception in 1995.

The American Kennel Club Canine Health Foundation (AKC CHF), Inc., a 501 (c) 3 charitable organization established in 1995, is the largest foundation in the world to fund exclusively canine health studies for both purebred and mixed-breed dogs. To date, more than $22 million has been allocated in health-research funds to more than 500 studies conducted to help dogs live longer, healthier lives. The foundation's Web site can be found at www.akcchf.org.

The AKC Museum of the Dog, established in 1981, is located in St. Louis, Missouri, and houses the world's finest collection of art devoted to the dog.

AKC Programs

The Canine Good Citizen Program (CGC), established in 1989, is designed to recognize dogs that have good manners at home and in the community. This rapidly growing, nationally recognized program stresses responsible dog ownership for owners and basic training and good manners for dogs. All dog that pass the ten-step CGC test receive a certificate from the AKC.

The AKC S.T.A.R. Puppy Program is designed to get dog owners and their puppies off to a good start and is aimed at loving dog owners who have taken the time to attend basic obedience classes with their puppies. After completing a six-week training course, the puppy must pass the AKC S.T.A.R. Puppy test, which evaluates Socialization, Training, Activity, and Responsibility.

Index

*for breed profiles, pages 16–193

Affenpinscher, 16

Afghan Hound, 17

Airedale Terrier, 18

Akita, 19

Alaskan Malamute, 20

American English
    Coonhound, 21

American Eskimo Dog, 22

American Foxhound, 23

American Staffordshire
    Terrier, 24

American Water
    Spaniel, 25

Anatolian Shepherd
    Dog, 26

Australian Cattle Dog, 27

Australian Shepherd, 28

Australian Terrier, 29

Basenji, 30

Basset Hound, 31

Beagle, 32

Bearded Collie, 33

Beauceron, 34

Bedlington Terrier, 35

Belgian Malinois, 36

Belgian Sheepdog, 37

Belgian Tervuren, 38

Bernese Mountain Dog, 39

Bichon Frise, 40

Black and Tan
    Coonhound, 41

Black Russian Terrier, 42

Bloodhound, 43

Bluetick Coonhound, 44

Border Collie, 45

Border Terrier, 46

Borzoi, 47

Boston Terrier, 48

Bouvier des Flandres, 49

Boxer, 50

Boykin Spaniel, 51

Briard, 52

Brittany, 53

Brussels Griffon, 54

Bull Terrier, 55

Bulldog, 56

Bullmastiff, 57

Cairn Terrier, 58

Canaan Dog, 59

Cane Corso, 60

Cardigan Welsh Corgi, 61

Cavalier King Charles
    Spaniel, 62

Cesky Terrier, 63

Chesapeake Bay
    Retriever, 64

Chihuahua, 65

Chinese Crested, 66

Chinese Shar-Pei, 67

Chinook, 68

Chow Chow, 69

Clumber Spaniel, 70

Cocker Spaniel, 71

Collie, 72

Curly-Coated Retriever, 73

Dachshund, 74-75

Dalmatian, 76

Dandie Dinmont Terrier, 77

Doberman Pinscher, 78

Dogue de Bordeaux, 79

English Cocker Spaniel, 80

English Foxhound, 81

English Setter, 82

English Springer
    Spaniel, 83

English Toy Spaniel, 84

Entlebucher Mountain
    Dog, 85

Field Spaniel, 86

Finnish Lapphund, 87

Finnish Spitz, 88

Flat-Coated Retriever, 89

Fox Terrier, 90

French Bulldog, 91

German Pinscher, 92

German Shepherd Dog, 93

German Shorthaired
    Pointer, 94

German Wirehaired
    Pointer, 95

Giant Schnauzer, 96

Glen of Imaal Terrier, 97

Golden Retriever, 98

Gordon Setter, 99

Great Dane, 100

Great Pyrenees, 101

Greater Swiss
    Mountain Dog, 102

Greyhound, 103

Harrier, 104

Havanese, 105

Ibizan Hound, 106

Icelandic Sheepdog, 107

Irish Red and White
    Setter, 108

Irish Setter, 109
Irish Terrier, 110
Irish Water Spaniel, 111
Irish Wolfhound, 112
Italian Greyhound, 113
Japanese Chin, 114
Keeshond, 115
Kerry Blue Terrier, 116
Komondor, 117
Kuvasz, 118
Labrador Retriever, 119
Lakeland Terrier, 120
Leonberger, 121
Lhasa Apso, 122
Löwchen, 123
Maltese, 124
Manchester Terrier, 125
Mastiff, 126
Miniature Dachshund, 74-75
Miniature Bull Terrier, 127
Miniature Pinscher, 128
Miniature Poodle, 150-151
Miniature Schnauzer, 129
Neapolitan Mastiff, 130
Newfoundland, 131
Norfolk Terrier, 132
Norwegian Buhund, 133
Norwegian Elkhound, 134
Norwegian Lundehund, 135
Norwich Terrier, 136
Nova Scotia Duck Tolling
    Retriever, 137
Old English Sheepdog, 138
Otterhound, 139
Papillon, 140

Parson Russell Terrier, 141
Pekingese, 142
Pembroke Welsh Corgi, 143
Petit Basset Griffon
    Vendéen, 144
Pharaoh Hound, 145
Plott, 146
Pointer, 147
Polish Lowland
    Sheepdog, 148
Pomeranian, 149
Poodle, 150-151
Portuguese Water Dog,
    152
Pug, 153
Puli, 154
Pyrenean Shepherd, 155
Rat Terrier, 156
Redbone Coonhound, 157
Rhodesian Ridgeback, 158
Rottweiler, 159
Russell Terrier, 160
Saint Bernard, 161
Saluki, 162
Samoyed, 163
Schipperke, 164
Scottish Deerhound, 165
Scottish Terrier, 166
Sealyham Terrier, 167
Shetland Sheepdog, 168
Shiba Inu, 169
Shih Tzu, 170
Siberian Husky, 171
Silky Terrier, 172
Skye Terrier, 173

Smooth Fox Terrier, 90
Soft Coated Wheaten
    Terrier, 174
Spinone Italiano, 175
Staffordshire Bull
    Terrier, 176
Standard Dachshund, 74-75
Standard Manchester
    Terrier, 125
Standard Poodle, 150-151
Standard Schnauzer, 177
Sussex Spaniel, 178
Swedish Vallhund, 179
Tibetan Mastiff, 180
Tibetan Spaniel, 181
Tibetan Terrier, 182
Toy Fox Terrier, 183
Toy Manchester Terrier,
    125
Toy Poodle, 150-151
Treeing Walker
    Coonhound, 184
Vizsla, 185
Weimaraner, 186
Welsh Springer
    Spaniel, 187
Welsh Terrier, 188
West Highland White
    Terrier, 189
Whippet, 190
Wire Fox Terrier, 90
Wirehaired Pointing
    Griffon, 191
Xoloitzcuintli, 192
Yorkshire Terrier, 193

AMERICAN KENNEL CLUB®

Advocating for the purebred dog as a family companion, advancing canine health and well-being, working to protect the rights of all dog owners and promoting responsible dog ownership, the **American Kennel Club:**

Sponsors more than **22,000 sanctioned events** annually including conformation, agility, obedience, rally, tracking, lure coursing, earthdog, herding, field trial, hunt test, and coonhound events

Features a **10-step Canine Good Citizen**® **program** that rewards dogs who have good manners at home and in the community

Has reunited more than **370,000** lost pets with their owners through the AKC Companion Animal Recovery - visit **www.akccar.org**

Created and supports the AKC Canine Health Foundation, which funds research projects using the more than **$22 million** the AKC has donated since 1995 - visit **www.caninehealthfoundation.org**

Joins **animal lovers** through education, outreach and grant-making via the AKC Humane Fund - visit **www.akchumanefund.org**

We're more than champion dogs. We're the dog's champion.

www.akc.org